Therapy With Substance

Therapy With Substance

Psycholytic Psychotherapy in the Twenty First Century

Dr. Friederike Meckel Fischer

First published by Muswell Hill Press, London, 2015

Published by Aeon Books Ltd 2020

www.aeonbooks.co.uk.

British Library CIP Data available

ISBN: 978-1-913274-30-6

Printed in Great Britain

For you, my dear Father
(4th May 1923 – 17th September 1953),
You showed me the way.

Contents

Acknowledgements xiii

Foreword.. xv
   Reference.. xxi

Introduction.. xxiii

1. **My Personal Background**... 1
   Stuck in therapy 1
   Breakthrough with breathwork 3
   Opening with substance.. 8

2. **My Training in Psycholytic Psychotherapy** 13
   First training weekend: MDMA, with 50 micrograms of LSD 18
   Second training weekend: MDMA.. 19
   Third training weekend: MDMA and 2CB.. 20
   Fourth weekend: MDMA and LSD 20
   Fifth weekend: the moment of death 21
   Sixth training weekend: the moment of birth 22
   Further experiences with Samuel Widmer... 22

3. **Developing the Setting - Towards My Model of Psycholytic Psychotherapy** 25
   First groups: meditators and explorers 26
   Mother Aya and the baking bread 27

4. **Psychotherapy and Psycholytic Psychotherapy** 31
   The individual before starting therapy... 31
   "Disorder"... 32
   The conditions that need to be fulfilled before starting psychotherapy 33

The unconscious mind 34

Trauma and dissociation 35

Does traditional psychotherapy really work? 36

Expanding consciousness to fulfil the therapeutic task 36

How does psycholytic therapy work? 38

Expanding my therapeutic viewpoint 41

The client-therapist relationship 43

5. The Psychoactive Substances 49

Descriptions, presentations and classification 49

Psychoactive substances as non-specific consciousness
amplifiers, catalysts and gateways to the unconscious 51

Perception, consciousness and expanded consciousness 53

The triad of dosage, set and setting – the controlled setting........... 54

The controlled setting, an overview 57

Arc of unfolding 57

MDMA and 3,4-methylenedioxymethamphetamine 58

The Effects of MDMA 59

What does it feel like to take MDMA? 60

The MDMA "ascent" phase 63

The MDMA ascent of a "college graduate" 64

The MDMA plateau phase 65

LSD; Lysergic acid diethylamide 65

How does LSD work? 67

A challenging emotional experience – the story of N 70

Commentary on the story on N 74

Unusual effects of LSD and other substances 77

The special nature of LSD 79

Inflow of the substance LSD 82

LSD report from an experienced client 82

The plateau phase of LSD 84

2CB; 4-Bromo-2.5-dimethoxyphenylethylamine 84

The ascent with 2CB 85

Reports of 2CB experiences 85

Entheogens: psilocybin, mescaline and ayahuasca 86

Psilocybin, psilocin 86

Specific effect of psilocybin 87

An early mushroom experience 88

Harman alkaloids and DMT: ayahuasca 90

Combinations of substances 90

The issue of self-intake 91

Integration 94

6. The Arcs and Tools of Psycholytic Psychotherapy 99

The first sub-arc: the external structure of a weekend 100

Friday evening – The intention question 100

The second sub-arc: the formal procedure for a session 101

Saturday – Preparation, administering and ascent 101

The plateau phase 102

The descent phase 104

Therapeutic tools 104

I. The therapist 104

II. The substances 105

III. Modified family constellation work 105

IV. Live-Body-Work 107

Theoretical principles 107

Live-Body-Work as a tool 109

V. The group 110

The development of the group into a tool 110

The group as tool 112

VI. Music 113

Why include music in a psycholytic session? 114

The function of the symptom 117

The importance of the expressed intention 118

The corrective new experience 118

The iterative integration process 119

An ascent with MDMA 120

Working on the plateau 123

Example 1: Working with modified constellation work 123

Example 2: Live-Body-Work 124

7. Stages of the psycholytic therapy 127

Introduction to the "work" 127

Selecting clients – briefing and contraindications 128

Learning objectives for effective psycholytic therapy.................. 129

From "beginner" to "school leaver" 129

The first session 130

The primary school pupil... 132

The secondary school pupil 137

The transition to school leaver.. 140

The school leaver... 143

8. Stations of the Learning Process in Psycholytic Therapy 145

Stations of the learning process 145

The main therapy issue 147

Example of a core therapy issue 147

Personal history – psychosomatics 148

Parents and family 150

Example: inner peace.. 151

Example: patterns 151

Example: when a situation experienced as being difficult
became an everyday sensation... 152

Psychosomatics.. 153

Epigenetics – transgenerational trauma and ancestors 154

Example 1: biographical and epigenetic (ayahuasca).................... 154

Example 2: epigenetic 155

Example 3: epigenetic 155

Example 4: transgenerational trauma 156

Early impacts: bonding patterns, from belief systems to
behavioural patterns.. 156

The origin of patterns in the embryonic and foetal phases........... 157

Example 1: patterns generated by trauma in very early
pregnancy – biochemical-psychic traumatisation......................... 158

Example 2: patterns generated by influences during
pregnancy and birth 160

The same client a few years later: belief system 160

Example 3: recognising the pattern of a belief system 161

Example 4 (another client).. 162

Example 5 163

Group issues 164

Critical appraisal and the limitations of therapy........................... 165

9. **Processes** **167**
The story of Y. 167
2006, 1st set of case notes: MDMA.............................. 168
2006, 2nd set of case notes: MDMA and LSD 168
2006, 3rd set of case notes: ayahuasca 169
2007, 4th set of case notes: ayahuasca.......................... 170
2007, 5th set of case notes: 2CB.................................. 172
2008, 6th set of case notes: 2CB, MDMA, LSD 172
2007, 7th set of case notes: 2CB, MDMA, LSD 173
2008, 8th set of case notes: MDMA 174
2008, 9th set of case notes: ayahuasca........................... 174
2008, 10th set of case notes: 250 micrograms of LSD ... 176
2008, 11th set of case notes: 2CB and LSD 176
2009, 14th set of case notes: 2CB and LSD 177
2009; 15th set of case notes: 2CB and MDMA 178
2009 16th set of case notes: MDMA and LSD 178
2009, 17th set of case notes: 250 micrograms of LSD ... 179
2009, 18th set of case notes: 2CB and LSD 180
Reflection on the process undergone by Y....................... 181
Mo's story 182
Report on the overall process 182
Reflection on Mo.'s process 189
Case notes: ayahuasca, Brazil.. 191

10. **Dangers, Risks, Side Effects and the Law**.................... **195**
Risks associated with the substances in the controlled setting...... 195
Health incidents 196
Dangers of taking the substances described in a
controlled setting 196
The significance of emotionally intense experiences in
psycholytic therapy... 197
The route to a safe self-awareness session 197
Dosage, set and setting are closely linked. 198
The client and dosage 198
The client's attitude 198
The client's level of knowledge..................................... 198
The client's level of ability 198

The combination of set and setting 199
The therapist and the dosage 199
The therapist and the client 199
The therapist and the environment 199
The therapist as "mountain guide": requirements of the therapist 199
Side effects of therapy 201
Risks and side effects of therapy with substance 201
Phenomena encountered while working with psychoactive
substances 202
Potential dangers for clients 203
The context of illegality 203
My personal experience of illegality 205
The advantage of illegality 207
The danger of errors 207
Failure and success 208
Supervision, intervision and exchange 209

11. **The Parallels of this Work with Shamanism, Healing and
     Spirituality** **211**
     Parallels with shamanism 211
     Healing 213
     Spirituality 213

12. **Conclusions – Looking Back and Looking Forward** **215**
     Looking back 215
     Looking forward 216

Bibliography **219**

Index **221**

Acknowledgements

In July 2013, I gave a lecture in Greenwich entitled "Towards Authenticity, Practical Psycho-integration, Setting, Tools and Vision". I was asked on that occasion whether I might put all of my experiences together in a book. This suggestion was to become a challenge, and one for which I would like to offer my thanks here.

To Dr Tim Read for initiating this project, for his help with the production of the book and for his editing of the English translation.

To Stephan Schumacher for his assistance with the German text.

Thanks also to:

You, Stan and Christina, for opening the entrance door to consciousness long ago.

You, my clients, friends, companions and fellow human beings for your engagement, collaboration and trust.

You, my teachers, for your willingness to pass on your knowledge and expertise.

You, Konrad – my husband, my friend, companion, fellow human being and trusted provider of a place of tranquillity.

All those who have worked assiduously on their own research topics, and on whose expertise I have been able to draw.

Those who have nurtured me through their critiques and questions.

That person who made it possible for me to write publicly.

I bow down in gratitude to that which is greater than me. I have been supported and fortified.

Foreword

Dr. Friederike Meckel Fischer's book entitled, *Therapy with Substance,* is a comprehensive guide for the medical use of psychedelic substances in the therapy of emotional and psychosomatic disorders based on years of work that she had conducted with her clients without official permission. It describes in clear and articulate language everything that is necessary to know for effective and safe use of this treatment modality and for the work with non-ordinary states of consciousness in general.

Dr. Meckel's book is being published with impeccable timing. It is being offered to the professional community and lay audiences at a time when we are experiencing a remarkable worldwide renaissance of interest into the scientific research of psychedelic substances. This is an unexpected and surprising change after four decades during which official legally sanctioned clinical work was made all but impossible by ill-considered legislation responding to mass unsupervised use by the young generation in America and the international hysteria generated and fomented by sensation-hunting journalists.

At present, new psychedelic research is being conducted at a number of American Universities, including Harvard, Johns Hopkins, University of California in Los Angeles (UCLA), State University of New York SUNY), University of California in San Francisco (UCSF), University of Arizona in Tucson, AZ, and others. Of special interest is the ground-breaking research into MDMA-assisted psychotherapy with veterans suffering from post-traumatic stress disorder (PTSD) spearheaded by Michael and Annie Mithoefer in South Carolina.[1] Because of the formidable medical, economic, and political problems associated with this dangerous disorder that are often resistant to traditional forms of therapy, the success of this project might open the door for psychedelics into mainstream psychiatry. Phase 2 clinical trials of MDMA-assisted psychotherapy for PTSD are currently being conducted or planned in South Carolina, Colorado, Canada, and Israel. New research projects involving various cannabinols, ibogaine, ketamine, and other psychedelic substances have been initiated worldwide. To understand the importance of Dr. Meckel's book, it is important to look at it in a large historical context.

In 1943, the serendipitous discovery of psychedelic effects of LSD-25 by the Swiss chemist Albert Hofmann[2] engendered an unprecedented wave of worldwide scientific interest in this substance and spawned a new discipline – modern consciousness research.[3] Never before in the history of science has a single substance held so much promise in a variety of fields. For brain researchers the discovery of LSD led to a golden era of research that also made progress in solving the puzzle of neuroreceptors, synaptic transmitters, chemical antagonisms, and the role of serotonin in the brain.

Psychiatrists saw LSD as a unique means to induce a laboratory model of endogenous psychoses and hoped that this "experimental psychosis" would help to solve the mystery of schizophrenia and bring a test-tube solution for their discipline's greatest challenge. This "experimental psychosis" induced by miniscule dosages – millionths of a gram or gammas – was also widely used as an unconventional teaching tool that made it possible for many thousands of professionals to spend a few hours in a world similar to that of their patients.

Psychotherapists reported LSD's unique potential to deepen and accelerate the therapeutic process and extend the range of applicability of psychotherapy to categories of patients that previously had been very difficult or impossible to reach – alcoholics, hard drug addicts, sexual deviants, and recidivists.[4] Particularly valuable and promising were the studies alleviating the emotional and physical suffering of terminal patients and relieve them from fear of death.[5] For historians of art, LSD experiments provided extraordinary new insights into the psychology and psychopathology of art, particularly various modern movements, such as surrealism, fantastic realism, cubism, and impressionism, and paintings and sculptures of various native cultures.[6]

The capacity of LSD to induce deep spiritual experiences brought fascinating insights into the psychology and psychopathology of religion – shamanism, rites of passage, ancient mysteries of death and rebirth, Eastern spiritual philosophies, and the great religious and mystical traditions of the world, as well as religious intolerance and religiously motivated wars and cruelties, such as the crusades, jihad, Inquisition, and satanic practices.[7] The fact that psychedelics were able to induce spiritual experiences spawned heated debates about "instant" or "chemical mysticism," focusing on the problem of the authenticity of these experiences.

LSD research seemed well on its way to fulfill all these promises and expectations, until the famous Harvard affair involving Tim Leary, Richard Alpert, and Ralph Metzner, and the unsupervised mass self-experimentation of the young generation and counterculture turned Albert Hofmann's "wonder child" into a "problem child." The administrative and political sanctions against psychedelics in the 1960s were effective only against law-obeying scientists, but failed famously to stop the street use of psychedelic substances. They encouraged a black market with dangerous products of uncertain quality and dosage and created an absurd situation where teenagers had access to more information about consciousness and the human psyche than mainstream psychiatrists and psychologists.

In 1966, Robert Kennedy, whose wife had been treated with LSD and benefitted from the experience, questioned the officials of the Federal Drug and Food Administration (FDA) and National Institute of Mental Health (NIMH) officials in his own subcommittee hearing on LSD. He was curious why so many LSD research projects were getting scrapped. He argued: "We have given too much emphasis and so much attention to the fact that it can be dangerous and that it can hurt an individual who uses it that, perhaps to some extent, we have lost sight of the fact that it can be very, very helpful in our society if used properly." Defending LSD research, he pointed out that it was bizarre to stop scientific research with psychedelic substances at a time when millions of Americans were using them. As a matter of fact, this situation should have made it imperative to acquire as much reliable information about them as possible.

The draconian legislation that killed serious legitimate research of psychedelics for four decades was not based on any scientific evidence and actually ignored the existing clinical data. So, for example, in 1960 Los Angeles psychedelic pioneer Sidney Cohen published an article entitled *Lysergic Acid Diethylamide: Side Effects and Complications* based on 25,000 administrations of LSD-25 and mescaline, showing that problems associated with psychedelics, such as flashbacks, prolonged reactions, psychotic breaks, and suicidal attempts were actually minimal in responsible use of these substances. They compared very favorably with other procedures routinely used by mainstream psychiatrists, such as insulin comas and electroconvulsive therapy (for both of them 1% mortality was considered an acceptable medical risk) and particularly with Edgar Moniz's widely used Nobel Prize-winning prefrontal lobotomy causing irreversible damage to the brain tissue.[8]

During the four decades when legal work with psychedelics was practically impossible, individual therapists and small groups decided to continue underground work with these substances, because they were convinced about their safety and efficacy when used responsibly and they refused to deprive their clients of their benefit. Ralph Metzner collected the information from such groups working with tryptamine derivatives in Europe and USA in his remarkable book *The Toad and the Jaguar*. The observations described in his book provide a solid basis for future research, particularly with the highly promising 5-methoxy-DMT. Thanks to the experiences of therapists working underground with MDMA, we have now legal studies showing this substance as an effective treatment for PTSD. Friederike Meckel's book is another example of invaluable clinical information obtained without legal permission.

After providing important general information about the nature of emotional and psychosomatic disorders, diagnostic criteria, the therapeutic relationship, and other important prerequisites of successful treatment, she offers a treasure trove of clinical data about the revolutionary changes introduced into psychotherapy by combining it with psychedelic substances and plant medicines. She describes the basic pharmacological agents used in this work – LSD, mescaline, psilocybin, entheogenic amphetamine derivatives MDMA and 2-CB, tryptamine derivatives, as well as plant medicines ayahuasca and Psilocybe mushrooms.

With each section of the book, the discussion of these compounds includes an account of its specific characteristics, psychological and physiological effects, instructions for optimal dosage, guidelines for its clinical use, and therapeutic potential. Dr. Meckel pays special attention to possible side effects, complications, and dangers of psychedelic substances. She makes a great effort to explain how the ratio between their potential benefits and risks critically depends on the quality and dosage and particularly on a complex set of non-pharmacological factors referred to as *set and setting* – who administers the substance to whom, with what intention and purpose, with what degree of experience and skill, and what is the physical environment and circumstances of the experiment.

The rich information in this book, mentioned above and illustrated by many case histories and clinical examples, is of great potential benefit for the future of psychedelic therapy and research. Recently, unexpected justification for the work of the therapists who had decided to follow their own judgment and conscience rather than misguided legislation came in the form of an open letter from a prominent former government official. After reading in the New Yorker Michael Pollan's article about the use of psilocybin in medical treatment, Dr. Peter Bourne who had been the White House Drug Czar during Jimmy Carter's presidency, wrote a remarkable letter to the editor of this magazine.[9] In it he expressed his regret about the Carter government's unfortunate drug policy and apologized to researchers who had continued to work with psychedelics in spite of a poor and erroneous administrative decision. This letter offers a sad commentary on how government funding for scientific research is heavily influenced by political and cultural values that are unrelated to science:

"With few exceptions, federal support for research on so-called drugs of abuse has taken into consideration only their adverse effects, reinforcing the bias of policymakers and funders. As a former director of

the White House Office of Drug Abuse Policy, I now feel a sense of shame at having failed to try to reverse the Nixon-Ford policy that placed most psychedelics on the D.E.A.'s Schedule 1 list, prohibiting their use. Congress would almost certainly have blocked this change, but had we been able to lift the ban on scientific research into medical applications, doctors would probably now have a far better understanding of brain function, and the unnecessary suffering of many terminally ill patients could have been alleviated. We should applaud the heroic scientists and clinicians that Pollan mentions, who are clearly committed to advancing the frontiers of science."

This letter might bring some satisfaction to the brave therapists who decided to be guided by scientific evidence and by their conviction that psychedelics were extremely useful therapeutic tools rather than irrational legislation engendered by mass hysteria. However, it cannot undo the damage that had been done to scientific progress and to many thousands of patients who were deprived of the benefits of psychedelic treatment. In the last part of her book, Dr. Meckel presents an extremely clear and convincing illustration of the factors and circumstances that prevailed during the decades when psychedelics were mislabeled as narcotics and misplaced on the Schedule 1 list.

She describes with unusual honesty her personal Odyssey in the form of years of unsuccessful therapy with traditional treatments and a large number of trainings that she had undergone over the years learning various conventional methods that achieve questionable therapeutic results. This complex and stormy personal history provided a baseline for her recognition and appreciation of the healing power of non-ordinary states of consciousness. After a long series of failures and disappointments, she discovered and experienced firstly holotropic breathwork sessions and then psychedelic therapy.

She underwent a three-year training for holotropic breathwork facilitators and, after having completed it, she became a certified practitioner of this method. Inspired by a powerful MDMA session that she had experienced with her partner and future husband, she decided to undergo training as psychedelic therapist. These experiences represented a radical turning point in her personal and professional life and convinced her about the enormous potential of non-ordinary states of consciousness. When administrative and political measures made legal research with psychedelic substances impossible, she decided to take her work underground instead of practicing with conventional methods that according to her experience were of dubious value for her patients.

Dr. Meckel's therapeutic Odyssey was then followed by a painful Odyssey of another kind – a confrontation with Swiss law when she was accused of illegal practice after one of her clients reported her to the police. Besides being engaged in agonizing, time-consuming, and costly legal procedures threatening her therapeutic license and personal freedom, she also had to face humiliating publicity in the Swiss media damaging her professional reputation.

She thus paid a great price for the help that she had provided to her clients and for the invaluable clinical information that she had been able to amass during a dark era in psychedelic history and in the history of science in general. At this time, the regrettable legislative error is being corrected thanks to decades of determined and unrelenting effort of Rick Doblin, President of the Multidisciplinary Association of Psychedelic Studies (MAPS) and his team. In the future, her book will hopefully serve as an important guide for the new generation of psychedelic therapists, as well as a much needed reader for lay audiences interested in information in this field based on scientific research rather than deceptive antidrug propaganda.

The potential benefit of responsible use of psychedelic substances transcends their importance as powerful therapeutic tools. The profound positive inner transformation of human personality that can be achieved in non-ordinary states of consciousness has an important collective dimension. It involves a radical reduction of aggressive tendencies, development of compassion and tolerance concerning differences in race, gender, and religion, emergence of ecological sensitivity and spirituality of a non-denominational, universal, and all-encompassing nature. If such a change could be achieved on a large enough scale, it could move humanity in direction of a global civilization and give our species better chances of survival.

Albert Hofmann, ethnomycologist Gordon Wasson, and Greek scholar Carl Ruck concluded on the basis of their joint historical research, which they described in the book *The Road to Eleusis,* that the sacred potion *kykeon* administered to the initiates in the Eleusinian mysteries was an ergot derivative.[10] Based on this research, Albert Hofmann believed that ritual use of LSD and psilocybin could one day be integrated into Western civilization and that this New Eleusis would bring to modern humanity spiritual and cultural benefits similar to those that its historical precursor bestowed on ancient Greece and its neighboring countries.

Stanislav Grof, M.D.

Reference

1. Mithoefer, M.C., et al. 2010. "**The Safety and Efficacy of ±3,4-methyle-nedioxy-methamphetamine – Assisted Psychotherapy in Subjects with Chronic Treatment-Resistant Posttraumatic Stress Disorder: The First Randomized Controlled Pilot Study**." *Journal of Psychopharmacology*, 19th July.
2. Hofmann, A. 2005. LSD: My Problem Child. Sarasota, FL: MAPS Publications.
3. Stoll, W. A. 1947. "LSD, ein Phantastikum aus der Mutterkorngruppe." Schweiz. Arch. Neurol. Psychiat. 60:279.
4. Grof, S. LSD Psychotherapy. 1980, Pomona, CA, Hunter House, Republished in 2001 by Multidisciplinary Association for Psychedelic Studies (MAPS) in Sarasota, Florida.
5. Grof, S. 2006. The Ultimate Journey: Consciousness and the Mystery of Death, Santa Cruz, CA: SarasotaMAPS Publications.
6. Grof, S. 2015. Modern Consciousness Research and the Understanding of Art. Santa Cruz, CA: MAPS Publications.
7. Pahnke, W. 1963. Drugs and Mysticism: An Analysis of the Relationship between Psychedelic Drugs and the Mystical Consciousness. Ph.D. dissertation. Harvard University.
8. Cohen, S. *Lysergic Acid Diethylamide: Side Effects and Complications*. Journal of Nervous and Mental Diseases 130:30. 1960.
9. Pollan, Michael (February 9, 2015). "The Trip Treatment." The New Yorker: 36–47.
10. Wasson, G., Hofmann, A., and Ruck, C.A.P. 1978. The Road to Eleusis: Unveiling the Secret of the Mysteries. New York: Harcourt, Brace, and Jovanovitch.

Introduction

In this book, which I have also written at the request of a friend who is committed to the subject that it addresses, I talk about the experience and insight that I have acquired over a number of years as a psychotherapist conducting "underground" therapy with the aid of psychoactive substances, and the development of the corresponding methodology. This work was abruptly ended when I was betrayed, arrested and subsequently convicted of an "Offence against the Narcotics Act". I nevertheless retained the knowledge acquired during my work, and I am now able to talk about it without fear of any further legal consequences.

The purpose of the book is to provide information for anyone interested in the subject. It does not encourage anyone to take psychoactive substances, lead a group or commit any kind of illegal act or offence against the law. Nearly all of the chapters contain terms such as "symptom" and "the unconscious" that serve to explain the model of psychotherapy that I am describing. I offer some explanatory models for various disorders and traumas and some reference is made to other authors in the field.

The first three chapters contain biographical material, introducing the reader to the background of this therapy. **Chapter one** describes my personal background. **Chapter two** gives the reader a highly personal insight into my training with Samuel Widmer. **Chapter three** provides a complete overview of psycholytic therapy from its beginnings up to the present day.

Chapter four looks at psychotherapy and psycholytic therapy as two distinct therapy models. **Chapter five** then leads on to psychoactive substances, and explains their typology, significance and effects illustrated by examples. **Chapter six** goes on to address the therapeutic work itself in general and specific terms and provides an overview of the various tools; how they are used, their function and significance. **Chapter seven** concerns the selection and preparation of clients and the "learning objectives" during psycholytic treatment; the process that I embody with the concept of "From beginner to school leaver".

Chapter eight is devoted to the therapeutic learning process, which is illustrated in **Chapter nine** with detailed accounts of the processes of two clients and a protocol. **Chapter ten** addresses dangers, risks and side effects; I also discuss the issue of illegality, but only to the extent where it serves the purpose of this book.

Chapter eleven looks at the parallels between my model of psycholytic therapy and the shamanic, healing and spiritual traditions. **Chapter twelve** reviews the therapeutic learning process again and adds my perspective as to how this process can best be brought to satisfactory completion.

CHAPTER 1

My Personal Background

This first chapter is autobiographical, describing my own personal journey towards psycholytic therapy.
This and the following chapters provide a concise and coherent overview of how my perspective developed and my method evolved.

My professional path led me to explore and employ unconventional methods of psychotherapy after I was brought face to face with the limitations of conventional psychological treatment. I do not want to over generalise and describe traditional psychotherapy as useless, so I will only discuss myself and my own experiences in this chapter.

In 1988, I fell in love with another man after 21 years of marriage. After a while it became clear to me that this man had only used our "relationship" to find his way out of his own marriage and that he wasn't doing it for me. This whole experience threw my life and identity into crisis to the point where I didn't recognise myself anymore. An immense feeling of inner disquiet, sadness and irritability came over me. The people around me must have been quite offended by my behaviour. I was quarrelsome, intolerant, neglected my domestic duties, questioned everything and complained a lot to my husband.

Strangely enough, I was a totally different person when I was at work at the hospital; balanced, cheerful, full of energy, willing and able to put everything into my work. Seen from the outside, I was two different people. Because I didn't know anybody who could help me in this situation, I realised that I needed to find a way of helping myself. So I decided that I had to become a psychotherapist. Looking back, I find it interesting that it never occurred to me just to go into therapy.

Stuck in therapy

Cognitive therapy seemed too superficial and technical, so I signed up for an introductory talk about training in "deep psychology-oriented psychotherapy". I stated professional interest as my motivation, having discovered in my role as occupational physician that most illnesses and periods of sick leave seemed to be triggered by problems between people. I was accepted into the training group on the basis of this reasoning. I managed not to discuss my own situation for the entire three-year period of training. I did not have the deliberate intention of giving nothing away – it just didn't happen, as if there was an invisible barrier inside me. This behaviour, which I later identified and began to understand in the course of my self-examination, didn't acquire the label of "post-war childhood identity" until much later. This post war syndrome had a powerful ethos – "Batten down the hatches, feel nothing and just carry on functioning." This was ultimately an important lesson for me about the "natural inability to open up", meaning that the most important issues tend not to be addressed in psychotherapy.

In addition to the theory and practical psychiatry part, I underwent group psychoanalysis for the self-awareness part of my training. The group was obviously a representation of society and/or family and their failed processes of social and human exchange. Now under favourable social conditions, formative social experiences were meant to unfold anew through interactions in the training group; they were to be made identifiable and intelligible, and corrected where possible.

This is a useful approach and I could understand it. It proved useful for a number of people in the group psychoanalysis, but I just sat in the middle of the group and remained unable to talk about myself, although people generally said I had a "big mouth". My heart would start beating wildly as soon as the session went quiet; it was as if I was no longer there in the room. When other participants talked vivaciously or argued, I was able to relax a bit and contribute to proceedings. Sometimes I found the sessions extremely dull, even when they lasted the whole of a Sunday. I counted the hours and was relieved when the prescribed 400 hours of group analysis were over. I was afraid – but above all I was afraid to admit that I was afraid of myself.

I had to complete 50 two-hour individual sessions in addition to the group ones. I was really glad to be able to sit in a comfortable armchair and look at the analyst instead of lying on the couch. I can hardly remember anything else about what went on in the sessions. I was probably quiet and somewhere else for most of it – a place that I was unable to name. I didn't even have a name for my absence. The term dissociation was not common even amongst therapists back then, and my silence was interpreted as resistance.

But I became very good at telling "my story". Since I was in training, I learned how to interpret my "symptoms" from my personal history. In choosing my husband, I obviously had been looking for a father substitute. I saw my diligence, ambition and record of high achievement as a highly developed superego – my unconscious controlled my behaviour. So what had sent me on this quest?

I provided no decent material for analysis. I didn't dream about anything. "Are you doing something else?" the analyst would ask me at regular intervals, followed by: "You keep changing yourself". I said nothing – for some reason unknown to myself, I didn't want to give anything away about my inner self in that setting. I think I felt that my problem was buried somewhere else in a deep-down layer that would never be accessed. Analysis hadn't worked through my resistance, nor had it changed my emotional state in any way. But I had learnt many things from psychotherapy, and became adept at using the professional jargon. My examination before the Medical Chamber was in 1992. I had learned the entire book of psychiatry by heart and came out with the top grade for theoretical knowledge.

Breakthrough with breathwork

During my training in depth psychology my former professor of gynaecology recommended "Holotropic Breathwork" to me, in order to alleviate my almost unbearable psychological state. Holotropic Breathwork, developed by Stanislav and Christina Grof, was an entirely different approach to psychotherapy that had a reputation for reaching the parts of the psyche that other therapies could not reach. I prepared myself by reading Stan Grof's book entitled *The Adventure of Self-Discovery*. I can now understand every single word of it, but I didn't get what Stan was talking about when I read it the first few times. But my first meeting and breathing session with him in Zurich in early 1989 pointed me in a completely new direction.

I follow Stan Grof's deep voice: "Now breathe deeper and faster; deeper and faster and allow yourself to be carried by your breath and the music".

I breathe deeper and faster, faster and deeper. I gasp, almost vomiting, my neck straining backwards. A powerful black drumming rips me momentarily into a dark tube. I am pushed from behind and squeezed through the narrow tunnel. It spins me out. I want to scream but nothing happens – there's something over my mouth. I land in the middle of a circle of men and women staring madly at me. I faint with fear. Black, all is black. Somehow, I remember that I have to breathe. I pant in and out again, finding myself – rescued – bobbing along on the high sea in a Moses basket.

While all of this is happening, I lie still and motionless on a mat under a big blanket, which I have brought along to the workshop as a precaution. As the music slowly becomes softer, I realise that I have survived the horror, that I have felt fear, truly felt it – but I have been through it and survived.

When I listened to the reports of other participants later in the sharing session, it became clear to me that this method had the power to set me properly on the path towards myself and my feelings. So I decided to train in Holotropic Breathwork and I duly completed the required training modules with Stan Grof during my holidays over the next three years. I was finally able to access the content of my emotional world during these training sessions in America. I was sad, I was able to cry again and I felt the impact of my father's early death for the first time. I encountered my loneliness and began to see how and why I had behaved as I did. Learning and achievement were not just the superego – they turned out to be a wonderful survival strategy. It showed me things that had remained hidden in my unconscious until then. For the first time, vivid memories accompanied my knowledge of my personal history. Here is an example of a breathing session:

I am four years old, alone in my room in the hospital, isolated. I have scarlet fever. My mother arrives. After a short time she says to me: "I have to speak to the doctor again, I'll be right back." She disappears and I believe that she will come back again soon. But she doesn't return. I wait endlessly, staring out of the window, tense and on the lookout for her. I have to give up hope at some point and go to bed. I fall into a deep hole, where myself and my feelings no longer exist.

Re-experiencing my past history, I understood my reactions of mistrust and disquiet when anyone fails to give me accurate information. I understood that I fall into a state of "non-feeling" in moments of feeling abandoned. It wasn't until years later that I was able to identify this as dissociation. These deep and enduring psychological consequences of trauma were not known to depth psychology in those days.

In spite of some of the difficult details that emerged during these sessions, it did me a power of good to slowly come into touch with these feelings. Above all, I was pleased to find that by re-living the sensations in certain situations, I was able to work through these experiences using my own insight and understanding. Nobody was persuading me, nobody was telling me I was ill or mad and nobody was asserting that they knew my inner self better than I did.

My training with Stan Grof ended in the autumn of 1991. When I returned from the closing seminar, I fell ill with scarlet fever again – this time at the age of 43. My kidneys packed up for two days, my fingers became swollen and painful to move, and breathlessness pointed towards an inflammation of the heart muscle. I fell into the same state of abandonment that I had experienced in the breathing sessions. The rest of my family were away. I lay down on the carpet in the living room, slowly breathing in and out with a continuous rhythm: circular breathing – a gentle way to achieve an altered state of consciousness.

I see myself in a cathedral with brightly-coloured windows. Clothed in white, I lie down in a dark brown coffin in front of a golden high altar. Light beams fall on the coffin through the window. I can hear choral music: "Te decet hymnus Deus in Sion... requiem aeternam ..." – Mozart's Requiem.

I am overcome by an endless feeling of happiness. A much longed-for feeling of tranquillity spreads through my body. I have done it: "I have died." I lie still for ages.

The beams of light are warming me. I look out from them into the dark empty church. I take a deep breath and find myself back in the living room.

All of my scarlet fever symptoms had disappeared. I felt fresh and healthy and went to mow the lawn. I had clearly entered an expanded state of consciousness and had been allowed to experience the healing powers of breathing. I threw the antibiotics in the bin and went back to work the next day. But I felt very raw and sensitive; I did not allow anyone to touch me and I was very careful about touching other people.

I had a series of experiences with the breathing, the content of which I was only able to interpret much later as mystical experiences. I could hardly understand Stan Grof's teachings at first. He was speaking to me in a language I could not yet comprehend, using expressions that I found extremely suspect: inner healing intelligence, transpersonal experience and cosmic consciousness. He spoke of mental experiences that were new and unfamiliar to me, lying beyond my powers of imagination. In spite of this, I was certain that I was on the right path, and one that I recognised from my childhood: I sat in church, understanding nothing but knowing that I was in exactly the right place.

As I went about my daily routine, I now had one foot in medical psychotherapy and the other in a terrain that I didn't really understand, but which seemed to be opening the way up for me into another dimension. I had an authentic sense of myself in this place, experiencing myself in states of distress and great joy. I looked within myself with an expanded consciousness. I experienced the incomprehensible in myself.

Stan Grof, a pioneer in the field of therapy using psychoactive substances, had spoken about his past work with psychedelic substances but I really didn't get what he was saying. I am sure that he doesn't remember suggesting to me at our final training meeting in 1991: *"psychedelic therapy may help you."* I had no idea at the time what that might mean. I am now certain that he sensed my on-going closed state, and was suggesting further self-exploration.

After passing my exams in psychotherapy and psychiatry, I obtained a post in a private clinic specialising in psychosomatics and psychiatry in 1993, where most of the clients were managers with alcohol dependency. I did intensive psychotherapeutic work at this "addiction clinic". Talking was my tool. My patients generally had an academic background and they tended to talk about themselves in a dry intellectual manner, telling me about their life stories and problems. I questioned what they said, trying through various interventions to bring them into some contact with the feelings connected to their memories. I hoped to offer them the possibility, through re-living their feelings, of gaining a better understanding of the roots of their addiction.

I was very struck that the events of the war played a powerful role for most of my clients; they were the 1935-1947 generation, many of their fathers had died in the Second World War and their grandfathers had lived through the First World War. Their childhood and adolescent years were influenced by the war and post-war period and, most importantly, a veil of secrecy was drawn over everything to do with the war years. I did notice this, but was not yet in a position to put these issues to any use in the therapeutic context.

Genuine contact with the emotions was very rare in talking therapy. If it did happen, most of the patients found the feelings unpleasant. They didn't want to cry or feel fear. If a few tears fell, they would wipe their eyes and change the subject. They loved it when I was able to offer them plausible explanations for their descent into alcohol, so they liked coming to see me. But how could the "Remember, Repeat, Process" requirement be met when the memory was not accompanied by the original emotional state? Could just talking about it really ever be enough?

Because a good 30 to 40 per cent of patients relapsed and came back to the clinic, I became increasingly dissatisfied with my work. I knew from my own process the value of re-experiencing deep feelings in the holotropic state of consciousness and how it had helped me to make my first steps towards integration. Through observation and comparison, I came to my first conclusions that the mother and father are important not only as caregivers and attachment figures but also from the patterns generated by their life and times, which have great significance for their children. I was sure that the bombing raids that Mother had experienced during her pregnancy had an effect on the infant's system and maintained their effect in my current client. But I still had no proof.

I came across a book entitled *Cockchafer fly!* that tells the story of a Viennese family after the war. An eight year-old girl describes the end of the war with the withdrawal of German troops and the Soviet army marching in. So there were other people dealing with the war issue, too! This led me to consider the effects of the wartime years through a systemic lens. The question driving me was whether it might be possible that the children of men and women of the war generation had symptoms that originated in their parents, and that they had descended into alcoholism because of this. I decided to train in systemic therapy. It was by lucky coincidence that I came across Gunthard Weber, who had done his training under Helm Stierlin – the founder of the Heidelberg Family Therapy.

But it was too early in the 1990s for any real awareness of the societal impact of the two world wars on the people affected – a kind of collective post-traumatic stress disorder. The term PTSD was still not part of the general body of thought back then. These findings didn't enter the public arena until the publication of Sabine Bode's book *Die Vergessene Generation (The Forgotten Generation)* in 2004. But epigenetic issues were to be of central significance in our psycholytic sessions as far back as the year 2000. Without even looking for it, we encountered the phenomenon of the transgenerational trauma and the presence of epigenetic symptoms when in a state of expanded consciousness. But we still had no technical term for such phenomena, so we used descriptions like: "I got that from my grandmother" and "I see through my mother's eyes". I felt alone in my observations and assumptions, and didn't dare talk about them because I had these insights using psychoactive substances.

From my experience of the breathwork sessions, I was already aware of the impact of prenatal and perinatal events on the development of the individual as far back as the beginning of the 1990s, and I tried to explain Holotropic Breathwork to the owner of the addiction clinic. But he just replied with comments such as "esoteric rubbish", telling me to stay away from him. Physical contact, such as putting your arm around a client in tears, was also taboo in traditional psychotherapy. And it was even less acceptable for a therapist to say anything personal about his own experience in therapy sessions.

Opening with substance

I had my first experiences with psychoactive substances in 1992, before starting psycholytic therapy training with Samuel Widmer, the co-founder of the Swiss Society for Psycholytic Therapy (SAEPT).

One of the participants gave me two little blue pills after a Holotropic Breathwork session in the USA – each 125mg of MDMA. I shared one of the pills with my friend Konrad on my return. This first experience with MDMA was to be crucial for us, bringing us to the firm conclusion that we should train with Samuel Widmer.

> *A wave grabs me, lifts me up to the crest of a wave, drops me into a trough and tumbles me out onto a white beach. I see myself from outside but feel myself in my body at the same time. I am filled with a certainty never felt before: I have come to myself.*
>
> *I look around. My father lies in a white-tiled toilet in the corner, covered in blood. I am not frightened. There is complete certainty: this is how it was! (He was murdered and I was told that he committed suicide).*
>
> *I now know without any doubt: this is the path to myself. My path towards my memories and innermost feelings – with this substance. The images have disappeared. I am flooded by a safe feeling of tranquillity. I am my breath, I am my body. Certainty with a "Yes!" truly felt.*

My husband experienced an opening up of his heart in this first session – a state that he has longed for ever since. He sensed a personal "status quo" at the time. He had split from his family. He now watched his wife from behind as she went on ahead. He realised that each of his four children was taking up a new position. And a number of phrases came as if from within that had a quality of absolute certainty and accuracy.

What a world had started to open up to us! I wasn't even aware that I had memories of my father. I had no internal image within myself... what he looked like, the places we had been together – nothing. But now I had experienced it, I realised that there was knowledge within me that I could tap into with this substance. I had decided – this is how I would be able to explore myself.

Now the depths that I had reached in the breathing sessions seemed like shallow waters to me. And what a contrast to talking therapy! It was increasingly difficult to imagine how talking was supposed to help the difficult clients at the addiction clinic. With hindsight, it seems to me that psycholytic therapy was the only method that could have penetrated the psyche to the depth required to enable them to properly heal. But for the time being, the conventional work at the clinic continued.

An outpatient called me up one night when I was on duty to talk about his suicidal tendencies. He didn't turn up to the planned therapy session the next day. Concerned, I turned to the clinic director. He threatened me with immediate dismissal, asking if I was now going to run around after every patient who didn't attend a therapy session. He told me that this kind of commitment "wasn't therapeutic". On another occasion, a client sent the team a case of sparkling wine when he was discharged from the clinic. The director shouted at me again; didn't I know this was a dry relapse? I should never have let the man go. I should actually have "punished" him for the gift. If *that* was supposed to be a therapeutic relationship, I wasn't sure I really wanted to call myself a therapist. I resigned without having another job to go to.

Following the abrupt end to my job in the addiction clinic in 1994, I moved to be with the man who was to become my husband. Working with a friend from the Holotropic Breathwork group, I started offering workshops four times a year in Zurich. All of our participants received a lot of personal attention and emotional kindness. Gentle physical contact for "trauma through omission" (traumatisation due to a lack of the attention necessary for the development of the individual – abandonment or neglect, for instance) was a way of helping them out of the trauma. We had an equally gentle approach to "trauma through commission" (infliction of abuse and pain).

Meanwhile I continued my psycholytic training group, where each member had to engage, talk about their inner experience and be present in the room. Body exercises were carried out before and during the sessions to facilitate and deepen the process. It was amazing to see what the substances brought to the surface in other members too. I thought I'd found the philosopher's stone and would have liked to help my difficult clients in this way too. But it was clear to me that this couldn't happen.

I saw the contrasts ever more clearly, finding it increasingly difficult to reconcile them. How could therapy be effective without depth or any contact inside or out? Apart from unrecognised psycholytic therapy, was there no other therapeutic tool available that I could use for my clients and myself? In one way or another, I wanted to access the unconscious psychic material of the people who entrusted themselves to me. I was driven by the firm conviction that there must be a learnable method that would render this possible.

I still hadn't found a suitable job so I used my time to continue my quest. I attended courses at an institute for body-centred psychotherapy. Apart from the fact that the institute directors wouldn't recognise any of my previous medical or psychotherapeutic training and wanted me to do another 600 hours of self-exploration to obtain their diploma, it also soon became clear to me that the body exercises and painting sessions employed there were not suited to bringing deeply-buried material out into the open. It only ever reached a certain depth, which still seemed too shallow to me. Years of trying out different therapeutic approaches followed. Time after time, I would think "This method works" – only to realise that it wasn't taking me to the depth that I wanted to reach. I was looking for the place that I had identified as my inner reference point and from which you could observe yourself and the rest of the world.

Carl Simonton's "Healing approach to cancer sufferers" brought me closer to the imagination and skill required for dealing with pain, anxiety and depression autonomously. With him, the afflicted person could be involved in the process of the disease and development of their own future prospects. Combined with the encouragement of hope, the unification of mind and body on which Simonton based his approach opened up a spiritual perspective. Jeanne Achterberg was joint leader at Simonton's workshops. She was a master of the art of healing visualisation. The special thing about her was that she accompanied the afflicted person only as an empathetic presence, leaving them responsible for themselves. I was introduced to the shamanic ritual of healing and the role and power of the "healing woman" with her. I attended a series of workshops organised by her and her husband in Palo Alto in the mid-1990s. Years later, I "rediscovered" and practised much of what she had spoken of back then in my own psychedelic sessions but while studying with Jeanne, I hadn't learned to access my inner self sufficiently to enable me to follow in her footsteps and make her method my own. While I was in Palo Alto, I also looked up the man who had once given me the two little blue pills, and was able to set up a contact with a supplier of MDMA through him so that I wouldn't have to look for a "dealer" in Switzerland later.

But I was still unable to apply the knowledge I had acquired in my further training – either at the addiction clinic where I still did stand-in work or in my own practice that I had started in 1997. My clients and I were simply not ready for it. People would have laughed at me if I had prayed with my clients or worked with symbols. I also learned about autogenic training and classic hypnosis during my psychotherapy training. I was able to achieve amazing things with posthypnotic work, and I liked to apply this method for exam nerves. But I didn't have the confidence to use hypnosis for anything else. It seemed to dig too deeply into the client's psyche, even when the posthypnotic instruction was discussed with the patient in detail beforehand.

So I expanded my classic hypnosis skills through a three-year course of training in the Milton Erickson hypnosis method. This method always helped a little, but only as much as the client allowed it to. I actually found that people were in a constant state of trance, and I realised over time that I would only be changing the scene of the trance. After a time, the way I asked questions and used my voice became so automatic that I was using the explicit form of the hypnotic method less and less. Instead, I explored the trance of the normal everyday state and sometimes the trance of the "problem state" with the client, trying to access reality (however it might be defined) from it.

I came across neuro-linguistic programming (NLP) through my dealings with hypnosis. Without going into detail here, I would just like to say that this method seemed too manipulative to me. I also felt that the objectives achieved were not really long-term – this was the experience of myself and my husband, anyway. But I still did an extra course of NLP for health professionals to make sure that I wasn't missing out on anything. The theoretical background of NLP contained much that seemed formulated to me. It consisted of findings that came close to the Eastern wisdom tradition: "The map is not the territory", "Everyone carries the resources they need within them".

For a while, I occupied myself with the similarities between transpersonal psychology and constructivism. But this urged me to go further. I was driven by the question of how and where I could continue. On the one hand, I was looking for a tool that I could use to push my way down to certain depths, and on the other hand, it had to be something that all my clients could use. I definitely knew what worked for *me,* but it soon became clear that the psycholytic path could not be a wide one. So I completed "coping" training with Rosemarie Welter Enderlin – family mediation training at the Marriage and Family Institute in Zurich, ultimately going on to train in systemic short-term counselling with Werner Herren in Aarau.

When I was finally approved to work as a psychotherapist in Switzerland in 1997 after four frustrating years of looking for a suitable job, I went on using the tools at my disposal for the time being. If a client stopped making progress with client-centred psychotherapy, I tried to use the session to steer them discreetly into a different state of "feeling" with gentle breathing exercises derived from yoga, which were obviously not as intensive as with Holotropic Breathwork. A few of my clients also dared to take the leap into Holotropic Breathwork and made good progress.

It had become clear to me that I needed to get involved with couple and family dynamics, and I had the incredible luck of obtaining a trainee position in systemic couple therapy with Hans Jellouschek. Working with him, I found that my conviction that a child perceives the world through the eyes of his mother or father was completely right and I learned with him to take this into account during therapy. I received nothing but excellent practical guidance and exercises; the training also expanded my viewpoint to the extent of seeing that each individual partner is taking part in their own film with their own sound track. The couple seeks out a "stage" and both partners act out their own part on that stage at the same time. This is then called a "relationship". It was obvious to me that before solving the "couple" issue people should work intensively on their own personal patterns first.

At that time, I had started to suggest, with great care and caution, psycholytic therapy to some of my individual clients. I researched everything I learned with Hans Jellouschek at the psychedelic sessions, and I was pleased to find that my insights in those sessions confirmed the value of what I was learning. After that, I extended my phenomenological knowledge with Gunthard Weber in Wiesloch, completing advanced training in family and system constellations, a further development of Virginia Satir's structural constellations. I had also looked at Bert Hellinger's key statements in many psychedelic sessions, especially those found in Christian culture: "Honour thy father and thy mother: that thy days may be long."

For me, the path of experience that leads via your father and mother to the rightful place in your own life and ultimately to yourself has become the longest and most informative part of my therapeutic experience with and without psychoactive substances. Even today, I see over and over again how liberating it is for the individual to find his or her own "rightful place". I closed the circle of my systemic therapy training with my third course of further training in systemic and family therapy at the International Society for Systemic Therapy in Heidelberg in 2001.

In parallel with the various training and further training courses, I also completed psycholytic therapy training with Samuel Widmer between November 1992 and the autumn of 1995, which I will talk about in the next chapter. I also had my first experiences with other psychoactive substances.

CHAPTER 2

My Training in Psycholytic Psychotherapy

In this chapter, I give a highly personal account of my training in psycholytic psychotherapy with Samuel Widmer.

This training took place at a time when the clinical use of psychedelics to augment psychotherapy was entirely legal in Switzerland for use by a small group of psychiatrists from 1988 until 1994.

Born at Christmas time in 1948, Samuel Widmer first came into contact with LSD at the age of twenty-two. As with my first experience of MDMA many years later, this experience left him with the strong conviction that it held a far-reaching significance. He learned how to handle substances in therapy from a friend, also starting with his own intensive self-exploration. Stan Grof had published his book *LSD Psychotherapy* in 1980, and many other researchers at the time were writing about their findings derived from the use of consciousness-expanding substances.

Widmer decided to become a psychiatrist and psychotherapist when he completed his medical studies. He developed his contacts with other researchers at home and abroad, co-founding the Swiss medical society for psycholytic therapy (SAEPT) with a number of other psychiatrists in 1985. A legal medication up until that point, MDMA was declared illegal in 1986 and classified as a Class A narcotic. But, in the face of enormous difficulties, SAEPT still managed to obtain an exemption permit for a small group of psychiatrists to use MDMA and LSD in their psychotherapy work and to offer the theoretical and practical training needed for working with these substances. This ruling applied from 1988 to 1994.

I became interested in this work at the time, totally underestimating the extent of the political antipathy at the start of the training. I read the book *Looking into the Heart of Things* by Samuel Widmer. As when I read *The Adventure of Self-Discovery* by Stanislav Grof, I didn't really understand what was being described. But, spurred on by the thought that I might be able to explore my own situation assisted by MDMA, I applied for a trainee position. Samuel Widmer and his wife offered me half an hour of their time one Sunday afternoon in the summer of 1991 for us to "get to know each other". I drove 600km from Düsseldorf to Solothurn to be there for those 30 minutes.

It was a friendly chat, and Mr Widmer explained the current situation to me, which I didn't understand, as the word "approval" meant nothing to me in the context and I didn't even know the various substances by name. He made me no promises. Time and again, I expressed my hope in no uncertain terms that I would be accepted into the training group, writing to Widmer at regular intervals to find out how my request to participate was going. My determination must have paid off. I fulfilled the necessary criteria because I was a medical doctor and a psychotherapist. Thankfully, Samuel accepted my then friend and now husband into the group as well. We knew that deep self-exploration would lead to far-reaching changes, so we thought it important to face it together. It was in fact during the course of this work that we got to know, love and respect each other. I am very grateful to Samuel Widmer for allowing us to participate as a couple.

Our training began in November 1992. The group met at the weekend once every three months at Samuel's house (first names are used in this type of work). At 6 pm on Friday evening, all 50 participants would be seated on chairs in a large, bright room. Most were from the healing and caring professions, but all were interested in self-exploration and personal growth above all else. At the time, none of the participants said they were doing the training in order to work with therapeutic substances. It was the second course of its kind; the first one had taken place between 1989 and 1992, so there had been some valuable previous experience in training psycholytic psychotherapists. Some of the people who had completed the first course were now helping as assistants.

Being German, a group of 50 people wasn't anything out of the ordinary to my eyes. As a doctor, I wasn't demanding in terms of support and attention, and it never occurred to me that a smaller setting might be preferable. A quiet discipline prevailed. People didn't speak all at once, and I didn't say a word – out of pure fear and awe. Participants got to know each other through exercises. We crawled about the room or wandered "aimlessly" about, for example, then had to stand still and look at or touch each other. This all happened without taking any substances, and was essentially no different from other psychology training sessions.

Then it was time for the "hot seat". Samuel asked a question or addressed an issue personal to one of the participants. Then he invited one of us to sit in the hot seat. You had to talk to the group from this position. The aim of the exercise was to learn "to speak of-the-moment", remaining authentic and in touch with yourself. In the second part of the exercise, group members were allowed to ask questions and make comments, or we had a discussion about the sequence we had just heard for feedback purposes.

I wasn't used to talking about and from myself. When it came to my turn, I talked about my unsatisfactory work situation. "You aren't doing a good job", commented Samuel shortly. I broke out in a sweat and felt dizzy. Within the space of a few seconds, I was confronted with the fact that Samuel had put my actual feeling and self-judgement out there in the room; that he sensed my uncertainty and that I didn't know myself at all. My instincts were activated in seconds – to somehow extricate my way out of this unpleasant situation, justify myself and preserve my self-image and my massive resistance to dealing with myself. But I couldn't get another word out. Samuel was a man of few words; he didn't over-talk things. I remained on the seat in my distracted state for a while and was then allowed to go back to my own seat. This was the first decisive moment on my painful path to self-awareness.

Briefings followed the hot seat session. This was all about core and core feelings. We learned about suppressed and suppressive feelings and the adaptive layer. Core feeling includes the characteristics of love. Core feelings are "pushed back" by conditioning and upbringing, and suppressed feelings emerge such as fear of abandonment, being rejected or feeling unloved. These feelings are extremely unpleasant, so they are pushed away by suppressing feelings – envy, jealousy and hatred, but also enthusiasm, diligence and other emotional states. In most cases, however, educators do not tolerate envy, jealousy and hatred, so the child develops an "adaptive layer", where all feelings are suppressed for the sake of survival. This adaptive behaviour can cause internalised psychosomatic disorders, externalised violence towards others or a lust for power.

We were told about the substance we were going to be taking the following day – its characteristics and peculiarities, normal dosage and associated effects. Part of our homework was to find out about it beforehand. This wasn't so easy in the days before the Internet, and I spent a lot of time gathering information. We received instructions on how to behave in the coming session, and terms such as set (the client's mental "constitution") and setting (the environment for the session) were explained. General issues such as: "What does it mean to be in a relationship?", "What is personal responsibility?", "How do I handle power?" and many more were addressed – always from the perspective of therapy using psychoactive substances.

Samuel's view of people and their "symptoms" differed from that of my deep psychology trainers. I began to look closely at the way he listened, trying to identify how he reached his conclusions. His direct questions always came from a highly accurate observation and a description of that observation. When he spoke, he spoke from within – even when discussing highly unpleasant issues. He was very direct in everything he said, and I was scared on most of the occasions that he spoke to me. Even though I wasn't exactly comfortable with it, his statements nearly always hit the nail on the head, so I learned a lot about authenticity in human encounters from this approach, adopting it myself.

The Friday session ended at 10 pm. We came together again on Saturday morning. Everybody was in his or her seat punctually by 9 am. We received the substance and we all took it together with a celebratory attitude. We remained seated for the next few hours. This "seated setting" was difficult for me. I had to fight against dizziness, nausea and fatigue. Anyone who couldn't maintain the seated posture was allowed to lie down on the rubber mat in front of them. Most of the time, we weren't given permission to lie down until the end of the session – the "descent" phase. I am now aware of the value of being seated; it required constant attention and centring. Whether you are able to stay seated and how you do so also gives a clear indication of your state of balance. I was always one of the ones who felt sick and went down on the floor first. My state could be described in a few words: uncentred, unbalanced and resistant to surrendering and opening up! I had such a huge longing to be able to open up and explore myself! I often felt completely despairing.

Participants didn't say anything or move, if at all possible. Samuel played a piece of music from time to time. I sensed that the music always came "at the right moment" – if things weren't working, it helped me to stay on the path towards opening up. To begin with, Samuel guided us with occasional instructions during the ascent – for the first one or two hours: "let it all go" and "be with what is". He also spoke of peace and the essence of love.

I was constantly lost in my thoughts. I was stuck in them; I would see a problem from my everyday life and get stuck with my search for a practical solution. I only noticed this at all after a while. Again, I tried to be with what is, but then lose myself as I pursued my next thought, and so it went on. It was clear to me that I was only looking within a superficial level of myself. I almost despaired at not being able to follow the instructions. It was only later that I realised that what I had experienced there was my battle with my outer layers. I had acquired a direct insight into the confusion in my head, my thoughts and my inability to stay with my thoughts and keep observing them.

Then I usually felt a little unwell. I would have preferred to lie down on the mat. Samuel noticed my disquiet and simply called it my resistance without actually entering into a dialogue with me. He was right. In later sessions, when I was able to make the transition from abdomen to rib cage and then heart chamber, it became clear to me that you feel nauseous if you do not give yourself up to the substance, the love or the feeling that wants to emerge. I was also resisting opening up – out of fear. "The number one guardian is fear", Samuel had said, with a nod to Castaneda. I tried to tell myself: "OK, you're frightened" – it didn't help.

I talked to myself again. Nothing happened. Again, Samuel said: "be with what is." I tried – I really tried to be with my fear. I wasn't afraid – I was all fear. And I became very sad. I was very familiar with these feelings from my childhood. That was how it had been; I could feel it very keenly and allowed myself to slide into this combination of fear and sadness. Then suddenly, I wasn't able to offer any more resistance, something collapsed within me and I gave up. There was a jolt to my heart at that very moment – so hard that I thought it might burst into pieces. The fear was gone; I was flooded with affirmation and a feeling of vastness and assent. Things should be as I had just experienced them.

Samuel said that we were now at the peak. I wasn't able to identify this place until later sessions, either. I can still clearly remember the phrase that Samuel came out with at the peak of the very first session: "If you do not live what you experience, it will turn against you." In that moment, I knew that these words would become crucial for me – and I also knew that I had to take this thorny path, whatever the cost. I was certain that I was on the right path at last.

There was a short break after about three hours. Nobody said anything so as not to drift off into a loud, superficial "exterior". We then continued on our journey. Sometimes there was an exercise, usually the one that we'd done on Friday evening. But I could clearly tell the difference compared to Friday evening in the shape of my heightened sensitivity to what was happening in the room and within myself. I was always afraid of really having to look at someone. Under the influence of MDMA, I managed to look someone in the eye or touch them briefly, but only when the substance took its full effect; after that, something put up resistance in me again.

Samuel sometimes addressed something that appeared in the room. "Friederike, what is keeping you from staying still?" Or he talked about the phenomena emerging in a session – fear, defiance, resistance. It kept going into the stillness again – or the inner chaos that we were meant to be looking at. I gradually understood that I was really only looking within myself and that I was confronted with my own state of consciousness. In nearly all of the sessions, I almost despaired at my inner confusion, my dark side and my sadness that seemed as though it would never end. I felt that I didn't understand anything but wanted to grasp everything. On one occasion (this was against the rules) I went over to Samuel, pummelled his chest with my fists and demanded him to finally tell me what was wrong with me.

"Everything is within you and you know it all", he responded, sending me back to my seat.

I understand now that I was surrounded by the atmosphere of my early childhood, but at that juncture I didn't understand anything and I felt really hopeless and over-extended. I wanted to understand everything but almost despaired at myself although I was working very hard. I wasn't able to identify this meta level until years later. I had the impression that my ways of thinking and seeing things were changing, thinking that I had already made progress in my cognitive process. I had no idea that I was only at the very start of a long process of development and change.

We worked with MDMA, LSD, psilocybin, 2CB, mescaline and combinations of these substances. It spanned 12 training weekends. As a beginner, it was often hard for me to follow the theoretical aspects of Samuel's talks. I was unable to identify the substance we had taken, nor could I feel the specific effect of the individual substance that he had just described. This meant that I spent most of the beginning of the session trying to control the chaos in my head. But I can still, to this day, remember countless insights and phrases expressed by Samuel. So I will now talk about some of the experiences I had in the training sessions.

First training weekend: MDMA, with 50 micrograms of LSD

... Samuel says that feelings come from below, the sexual ones first. Nothing happens with me. It stays black. I wait. The bleating nanny-goat in my head announces: "There's nothing in you, you feel nothing ..."

Samuel speaks of acceptance. I would like to accept that I am empty and black inside. My inner voice says: "This acceptance is your inability to fight to the end and make a decision. You don't accept, you are resigned."

I have always resigned myself to everything that has come along. I now ask myself and the inner nanny-goat: "Will it be the same here on the chair, too? Do I now have to resign myself to it? What is acceptance then?" I can't answer my question and my voice doesn't come back. I give up. I remain seated: "So I'll just sit here on the chair in the dark for eight hours. OK, and now you can shut your mouth."

I gradually begin to notice that I am the one who is rampaging around in a circular tub. I can see myself: I hate, trample, hit, bite, everything is red and black. I am able to go in and out of the feeling and look at myself. I hate what I am doing now, always doing and saying things I don't mean at all. I feel an old hatred; it is deep down, like the Devil's rage. I see the members of my family. There is my unbridled rage at not being understood and not being able to make myself understood. More and more of the hatred keeps rising up within me. I am hatred. All at once, I am glad that it's like this. Grateful to my hatred – for the fact that it shows itself.

The break is over. Church music. I feel sick. The music turns into icing sugar. Piece by piece. It is endless – it won't stop. Boys without a bass, lifeless vibrato. I sit and sit, waiting for it to stop. I realise an awful thing: my life is like this – I sit and wait for something to stop, but actually miss the start of anything. So this is what I have to chase after it's finally over.

An image stays with me: I see myself as and feel like a coin slowly rolling along on its edge. We are finally allowed to lie down. I will encounter the coin and its symbolic value again and again in later years.

Second training weekend: MDMA

After the exercise on Friday evening, it is clear to me that it is ultimately always my own decision whether I choose to go or stay, accept or not accept or become a victim. I am often unaware of this. Even not deciding is a decision in itself. Samuel says that whatever happens is the right thing. This calms my fears a little.

Helplessness surrounds me right and left like a coldness. I am isolated by coldness. A phrase comes to mind: you don't need a father anymore. They are all dead, anyway. Nearly all of my male acquaintances come to mind at the same time. I bid them goodbye without emotion.

Samuel talks of contractions that have just finished. I don't feel this. He says that we are on the plateau now. I am still not able to see this.

I can feel my heart: a rectangular wooden door opens, with a bright light behind it. It takes a while for me to notice that I am holding a dialogue with God. He is speaking as if from within me and from outside at the same time: "I am the power – you are the power, I am in you, you are in me." This repeats a couple of times. I am now sitting quite still. The parable of the Vine and the Branches comes to mind: "I am the vine; you are the branches. If you remain in me and I in you, you will bear much fruit; apart from me you can do nothing."

An image has remained: one large and three small pieces of my heart have broken away and are lying on the ground. Over the next few weeks I remembered the many church services that I had heard in my role as organist, and many Bible texts come back into my mind, which I can now understand at a different level. This reconnection with a part of my youth does me good, making me a little grateful that I was able to spend my time in that way. It is not until years later that I re-encounter the broken pieces of my heart and am able to understand what the image is saying.

Third training weekend: MDMA and 2CB

Samuel says: you will be able to identify the structure of resistance. You will notice that which expresses itself in you psychosomatically.

I experience a feeling of banality that I cannot describe in words but which I have experienced over and over again in everyday life. I realise that it can only be about me staying with myself. Everything unrelated to me, that isn't "me", immediately makes me feel sick and ready to throw up. This banality is my life. If I fail to access the core and just live in and carry out my allotted role, everything will remain banal. I'll wait out the banality and take the smart approach.

I feel sick. I would like this feeling of nausea to be a factor for me in insignificant moments, causing me to separate myself off. I wasn't able to identify either the structure of the resistance or any psychosomatic elements in this material at that point in time or during the sessions, even though I wrote these exact sentences in the case notes.

Fourth weekend: MDMA and LSD

Friday evening is all about power and will.

Then we worked in pairs during the plateau phase on Saturday. I would have liked my counterpart to let out their aggression – as a kind of exercise for me. What did come was related and familiar to me: a shadow looking like an angel now and then. (A friendly figure looking at me but I couldn't touch it.)

Unable to be clearly conscious of it, I had located the phenomenon of projection in my counterpart. When I took ayahuasca many years later, it also became clear to me why I had made a point of choosing it.

We worked with the "talking stick" ritual that weekend. Only the person with the stick in their hand was allowed to talk, giving them the power in the room. Samuel instructed us to endure any feelings emerging in the group discussion and stay with them at all times.

There was a debate about power between Samuel and one of the participants: I observed myself while this was going on: if I can manage to just look and listen for a moment, I can understand both sides.

Fifth weekend: the moment of death

During the breathing exercise prior to the session, I encounter a sense of despair, the scale of which was to preoccupy me for many more years: I would like to meet my father again, see him again and touch him. I write: "40 years unconscious is a long time."

This weekend is to be all about the moment of death. ... I understand why I remain totally cool in unbearable situations, cut off from all feelings. (At the time, I wasn't aware that this was all about dissociation-related phenomena following severe trauma.) Anybody mad with pain has to hold his or her intellect together. Like a gift, I get the sudden feeling of being able to accept the separation (from my father) in retrospect. I surrender. Only now do I think about the issue: it's about dying.

Whatever comes to mind: I detect my intention of reaching the truth and dancing in front of the door (of isolation) there. I am amazingly clever. Every meaning is cancelled out by the meaning of the next realisation; even the realisation of meaninglessness is still a trick, an attempt to avoid death. All is intention and power within me. I make an attempt to simply lie down, stop breathing and die. It doesn't work – I still have some kind of intention. Countless qualities of feeling and attitudes to life– from the holy Friederike right up to Oberschwein (Super-Pig) – they are merely attempts to run away. If only I could be pious ... Nothing dies.

I look over at Konrad. He is lying on his back with his eyes closed and his hands folded. I now sit by him. He is now a corpse, and I can't touch him. But he can't just die! I know how widows feel. The pain rips into me – I have to leave him, let him go, leave him behind, all alone. The candles in the pillars at his head are not burning. Suddenly, I am able to release him as if from myself. I affirm this. He moves his hands at that moment. We look each other in the eyes, crying and laughing.

In the group discussion, Samuel tells me that it's my problem that I am already dead and feel at home with the dead.

I turn to water and dissolve during the integration phase. I will also re-experience this moment of dying again over the next few years, acquiring an ever deeper understanding of it. (Worth reading in this context: Samuel Widmer: On the Moment of Dying in our System).

Sixth training weekend: the moment of birth

Samuel says something about the "medication", talks about the stations we have been through and about order at the various levels. Examining my conscience with regard to the order in the chakras – taking stock of the moment – shames me. I still haven't got anywhere. I start to feel a little queasy just when Samuel is saying that some people will still be dealing with psychosomatic phenomena under the effect of the medication.

After taking the medication, I begin to understand what Samuel might mean by order in the lowest chakra, and feel my pelvis open up at this. Still lying down, I can let something like an appetite for power go. Something flows into my chest area.

I start coughing and wheezing. I try to go through memories and feelings connected to coughing. I go to V. and Samuel. V. asks me about whooping cough. Yes, but that's not it. It's painful, terrible and funny– nothing is right. It becomes clear to me very slowly: I'm coughing for my life. A wafer-thin layer lies between me and the air, sticking to me firmly. I have no more feelings or thoughts inside me. I am the coughing and the breathlessness.

Now back in my seat, Samuel comes to me. He takes my head in his hands and moves it back. A huge pair of scissors and blood appear before me. I am flooded by a feeling of gratitude I have never felt before: "Thank God"; a second of knowing for certain that I am in the hands of the right doctor allows me to surrender myself. I am being born and can finally give a cry. I have never taken a breath so consciously before.

When I asked my mother later on, I found out that I was born with the amniotic sac and foetal membranes – the "caul", as it is referred to – over my face. I had the near-death experience connected with this birth episode years later in the Amazon.

Further experiences with Samuel Widmer

Each training weekend had its own theme and learning content. Although I don't have any written documents left about the 500 microgram session, for which we all had our own escort, I still have a clear memory of the experience. I passed the point of madness in that session:

Thoughts are racing through my head. I can't hang on to any of them – nothing stays put. Images of tin and plastic objects, wrecked cars, dolls' arms and grimaces in space roar past me. I feel like death warmed up, everything is highly unpleasant and I would like to get away from the experience. I start to struggle against the flow of images and thoughts, trying everything I can to create order. I pray, promising to behave properly. The images become quicker and more intense, my thoughts intertwining into a sticky mass of thoughts. The more I want to create order, the stickier it becomes in my head. I become one with the mass, the thoughts flowing together into a brown mud. I struggle, defend myself, get annoyed and then become full of rage. My will has left me. On the outside, I am totally submissive and quiet, but there is a battle raging inside me. I am overcome by panic. I'm going mad and I don't want to. I fight the madness. Now it becomes a fight against every-thing. Who has the power here? I want, I want. I want out of here. I want order. I want it to stop. I ...

I flag at some point – I just can't do it. I cry. I give up. Then I go mad. I have done it to myself, I wanted to know what it's like. Yes, I'm going mad. Yes. – Right at that moment, the thoughts and images cease. I enter a completely empty space – tranquillity, emptiness – and there is nothing there. I open my eyes and see my colleagues. I have the impression of being completely level-headed, as if I hadn't taken anything. I am just there. Time and space are one. No past, no future, only present. I have arrived. Thy Will be done, not mine.

I experienced both of these points again 20 years later when I was on remand. The experience with Samuel Widmer protected me from going mad or giving up.

I felt constantly confronted by my hidden feelings and thoughts. I saw that I had developed a false personality. I was ashamed almost every moment of the day, I saw through all my tricks of self-deception and oth-ers' deception of me. I didn't know who I was and I didn't know how to conduct a relationship, or even what a relationship actually was. I only knew one thing: I wanted to discover who I really was and how I func-tion, and I suspected that there was something important behind my madness.

So I stuck with it, even though I sometimes had to force myself to go to the weekend sessions. The Saturday session generally ended at around 8 pm. Then there was something to eat and we all said goodnight at around 10 pm. We then mostly went off to our hotel and talked about the insights we'd had. We were back in our seats again by 9 am the next morning when the sharing started. Anybody who wanted to would talk about their session – Samuel added comments or explanations, and you could also ask questions. The weekend finished at around 1 pm. Each participant had to send their notes to the other participants – meaning that we had to write our own notes and read 49 other sets by the next meeting.

The training with Samuel Widmer was a lot more comprehensive than I describe here. I have been able to draw on the content of the training again and again – whether in terms of self-exploration or group leadership. The wisdom that Samuel Widmer imparted put me on the path to my own self. With hindsight, I am often unable to distinguish whether I had learned something from him or discovered it for myself. It is not an important distinction; I sometimes came to the same or similar conclusions as he did. Our ways parted after the training: he subsequently went down the path of Tantra – for which he ultimately acquired the reputation for being a "sex guru". I went on my own path, but he laid the foundations of the principles of psycholytic psychotherapy. I went on to adapt the setting in my own way, but the basic idea behind it is the same: quiet observation and self-awareness through staying with everything that manifests itself. I learned from him to stand by what I do. This is at once the consequence and the condition of the work.

The training lasted from August 1992 to the autumn of 1995, ending with a week of intensive work, including Sufi–swirling and breathing. I didn't seek any further contact with Samuel after the training ended. Although there is no doubt that he offered a valuable training, his reputation became increasingly controversial and there was a period when it was awkward to be associated with him. While there are some aspects of his work that are not to my taste, I remain deeply grateful to him. I acquired the crucial knowledge and experience from him that motivated me to take the necessary steps towards finding myself and establishing my approach. The foundations had been laid, and I could now develop my own personal path.

CHAPTER 3

Developing the Setting - Towards My Model of Psycholytic Psychotherapy

I hadn't completed the Holotropic Breathwork and psycholytic therapy training with a view to using it professionally. I only started with the psychotherapy because I hoped I could help myself through it. I had looked for a means of finding out where my difficulties come from, and especially how I might start being and feeling happier again. I had grown up with the firm belief that I would have to train in some way in order to be capable of helping myself. Instead of buying milk at the shop, my then husband said that I would rear a cow and milk it myself in order to drink a glass of milk. In a certain sense, he was right.

After I passed my psychotherapy exam in 1992, I had a brief job as a doctor specialising in industrial medicine and psychotherapy at a health clinic in southern Germany. But the clinic was closed down and I had to look for another job three months later. I felt fortunate to be able to work as a psychotherapist in a private clinic and, without making a conscious decision about it, I gave up my career as a doctor for industrial medicine and doctor of medicine for good. I resigned from the clinic two years later and moved to Switzerland. I had no success there in obtaining a post as an industrial doctor or a psychotherapist. My training in Germany was not yet recognised in Switzerland at the time and, now at the age of 47, I balked at the idea of cramming for yet another State examination. With the help of a lawyer, I managed to obtain a special permit to open my own psychotherapy practice in Switzerland in 1997. I wasn't allowed to use my academic qualifications in conjunction with the title of psychotherapist. The Swiss Psychology Association wouldn't accept me because I was a medical doctor and the Medical Association wouldn't accept me because I was a psychotherapist. So I fell between two stools and ended up belonging nowhere.

First groups: meditators and explorers

Due to the sudden death of a facilitator, I was able to co-lead a Holotropic Breathwork workshop in the mid-1990s in Germany and I talked about my experiences with substances with some enthusiasm. This led to me being asked whether I could facilitate such an experience for some meditation students who were "stuck" on their meditation path. I was glad to oblige, and some of these meditators came to me again and again. After a brief introduction, I gave them a capsule of MDMA, had them lie down and played a gentle piece of music at a low volume now and then. I sat with them all the while, leaving everyone to their own process.

The meditation students were always highly disciplined. They talked to me a little about it when the effect of the substance had worn off. I hardly ever said anything about their experiences – I was there just to accompany them. Their teacher or master was their contact for their inner processes and realisations. As time passed, more people came to me wanting to try an experience with a substance, and we agreed a time together. All I did was to provide the substance at these meetings, accompanying them in silence. Group participants came on a Friday evening, the session was on the Saturday and everyone went home again on the Sunday morning.

I met a man at another Holotropic Breathwork weekend who asked whether he and a couple of friends could try "self-exploration with drugs" with me. I felt a slight hesitation but didn't pay any attention to it and said yes. So it was that three men came to see me in the late nineties. One of them particularly wanted to write a book. So I began to see myself more and more in relation to a small group and tried to give the encounters a certain structure. I also did a few exercises that I had learned with Samuel, attempting to create a similar atmosphere.

None of the group participants were a patient or client of mine. I didn't know their personal history, nor did I ask them about any problems in their everyday life: I was a "self-exploration facilitator" with the role of managing the setting – the music, the space and the substances. A number of the participants were far more advanced than me in therapy terms, and I was able to learn from them in the debriefings. They were competent, friendly and interested. We met as friends and had a good time together. Some of them eventually brought their partners with them, and the group expanded.

The sessions changed; I introduced sitting up, where I just worked with one person to start with, while the others stayed with their own process with their eyes closed. Because the issue was mostly about fathers and mothers, I also led sessions exploring some general issues for a short time. Then we tried a period of sitting up for a brief period, with everyone saying a little about where they were and how they felt. But this only interrupted the "introspection," and wasn't very helpful. We therefore extended the exchange periods, especially as a few of the participants had found that assistance in getting through a difficult patch could be helpful. I found that the better the clients' understanding of how to be with the substance, the more they began to appreciate the individual work and make use of it.

I personally always felt like an outsider during the initial sessions. I would try to communicate with the people when they opened up, but always felt that I said the wrong thing. I couldn't access them on their level. So I didn't feel like I was being any help, but only a hindrance to the process. I therefore made the decision to take a little of the substance myself. This was challenging to begin with, as I had to change the CDs, remain seated, talk and follow the process of each individual, feeling responsible for everything going well. But I found it easier to remain in balance with each new session. The most important thing was that I was reaching the people present at their level of experience. My perception of the on-going processes became more acute. Having familiarised myself with computers, I prepared the sequence of music beforehand by burning the music to a CD.

Extremely difficult issues came up in the group; thoughts of getting a divorce, disputes and drastic events. We sometimes felt as if we were pitching on the high seas in a little boat. I still wasn't the "therapist" yet. I was leading the sessions, but we were all more or less equals. I always expressed my opinion very clearly and quite undiplomatically, which could lead to problems years later. By today's standards, my level of self-awareness was only a tiny bit above that of the other members of the group. Just as it is almost impossible to imagine as a literate adult what it felt like when you could not yet read or write, I have hardly any sense now of how I worked back in the beginning. As with my medical and therapy work, I simply did what I could.

Mother Aya and the baking bread

As time passed, fewer and fewer meditation students came to me, and then they stopped altogether. The shape of the self-awareness group changed totally; it now consisted of my own selected clients. I knew them and their personal histories and problems with everyday life, and my role was as a therapist. They had been in traditional therapy with me before the substance-assisted therapy started, and stayed in therapy while the psycholytic therapy was going on. They hadn't travelled from afar just for "a workshop".

The evolution of the setting for my psycholytic therapy groups was closely linked to my own inner development process. My husband and I visited the Amazon region again and again from the year 2001, drinking ayahuasca when we were there. At the first session, I asked Mother Aya to show me my spiritual path. She only said one thing to me: "Bake your own bread." I didn't understand the message and asked the same question the following evening. Mother Aya seized me like a demon: "I told you: 'bake your own bread'." Then she ripped me from my body, showed it to me from the outside and said: "It is only the vessel. The essence is within. *That* is what you have to work with."

Mother Aya showed me separated-off parts of my personality, which I was able to re-appropriate for myself. In my inner eye, she showed me that each individual experience is stored in every cell, and I felt her healing me at a cellular level with pure energy. She had me look inside my brain and locate the well of forgetfulness. She threw me into deep pools, forcing me to open my eyes and look around. She taught me how to ask questions and wait for the answer. My husband was next to me and I was able to accompany him a little on his own path when he had the feeling he was dying. I learned to see what was happening within him – Mother Aya taught me how to look with my heart.

In particular, the instructions that I received via ayahuasca – but also experiences of other substances too – led me physically, emotionally, psychically and spiritually through experiences towards realisations that were gradually reflected in a change to my way of thinking, living and working. This is not the place to go into the individual details. However – I did start baking my own bread. It was when we returned from our first trip to the Amazon region that I first had the idea of using elements from the constellation work during sessions with MDMA. I put mother and daughter opposite each other. A sense of peace slowly entered a relationship that had been very difficult before. Mother and daughter agreed wholeheartedly about what had happened in the past. The other people present were moved and touched by the process and the inner embrace. A number of participants went through similar experiences merely through their respectful presence. Modified constellation work became an important tool in my psycholytic therapy work.

When we were in the right setting, we remained silent for a while after reaching the peak, with me talking here and there about issues that had emerged the evening before and sharing my own realisations. Then I opened up the discussion. Anyone could speak. When one person spoke, the others would remain seated in silence. Some people talked about realisations they had made: "I saw that everything comes from love." Another participant said: "I recognised the fact that I belittle my partner." I then asked how he did that exactly. People listened, made comments or elaborated on the issue, saying how they showed disdain for their own partners.

At some point during this phase, someone would announce: "I'd like to work." Everybody remained seated in the circle. We would then do constellation work around the issue; anyone in the group could be the protagonist. This enabled us to identify many life events and their complexity and eventually arrive at a satisfactory solution. We discovered hidden systemic connections that we would not have seen without the constellation work. We continued working with this method and our perceptions became more acute.

We not only initiated biographical and systemic processes with the "modified constellation work". We also – unintentionally – nurtured the ability to remain centred, guide our attention and simply observe inner processes without intervening. Over time, we learned to do this with the various substances and at higher dosages. We penetrated deeper and deeper through the layers of human existence and evolution. We began to perceive our perception. As if through a slow motion microscope, together we explored how the interpretation of the initial perception becomes the lens of our overall perception and we learned how our beliefs and subsequent behaviour evolve from this.

One participant wanted to explore a specific unpleasant feeling that kept recurring. I asked him to focus on the feeling and blot everything else out: where are you? What can you see? What do you perceive? How old are you? He looked around himself carefully and while he reflected on himself, I remained in contact with him. Everyone else just observed the process but was allowed to intervene if they felt that they could make a contribution or if the issue affected them.

The participant described what he saw, heard and perceived – and I used words to help him explore and describe what he perceived in even greater detail. I accompanied him into the same vibration and perception, observing my inner emotions. I managed to establish where he was at some point. It could be in a variety of different places: the womb, a certain dissociative state – it was never the same, and my role as witness always demanded all my attention. When we had found the location at which the unpleasant feeling could be perceived with its inner emotion, the aim was to find out what the feeling did to the person. What reactions had been produced during the original experience – both within the body and at the mental level? How was this expressed in any given situation today?

Bodywork sometimes evolved from the observation process, such as reconstructing the birth process. Essentially, bodywork came partly from the observation element of the modified constellation work and partly from Holotropic Breathwork. Situations and moments were re-adjusted and "acted out in a controlled way" in the bodywork to the point where the person accessed the desired or separated off feeling.

Bodywork and the ability to engage in processes at a deeper level evolved into a way of processing anxiety-laden and traumatic experiences. We called this "Live-Body-Work". With this work, which readily accesses the layers of psyche where the trauma is held, we break the link between the feeling and the event that triggered it, removing any dissociation. I termed this "applied neuro-psychotherapy".

Modified constellation work, Live-Body-Work, music and the group itself had a powerful influence on the setting in the final two or three years before my psycholytic therapy work came to its abrupt end. Alongside current therapy methods, they formed the basic structure for my substance-assisted psychotherapy in its mature form. It was noticeable that using these tools both deepened the process and sharpened the tools themselves, meaning that the potential of a substance could be mined to an even greater degree.

CHAPTER 4

Psychotherapy and Psycholytic Psychotherapy

This chapter looks at the individual before going into psychotherapy. The concept of "disorder" is discussed.

We consider the conditions that need to be fulfilled before taking the important step of starting psychotherapy.

We outline the concept of psychotherapy and its general role. We also address the concepts of "the unconscious", "developmental disorders", "trauma", "dissociation" and the incidence and consequences of all kinds of psychological disorder.

We discuss the issue of the extent to which the role of psychotherapy can be fulfilled through traditional methods.

An explanation is provided for how psycholytic therapy may work.

We describe the continuous nature of the therapeutic process and focus on the developing relationship between therapist and client on the one hand and the role of the therapist on the other.

The individual before starting therapy

Going into therapy is definitely not a straightforward matter. Just looking in the business directory or asking the family doctor, friends or colleagues to suggest a therapist is already a huge step. Worse still, hearing from partners or colleagues that they think you should see a psychotherapist could make an already unhappy individual feel that they might also be mad.

Actually sitting down with a therapist hopefully marks the beginning of the end of suffering. But the commencement of therapy often starts by intensifying the suffering, as the individual detects new and somewhat disturbing depths. At the outset of the "inner journey towards the self", the individual is also unaware of what the (happy) outcome might be. Anyone who even dares to embark on the "adventure of self-discovery" therefore already deserves a certain amount of respect.

What can have happened to make an individual look for a psycho-therapist, register with them, make an appointment and attend for the first time?

First of all, he or she will have realised that, in one of the many different areas of their life, their psychological condition has altered in a direction where something is not or no longer right. They have to identify this "unease" as such, then define it and give it a name. At first this is experienced as a "state of disturbance" and an "unpleasant" state of mind, which can no longer be ignored. Perhaps they are shunned by those around them, feel isolated or suffer from a sense of being avoided. Things just aren't going well and they know it; they try to puzzle it out and address it, searching for the answer in the external world. Perhaps they don't get on with the new boss or they can't deliver the desired performance at work anymore. They develop anxieties, they "can't do it any more" and their drive is greatly diminished. Perhaps they are unable to connect within their environment or become part of a relationship or community where they feel that they belong. Perhaps a relationship has failed yet again for the same old reason. Perhaps they even question the meaning of life.

They are deeply "alienated" from their essence, are no longer in touch with their inner self and have lost their sense of purpose and meaning. This is why everyone in the course of psychotherapy asks the question that is at the root of all things: "Who am I?"

"Disorder"

A disorder is obviously not an "entity in itself". Nearly all difficulties manifest themselves in relationship to others, arising between two or more individuals. Disputes, misunderstandings, grief – an infinite number of external concepts can be found to describe the status of such relationships. If an individual would like to feel well in themselves, "hang in there" – in a relationship, society or the workplace – if they want to feel that they are not excluded but want to be included, they must somehow be attentive to their disorder in order to be able to focus on and return to a "normal state of being" or even achieve it for the first time.

What defines a disorder is mainly associated with the family and their culture. What does the family define as a disorder? What points of reference does the family use?

Regardless of any specific circumstances, every family has its own way of going about things. Ideally, any child within a family is surrounded by trustworthy individuals, usually the mother and father, who give them guidance and support in various physical, mental and spiritual realms of life. Through guidance, rules and polar responses such as praise and chastisement, attentiveness and avoidance, the child has to learn how to behave correctly in all relationships within the society into which they were born, so that they may continue to belong. If this happens using the tools of practical everyday life, namely clarity and precision, the child will mature into an individual who is capable of a relationship, love and a role in society that gives meaning to their life.

The conditions that need to be fulfilled before starting psychotherapy

It is important that somatic reasons for the state of psychological distress are excluded beforehand.

The "individual in distress" must develop his own desire and set himself the goal of feeling well in himself again, of achieving harmonious relationships, or of feeling like a valuable individual in the workplace again. Put succinctly, it is all about "belonging again" in every relationship. **Ideally, suffering should be a stimulus towards an intention to change.** This would be the best motivation for seeking a therapist. The individual would need to formulate their intention to change as a key goal and be able to trust that the therapist will provide the necessary expert help and support. Depending on the context, this step makes him a client or a patient. The trustworthy individual is a "professional" and then a therapist. This also requires the appropriate response from the therapist – that of engaging with the client, taking their words seriously and supporting the client in accordance with their own professional expertise.

The task at hand consists of achieving the goal, and the therapist assesses whether they can complete that task. The goal is re-assessed as work goes on with the client and has to be altered under certain circumstances: we then find ourselves in a "therapeutic alliance".

Before psychotherapy can begin, the client must therefore acknowledge: "Things aren't going very well, I need help."

The general aim of psychotherapy is to effect change in a client's life. Their suffering as a result of traumatic events and/or their difficulties in personality development will determine the direction of such change. A major aim of psychotherapy is to process all types of disorder – neuroses, wounds, resentments, painful experiences, traumatic events and their consequences, post-traumatic stress disorder and the reintegration of dissociated aspects of personality. In terms of classic psychotherapy, this means

confronting the unconscious and its inner contents. The aim is to clarify the causes of the current state of suffering so that it can be resolved. This in turn leads to new ways of behaving and relating so that the individual becomes more "functional" with improved capacity for loving and working.

The unconscious mind

We know that we only use a fraction of our conscious mind and that much of our psychic material is located in the unconscious. Our perception of the world and our interpretation of this perception, which is the basis of all of our actions, is generated from and shaped by the unconscious. The term "unconscious" means that the material that produces these interpretations is not accessible to the conscious mind in the form of memories or explanations. Very early influences and core experiences, especially from the time in the mother's womb and the process of birth are "stored" in the unconscious. Due to the immaturity of the nervous system, they do not become interlinked via the neurones – or only to a very limited degree. However they are "stored" in the unconscious at both body (cell) level and in the brain, forming coherent traces of experience. These traces persist and manifest themselves in later life as reflex patterns that are triggered by stressors with a similarly threatening emotional resonance. This repetitive pattern where very early trauma is resurrected by stress continues to affect our lives, without us being aware of it.

In this respect, I suggest that the unconscious can be likened to the body's pair of "spectacles", a lens through which we perceive. Whatever we perceive initially represents the world; but the stored residue of early traumatic experiences continues to model and define our perceptions. The focal power and colouring of our spectacles determines how we interpret what we see, constantly recreating the world about us based on that early conditioning. But we do not notice that we are wearing these spectacles. At worst we remain in an uncomfortable state, where we are unable to adopt an external perspective of our disordered function. This causes us significant problems as we formulate our reactions and behaviour from this state. Some people have likened this condition to being a person with one arm who cannot know what it is like to have two arms.

In time the unconscious but ingrained elements of this behaviour start to become identifiable from the external viewpoint of the therapist through close observation and can be formulated as a working hypothesis. Personality disorders do not allow the person to obtain their own external view. With less severe disorders such as neurotic disorders it is possible for the client to be aware of the presence of their own pair of spectacles and generate their own external view.

I subscribe to the view that the cause of nearly all psychological disorders can be traced back to these early imprints. They occur because the organism is unable to down-regulate its reactions to the severe impact of stress via its own organisational systems. As a result of this dysregulation, the organism remains in a state of elevated arousal which has a crucial impact on psychological development and probably leads to developmental or attachment disorders. These patterns are laid down as an internal template that continues to influence emotions and behaviour, so that they are experienced and played out over and over again. I will go into this in detail in a later chapter.

Trauma and dissociation

In the course of a severe traumatising experience, the neural signals that we experience as sight, sound, smell and touch are not stored as "coherent traces of experience" or memory. These memory fragments become separated from each other – dissociated. The level of this separation depends on the gravity of the trauma, but when the trauma is experienced as severe and terrifying, the degree of dissociation is significant. Generally speaking, part of the experience is incorporated within the sensible and functioning ego part of the psyche, which serves to shape everyday life. This allows a child to develop and mature following traumatising experiences and often function "normally" in adult life. The person identifies with this ego part.

But alongside this there is still the dissociated part of the memory trace, carrying the physical reactions, the emotions and the psychic residue of the trauma within it. If this dissociated element is not acknowledged consciously **and** incorporated, it will remain practically unchanged throughout life. The residue of this memory trace forces itself into the waking consciousness again and again, especially when it is triggered by something in everyday life that acts as a reminder of the original trauma in some way. The conscious ego part instinctively tries to suppress the unbidden but forceful memory – feelings that might be connected with fear, numbness or rage. Often this unconsciously stored material "disguises" itself, manifesting itself as panic attacks. Unconsciously, the person learns to avoid trigger situations that would otherwise make the emotions reappear just as if the traumatising event was happening again. Many strategies are developed, which can range from alcohol consumption to Zen meditation. The most common avoidance strategy is some form of addiction.

Does traditional psychotherapy really work?

Truly effective and sustained changes in feelings, mood and behaviour can only really be achieved if the unconscious, pre-conscious (psychic material that can be remembered again through questioning and association) and conscious psyche can be drawn carefully into consciousness and processed in such a way that changes become externalised in the everyday world. In simple terms, the client must first take notice of what he thinks and feels, how he behaves and the manner in which he affects his environment. He must first be aware that there is an aspect of his way of being in the world that is not working well or that harms him and his relationships in the same way over and over again. Sometimes the key task is to learn a new way of being watchful.

If the client is able to develop this watchfulness, he will be able to see and recognise his own actions and behaviour and how he has shaped his life through this formative psychic substance of the unconscious. If he starts to become aware of this, and if an understanding has been arrived at, he can begin to develop and try out different reactions and behaviour independently. In the widest sense, Jung named this process of gaining conscious awareness "individuation". This involves growing up, recognising the dark side of our psyche and uncovering our projections. It involves developing the capacity to make our own decisions in everyday life and take responsibility for them.

Expanding consciousness to fulfil the therapeutic task

The therapeutic task of helping the client to face the unconscious always took me to my limits as a psychotherapist using traditional methods. I did not seem able to uncover the real depths of the unconscious when working with my clients, I only ever gained access to what seemed to me to be superficial material from their personal history, which I then interpreted. This did indeed lead to the clients achieving cognitive insights and certainly being in touch with their emotions, but they never achieved the deep changes that I was hoping for and that seemed necessary to me. During supervision sessions we often talked about the issue of resistance. The professional jargon describes "obstacles to the progress of the therapy" as resistance.

With increasing experience, I stopped working against this resistance and tried to harness it to the therapeutic task. I gradually learned to interpret resistance in all its manifestations as a wonderful achievement of the organism, which pursues the aim of maintaining life and enabling the individual to flourish despite unfavourable circumstances. During my additional systemic training, the concept of resistance was "eliminated" in this traditional sense, and the individual was seen as his own best "expert adviser". All behaviour was allowed to be the absolutely correct and "right" reaction to an individual situation, even if the same behaviour had harmful effects in later life. Behaviour often reflects the symptom, which I will discuss elsewhere.

It then became necessary to recognise the usefulness of this "right" behaviour (now a symptom or disruptive factor) "at that time" in order to discover the formative event behind it and then work through and resolve it.

During the course of my daily work and my increasingly critical appraisal of traditional psychotherapy, it became clear to me that the solution to the conflicts and traumas stored in the unconscious was never going to be found through mere conversation and the retelling of events. We know from research on neuropsychotherapy that unconscious processes take place in the subcortical areas of the brain such as the amygdala. And we know that subcortical processes cannot be brought into consciousness. According to research on psychotherapy, this is impossible because they are not available in a form that can be verbalised. My findings do not concur with the research on this point. I have found that subcortical processes can in fact be brought into the conscious mind with the help of psychoactive substances and rendered into a linguistic form by the self-reflecting ego, the current adult ego and thereby enter our everyday consciousness. The same applies to "infantile amnesia" as postulated by Gabrielle Roth. Everything can ultimately be remembered, especially if it is of any relevance to the person affected.

At that time, I felt compelled to access this deep layer of the psyche in some way or another to explore it. I did not do this just for myself, but for my clients too. Based on my experiences with Holotropic Breathwork and my first sessions with psychoactive substances, the route of expanding consciousness seemed to me to be the only viable way forward.

When I began my process of self-examination in 1989, today's trauma therapies were not yet "on the market". Ego state therapy of Watkins and Watkins, Dr Peter A. Levine's research on trauma, the findings of Dr R. S. Nijenhuis on structural dissociation and the polyvagal theory of Prof. Stephen W. Porges were still only at the development stage and neither known nor accessible to the public. I came across the first book in German written by Peter Levine by accident in 2005 – to my delight, the findings were aligned with what my clients and I had seen in our sessions; trauma is stored in the body, hindering further development.

Concepts such as epigenetics and trans-generational trauma were not yet in circulation. The authors of the war and post-war generation, Sabine

Bode and Hartmut Radebold had not yet given public expression to the significance of this period of collective trauma. Trauma-related body therapy methods such as Eye Movement Desensitisation and Reprocessing (EMDR) and Tension and Trauma Releasing Exercises (TRE) were not part of everyday therapeutic methods. Back then, the prenatal psychology of Ludwig Janus was even side-lined as being esoteric. When I heard Professor Janus talking in the early 90s about a man who had lived and relived his mother's attempt to abort him, I could not believe such memories to be possible.

Wide-ranging research in these fields has recently produced amazing results, offering new opportunities for accessing unconscious psychic material about and especially via the human body. Back in the early days of my own therapeutic work, people still laughed at me when I talked about body memory. People in highly conservative and uninformed circles also still assume today that there is some kind of sexual abuse behind the use of body work in psychotherapy.

And we cannot forget that the Internet was in its infancy and it was not an easy matter to keep up with the latest information. To access information on psychedelic therapy, I had to travel to conferences, buy books and seek out contacts. This was taxing, costly and time-consuming, and I always felt that I was trailing behind the cutting edge of knowledge.

Consciousness expanding methods were serving more and more as a key to researching my own psychological processes and lighting the darkness of my overshadowed childhood, leading me to the repressed wartime and post-war patterns through which I made my life grey and cheerless. The fact that you could employ psychoactive substances was a sensational discovery for me – yes, I can look back now and say that they were life-saving factors for me. My two-year older and seven-year younger sisters are both severely depressive. The older one has been retired since her 40th year and the younger one can no longer practise her original profession due to depression.

Now as then, the use of a psychoactive substance to expand consciousness seems to me to be **one** possible effective therapeutic tool. It incorporates a process requiring both sides – client and therapist– to engage with all of the consequences. For me, expanding consciousness in this way with the possibility of gaining insights from the deep psyche was the ideal route, and one that became available with the help of psychoactive substances.

How does psycholytic therapy work?

One search engine takes us to the following definition: "**Psycholytic psychotherapy** is a psychotherapeutic treatment method in which the consciousness-altering qualities of psychotropic substances are used to support therapy. This is where cerebro-physiological processes relax the psychic defences, allowing better access to suppressed feelings and hidden capacities."

Another search engine gives the following result: "Psycholytic therapy is not seen as a stand-alone therapeutic method, but as an aid to deep, psychology-based psychotherapy, as for psychoanalysis. It is designed for patients resistant to therapy, whose resistance could not be overcome by traditional procedures. The diagnostic target groups are neuroses, personality disorders and psychosomatic complaints."

Psycholytic therapy is not therapy under or with substances. The substance is merely the key to the realm of the unconscious. The effects of various substances enable the client to gain access to his unconscious psychic material, suppressed feelings and much more. The task of psychotherapy can be accelerated by this method. However, due to the specific way in which the substances take effect, no strict comparison can be made between the two therapeutic methods.

There is neither "therapy" nor "psycholytic therapy" as such. Each evades any objective definition or attribution such as "This is how it is" or "This is how it is done". Each form obviously has its tasks and goals, each relates to two individuals described as therapist and client or therapist and patient. Both therapeutic routes show similarities, both require rules, both processes have a beginning, middle and end. Each route is based on a therapeutic concept, and maybe even a philosophy of life, too. Each of these two therapeutic directions has their own intrinsic characteristics, but we are still merely describing operational concepts. Whenever I write about traditional or psycholytic therapy, I primarily reveal something about myself by using specific terms. Strictly speaking, with regard to questions such as how a substance works, how it provides insight into the unconscious and much more besides, my answer tells the reader nothing about the substances but about how *I* experienced them, and how I experienced the "therapy" *myself*. The reader can also learn from me how other people with similar thoughts and experience to mine describe and rate psycholytic therapy. But ultimately I can only talk about myself here. My experiences and I are identical. Only I appear in my observations and experiences. This means that nobody else can observe the same thing as I do. These comments represent perceptual phenomena that are easily lost in the act of description.

Psycholytic therapy has a different effect on each individual: for one individual, it may be a release from the inner prison of a traumatising life situation. MDMA is currently used in clinical trials to treat post-traumatic stress disorders in many countries – and is once again being declared as a very suitable treatment. With MDMA, some people feel that they have come back to their own bodies again for the first time. For another individual, psycholytic therapy becomes a way towards understanding their own self within their burdensome life history, and for yet another it is a way towards self-knowledge, leading them into more spiritual territory.

Like traditional psychotherapy, psycholytic therapy brings about what the individual is ready for. The process may seem mysterious and meandering but the thrust of psycholytic therapy tends to lead to a spiritual path. If you were to put psycholytic therapy into a psychological category, you would put it close to humanistic and transpersonal therapy. Any therapy, including psycholytic, occurs and exists in a context. It evolves through action with the aid of general and specific tools. It has its own course and contents and its own consequences and effects on the system. It can be practised in very different ways. The wide framework of "therapy" remains, but each individual form has its own intra-individual substance.

When psycholytic therapy begins, it is structured differently from the start of traditional therapy. As long as psychoactive substances remain illegal, anyone embarking on this venture has to confront the issue of "illegality" first. This can be seen as a benefit or a disadvantage. If the motivation is geared towards therapy and a desire to engage oneself and not towards hedonism, curiosity or voyeurism, illegality can even be seen as an advantage. The willingness to dare to do something unusual to resolve one's own suffering or to achieve self-knowledge suggests determination and commitment. Someone really wants to know, is desperate and has already tried many different things. Psycholytic therapy is often exactly that – a final attempt to access unconscious psychic material in order to put an end to the suffering that dominates a person's life.

Conducting psycholytic therapy, especially illegal therapy, requires a setting that goes beyond a regular hour of therapy. Taking a psychoactive substance requires preparation. Sufficient time needs to be allowed for the session itself and the programme for follow-up work also needs to be agreed. This is why my therapy took place at the weekend. The location needs to be suitable for the intrapsychic process. The entire external framework is ultimately designed around the consequences of taking a psychoactive substance. Sessions are not as frequent as for traditional therapy, but the intensity of the individual sessions is far greater.

The action of such substances can have far-reaching consequences for the individual. The ability to be "on a substance", and learn to observe the inner self under its effect in a composed, centred and disciplined way, increases with practice. This means that the client takes responsibility for what happens. If the use of the substance is successful (see "From beginner to university graduate") the experiences gradually change with the increasing capacity for introspection. Cognitive processes grow deeper and intrinsically more coherent. If insights occur repeatedly with persuasive power, they evolve into everyday knowledge. The process follows a course that runs from a dawning comprehension of biographical events to a deeper self-understanding, and later on perhaps to a more profound understanding of the world. I find that this is reflected by increased authenticity, reinforced self-belief and greater emotional stability. I have found that the deeper the understanding and the higher the degree of integration – the more distinct the change in personality traits. Similar changes are also observed within the framework of traditional therapies; but it is my experience that changes effected through psycholytic therapy are more marked and sustained.

The openness facilitated by the anxiolytic effect of the substances changes relationships. First of all, this affects relations in the therapeutic context itself; the relationship between client and therapist takes on a different colouring. I will come back to this subject later. Interactions between group members become anxiety-free and authentic. Later on, this openness and the capacity for closeness are naturally transferred to the "life outside", so that the individual who has undergone psycholytic psychotherapy becomes more able to generate and sustain rich and fulfilling relationships and co-exist harmoniously with their fellow humans.

In my opinion, the most important components of psycholytic therapy are still the numinous or mystical experiences that can occur at any time through the effect of a psychoactive substance. I consider these high impact experiences to be the key drivers of change in psycholytic therapy. I will reflect on this later.

Expanding my therapeutic viewpoint

My original training was in depth psychology, and my concept of therapy stems from that. But it has condensed and transformed in tandem with my inner development and my perspective has widened considerably. I have added other therapeutic concepts over time, and I am now at home in various "therapy languages". I might have learned the vocabulary of a foreign language at school, but thanks to my residence in the United States for several years, I have moved beyond "speaking English" to English as a second language. In a comparable way, a therapeutic theory is internalised to the point where the theory can be abandoned and the underlying essence comes into effect.

The closer I came to this essence, the clearer it became to me how similar the basic concepts of the various theoretical schools are to each other. Where the shaman talks of lost parts of the soul and the psychiatrist of dissociated parts of a personality, the neuroscientist explains dissociation as the consequences of extreme overwhelming stress, where only the reptilian brain reacts, but the limbic system and the cerebrum can no longer "cooperate". They are ultimately all expressions of the same phenomenon. Unfortunately, terminology and approaches are still disputed within the therapeutic community. In spite of this, major similarities can also be identified here if you look carefully and apply accurate interpretation.

Like all therapists, I begin psychotherapy with a detailed exploration of the presenting problem and the personal history. Even at this early stage, my years of experience often enable me to get some idea of what the client's hidden issue might be. We then work out the task together. Again based on long experience, I start to see various routes forward and this process has become faster and clearer than it was back when I started. I discuss the hypotheses acquired in this way with the client. We follow this path, always reconsidering whether we are still keeping to the task or whether another issue has come to the fore instead.

My understanding of the terminology that I acquired during my training has changed over time. The "angry mother" and "angry father" no longer exist within my concept bank, for example. When a person describes the mother as "good" or the father as "evil", I identify and explain this as a description of their own experience and not necessarily as an objective characteristic of the mother or father. In due course, the client is able to identify the way of seeing things exemplified by his parents' reaction to his childhood behaviour as the world as experienced by his parents. The underlying issue is therefore "How biochemistry engenders feelings" and how such feelings are (have to be) captured in language, experienced in the form of patterns and then "packaged" in terminology. My fundamental research therefore focuses on how the client fared emotionally when he experienced the mother as being good or the father as being evil or nasty. This also means that, in my conceptual system, nobody is *blamed* for a disorder, no specific person is demonised and behavioural abnormalities are not simply held to be the responsibility of one particular person. However helping a person to become more aware of their personal responsibility for perception and its interpretation is absolutely essential as the first behavioural correction. It is the most important lesson at the beginning of the therapeutic task.

The fateful aspect of many disorders is an important issue, especially with so-called trans-generational reactions to trauma. As described in the relevant part of the text, I see these so-called disorders mainly as "hereditary defects" occurring or inherited at a very early stage. From the perspective of this basic assumption, the thoughts and behaviour of an individual with respect to himself is always understandable, logical, correct and "normal". Problems arise where this normal reaction of an individual in an interaction with another person is pathologised or experienced as disturbing. In most cases, the person says: take me as I am ... from experience, the thing that pollutes the relationship is always the same.

Viewed on a meta level, my therapeutic viewpoint has widened continuously. The result is a holistic way of seeing things, in which the unity of body, mind and spirit move into sharper focus as a guiding principle. Above all, I have learned to emphasise the importance of empathetic kindness, compassion and understanding.

The client-therapist relationship

"The central factor in psychotherapy is the patient-therapist relationship"; I am sure that all representatives of all therapeutic schools of thought would subscribe to this guiding principle. We need to add the following with regard to psycholytic therapy: "The therapist's self-perception and role change with and throughout the psycholytic therapy."

Instruction manuals about the "patient-therapist" relationship refer to universal rules of behaviour that provide boundaries and define roles. But, despite their necessity, rules always have limiting and restricting qualities. Rules are artificial and invented by humans. For example, we have the "meter" as something that we humans have invented to determine the measure of distance – but there could be many other possible ways of determining distance. Similarly there is no such thing as *the* patient-therapist relationship as such. Deviant behaviour only contravenes a personal concept and we may lose sight of the individual if we follow the rules pedantically to the letter.

A psychotherapy session is a laboratory situation. Life doesn't happen there. It is remembered and described there and even changed by the telling. This is why new and different ways of thinking are required in order to facilitate changes that happen in the world outside the therapy session.

It is said that the therapist is not supposed to have a relationship with the patient based on friendship. But what happens if the client needs just that in order to heal; someone who is a friend to him until he dares to take the leap into another relationship? Someone he can try things out on and learn what one does and doesn't do as a friend? A female friend to whom he can confide without any obligation or fear of criticism? Where is it written that the therapist can't be this, too? A trusted person they can call if things are "really bad"? Or who can send him an encouraging text message if they know that he has to deal with a difficult situation?

Not that I want to tear down or criticise everything that goes on in a therapeutic setting. But during my many years of therapeutic experience, I have found that progress and change in a client's life could be even more effective and sustainable if I could support him in other contexts and was able to gain an insight into his "everyday life", even though it might only be a small one. What he didn't or couldn't tell me was often visible and important here. The environment and my observations provided valuable indications of what the client was unable to tell me precisely because of the disorder. A one-sided description of a problem is a stumbling block that cannot be underestimated; due to this phenomenon, the client's task can often turn into a trap. All you have then is a disappointed client and an "incompetent" therapist.

Because all individuals have their own perception of things and because we all ultimately communicate using terminology, I am a different person to each different interlocutor. I am what they see, want to perceive and can perceive in me. They will judge and react to me according to their inner intrinsically logical and meaningful criteria. If they do not like what I say or how or when I say it, they will condemn and damn me, maybe write something about me, look for another therapist and forget me. If they like what I say and how and when I say it, they will praise me, maybe write something about me, stay around me or remember me forever. When it comes down to it, their behaviour is only peripherally connected to me. But if I decide to engage with them, then it is very much to do with me.

As I have said, my counterpart's position determines who I am to them. This also applies to me as a therapist. The more projection-free I learn to be, the more the client will be the person that they actually want to be to me. The less projection-free I am, the more likely they will become a person who unconsciously reminds me of someone else. At any event, we all enter a mutually shared system in which we receive and engender reactions on a number of emotional and mental levels. Over the course of time, every one of us continues to redefine what we are to another person via our reaction. This requires me to take a basic stance in terms of my interaction with the individual. Do I want to engage with them – do I want to listen to them, do I want to follow their thoughts and feelings, do I also want to reveal my own to them and enter into a time-consuming dual relationship of equality, do I want to show them my newly emerging sympathy or antipathy or my approving or disapproving stance and get into what might be a demanding discussion? Do I want to immerse myself in a system and all of its issues, holding up a mirror to them with a certain ruthlessness if they open up to me? Or do I want to keep out of these issues as a "professional" and keep my distance? Where does it say how far therapeutic closeness is allowed to go, and to what extent the therapist needs to keep their distance?

In the health insurance regulations? In the basic ethical principles of a therapy originating in another level of consciousness? Where is it stated how closeness and distance have to be experienced in individual cases? What use is that to the client? Where is the focus? Who would presume to judge or condemn?

I alone must ask and answer the question as to whether I and my own opinion should be allowed to be in the client's life or whether I should just "accompany" the client with and in therapy time. I have to be clear about what I am prepared to do in each individual case.

The client should also examine how far they wish to engage with me as a person. When it comes down to it, we are mutually dependent. If there are two of you and one doesn't want to do something, there is either a power struggle, where one is the winner and the other the loser, or you both find something different if you really want to do something together.

As such, these intentions are not in the room *per se*, but they are always a reaction to how the interlocutor is perceived through the memory and the personal pair of spectacles. Right from the initial point of contact, a system of mutually dependent interactions comes into play, generating relationship-shaping behaviour at all times.

In everyday practice, this means that I listen very carefully to how the client describes their problem of conflict. How do they present themselves and their opposite party in the conflict? How much self-examination are they willing to do and how capable are they of doing it? Are they ready to change their behaviour? As a general question: are they ready to pay the price of change through therapy? Will they want to take responsibility for completing the process of change or will they "blame" me for any changes? Or do they just want to be released from their suffering? Will they do their homework assignments? Are they ready to face their pain? Are they ready to face their own unpleasant side?

It is hardly ever possible to answer these questions conclusively when therapy begins. But a guiding trend usually crystallises quite rapidly. If the therapy is more of an exploration to begin with, I have to be clear about the status of the relationship and communicate this as I go along. I first encourage the client to express what is there, and they must not only know but also feel that I like them – exactly as they are now: "I am glad that you are telling me" and "I simply take you as you are. I am a shoulder for you to lean on". But I must also be the one who provokes and opposes. In order to be of any use to the client, in addition to a warm heart, every therapist has to have an intelligent mind, analytical understanding and readily accessible background knowledge.

These observations apply to traditional and psycholytic therapy, but the use of psychoactive substances has changed some of my personality traits and perspectives on these points. Over time, various changes have naturally infiltrated my everyday therapeutic work. With regard to the fact that I need a connection with every client, I have made my own autonomous changes to the guidelines that were not explicit in my training but only ever implicit. The most powerful change is therefore evident in the relationship between the individual client and myself. For me, natural openness and the possibility of closeness are now basic prerequisites for any interpersonal encounter.

Emotional openness to the psycholytic therapy sessions led to individual closeness, which became even greater as the group lived and worked together for the whole weekend in my house. Our shared experiences, sometimes taking us into difficult waters, brought everyone together – the clients with each other and myself with my clients; we became friends. But nothing fundamentally changed about my position or my concept of myself as the therapist.

Psycholytic therapy inevitably boils down to a meeting of hearts, which isn't achieved in a traditional setting and is perhaps even avoided. The capacity for openness and allowing emotional closeness becomes part of the personality over time and is no longer just an "effect" of the substances. This meeting of hearts also has consequences in a therapeutic context. It lifts barriers between therapist and client – an encounter on an equal footing develops between two people for which both are responsible. It can also result in a struggle for authority, which they must also see as an issue and take responsibility for.

In any case, emotional openness allows everyone involved to become closer to each other. As the capacity for communicating with one another openly and honestly increases, something else evolves too – this is a form of love that demands honesty and composure. Love is not a sweet feeling, but an anxiety-free, clear, open, trusting and empathetic state. Only this will enable the individual to engage with himself and others. In my view, this kind of relationship between two people is the truly effective component of any therapy.

Another effect of psychoactive substances is that, facilitated by the setting, the client becomes his own primary point of reference as he contemplates what is occurring within himself. He learns something about himself, succeeds in understanding that he has a feeling about himself and, yes, he comes face to face with himself. "I am the one who is feeling the pain", "I am the one who is observing", the self-reflecting I acknowledges. It all takes place within the client. This changes the role of the therapist. They are primarily there to maintain the outer framework – the setting – shaping it in a responsible manner to ensure that everybody feels safe and can pursue their own processes. They take clear leadership of the group, the inner framework, and this also encourages the willingness to engage in the internal process. They become a supporter and companion for the individual process. They cease to know better, but rather follow the client's own process during the therapy, they provide empathetic support and keep the goal of therapy in sight. They may confront and question but they never remove themselves from the process. If I had to sum it up in one sentence, it would be: "They enter into a relationship."

CHAPTER 5

The Psychoactive Substances

This chapter explores the range of psychoactive substances for therapeutic use, their different effects and characteristics, with reference to prominent pioneers such as Albert Hofmann and Stanislav Grof.

I discuss key terms such as "non-specific consciousness intensifier, catalyst, gateway to the unconscious" and more.

We establish the meaning of the concepts of "perception, consciousness and consciousness expansion" in terms of our setting.

I emphasise the importance of guidelines for the use of psychoactive substances in a controlled setting:

- The triad of dosage, set and setting, the controlled setting
- The arc of the unfolding common to the substances
- The substances that I use in my practice and their mode of action, giving examples
- The justification for self-intake
- A summary of the stages of integration

Descriptions, presentations and classification

Above and beyond one's own experience, it is extremely difficult to obtain much information about "psychoactive substances" that is couched in neutral terms. When you enter the term in a search engine, you receive definitions that refer almost exclusively to illegal drugs. Therefore, psychoactive, psycho-integrative, psychotropic, psychedelic, psycholytic, consciousness-expanding, consciousness-altering substances are also illegal drugs, intoxicants, narcotics and addictive substances, but also remedies, sacraments and instruments of the Devil. Whatever the name used, it primarily says something about the person or group of people that uses it, and often has little to do with the actual substance that it refers to. To use the words of Wittgenstein: "The meaning of a word is its use in language."

Due to its origin in a certain context, the terminology used is also taken over by semantics. Each concept creates an intermediate world in the mind of the hearer, which is activated associatively when the term is used, resonating with it and determining attitude, stance and judgement. It would not work, for example, to refer to the sacred context of using a substance in a Court of law. Generally, the use of inappropriate terminology results in going down tedious, well-trodden avenues of discussion, widening the gap between polar positions.

There is a whole raft of articles on the Internet, mainly providing information about the history of drug consumption, its use, classification, health aspects and the legal situation. Speak to the average citizen without any experience of "drugs" – except for alcohol, tobacco, psychiatric drugs and other medications – about "psychoactive substances" and they will mostly trot out a series of sweeping statements that have been generated by the media. They associate "drug consumers" with drug users, drug addicts, mainliners and junkies – "social misfits" who end up living under a bridge. The tabloid press create and sustain this image with headlines like "Druggie goes berserk and jumps out of window".

"Drugs" are discussed with relative impartiality when it comes to the ritual use of psychoactive substances in "primitive" cultures. An infinite number of lectures on this type of "consumption" are introduced with words like: "The use of psychoactive substances can be traced as far back as the Neolithic period ... The cultivation of opium originated in the Near East ..." All of this is far from having much relevance for the present day. But psychoactive substances do exist in today's society, and cannot be airbrushed out or banished in the face of the obvious inherent human compulsion to expand consciousness beyond the bounds of our consensus trance. Amongst other things, it was the certainty and conviction that consciousness expansion is absolutely necessary, given the desolate state of our world, which motivated me to write my experiences down in this book.

Psychoactive substances can be classified according to their biochemical effects. But in terms of interpretation and evaluation, they are still only that which we project onto them. I will therefore not be talking about the extent to which taking them becomes a self-fulfilling prophecy. "Psychoactive substances" are substances that each have a specific effect on the brain and are graded according to their effect on the central nervous system. A distinction is made between those with a subduing or stimulating effect on the central nervous system and those with an hallucinogenic effect.

The latter are described as "**hallucinogenic / consciousness-altering**" in articles found on Google. These substances are: LSD, MDMA, psyche-delic mushrooms, 2CB ... and more.

When I talk of a "psychoactive substance" in the context of this book, apart from the basic characteristics, I am imparting my own understanding of psychoactive substances; which substance I used, the intention with which I used the substance and the results and experiences that occurred in the context described. I am obviously not the only person who is convinced of the benefit and blessing of expanding consciousness with the aid of psy-choactive substances and I am not the only person who has used them in psycholytic therapy.

Psychoactive substances as non-specific consciousness amplifiers, catalysts and gateways to the unconscious

I uphold the view expressed by Albert Hofmann, Stanislav Grof, Ralph Metzner and many others that a psychoactive substance is a non-specific consciousness amplifier or intensifier, a catalyst for changes to the percep-tion and the psyche. We find that these substances act as a gateway or por-tal to the unconscious, functioning as a valuable aid to deep psychology. Humans have used these aids for thousands of years – since long before there was any such thing as deep psychology – to access those areas of the conscious mind where answers can be found only if the right questions are asked.

Non-specific means that the substance itself does not have any intrin-sic quality that brings out the same psychological material in all people. In terms of biochemistry, it acts on all individuals in the same way. Amongst other things, MDMA acts on the amygdala, which it effectively puts "out of action". This brings freedom from anxiety, so that stress-triggering psy-chic material can be remembered, looked at and integrated without re-release of stress hormones. The kind of material emerging from the unconscious in the course of a session can only be explained and under-stood in direct conjunction with the triad of dosage, set and setting, which I will look at before I introduce the individual substances. Depending on the conditions, the result can be healing insights or confusion and alarm. In this context, *intensification* means that the insights, experiences and mem-ories – especially those that have been previously inaccessible to con-sciousness – not only become available, but are illuminated with some clarity.

Psychoactive substances may be a curse or a blessing, but this is entirely in the hands of the user and not the substance itself. Walter Lechler said on this point: "It is not the drug, it is the person." Viewed in this way, psycholytic therapy is no different from regular therapy, but one where the process taking place is expanded, deepened and enriched with the aid of the substance. Unconscious elements of our psyche can be rendered conscious through the use of such a substance, and this consciousness-raising provides the opportunity for a lasting change in feelings, and therefore actions.

However, the use of this "gateway to the unconscious" requires both sides – client and therapist – not only to engage with this instrument but also to treat it with respect and exercise a responsible approach to it. A psychoactive substance is not a medication with a specific action – it has almost no psychotherapeutic effect *per se*. The actual psychotherapy is the decisive factor, and the substance is only the key that unlocks the doors of perception. For this reason alone, the effectiveness of psycholytic therapy cannot be assessed according to the usual criteria to measure effectiveness. And for the very same reasons, you cannot assume that taking it *per se* will solve a specific problem in the same way as a specific medication will make a headache go away.

Psychoactive substances work by bringing material up into the conscious mind, so that it can then be brought into psychotherapy for processing. Nor can you expect someone taking it to feel better right away. The opposite often happens first; one client told me: "I can now feel something; I am only just realising that things are bad and I can also feel *how* bad they are." In such cases, this is not an undesired side effect, but a sign of effectiveness; the client is learning to feel, gaining access to unpleasant feelings that had been previously repressed.

I would like to emphasise again that I am not just talking about supporting the therapeutic approach in a controlled setting. It is probably not common knowledge that the first step is simply to learn how to be with a substance in order to gain some familiarity with it. Only through practice and keeping to the rules of practice can this instrument be used as a therapeutic aid so that it becomes a long-term facilitator of profound knowledge and integration. It is also unrealistic to think – though traditional therapists might claim so – that a therapist can take on the task of conducting substance-based therapy from outside by staying in the "normal state of consciousness". Given the altered quality of the thinking under the influence of a substance, it seems to me that, with regard to the requirement to pick up the client where they're at, it is an imperative of psycholytic therapy for the therapist to be able to follow the client's experiencing process. The quality of the thinking is more associative, networked and more similar to primary thought processes. The therapist needs to understand these as well as any remarks arising from the analytical/logical thought processes of our normal state consciousness. The therapist needs to work in both of these worlds and if they cannot do this they will hinder the process appreciably. I will talk about the subject of "self-intake" again later in more detail.

Perception, consciousness and expanded consciousness

The substances that I used to *expand consciousness* reflect my primary objective of knowing oneself through exploring the unconscious. In order to present my understanding of psychoactive substances, I must first explain my use of the terms "perception", "consciousness" and "expanded consciousness".

Perception is a relative process, where a comparison is made with a kind of zero potential within the individual. The comparator is the "I", or that which the conscious mind designates as "I". If we assume that the normal state is a neutral zero potential within me – a specific ego state – perception is the difference between zero potential and perceptual information.

As regards the terms **consciousness** and **expanded consciousness**, there is a wide range of philosophical, religious, psychological and scientific definitions and explanations for them. I will therefore restrict myself to recounting the knowledge that I have acquired from my own experience. Limiting myself to what my clients and I have found and "explored" during the course of our work together therefore seems to me to be a position that releases me from the pretension and burden of providing a theoretical underpinning, whilst still remaining true to the aim of this book.

At an advanced stage of self-examination, we acknowledge and express in language that consciousness occurs when we perceive that we are perceiving and are able to identify with words what and how we are perceiving. It was all about the ***perception of perception***. This inner observation put us in touch with the phenomenon of consciousness.

In my experience, consciousness also exists outside of us and outside of our brain. I refer to experiences that allowed me to observe the moment that I was created, two near-death experiences under the influence of ayahuasca in Brazil and my experience of entering into a state of pure consciousness – which I came out of as soon as I observed and named it. I also refer to the experiences of my companions.

In my opinion, these substances don't actually *alter* consciousness, but enable us to penetrate into an all-embracing state of consciousness that is beyond our "everyday state of consciousness". It is as if we were moving away from our familiar landscape, deeper and deeper down into alternating landscapes opening up beneath us and merging into one other. The further we become immersed in "big consciousness", the more clearly we see ourselves as embedded in a Big Whole, where we have always resided without being aware of it. According to my experience, total immersion in "big consciousness", "the dissolving of the ego into the Whole" is the process of dying. Every one of us has opened up different channels in the Here and Now, connecting us with "Whole Consciousness". Another way of looking at consciousness is as a large space with different things in it, but only a small area is "illuminated" when we are in our normal state. However in the "expanded mode" – depending on the substance, dosage and management – larger areas of the space are "illuminated" and consciously perceived.

Or you could say that taking a psychoactive substance increases the ability to remember, think and interpret. Perhaps we engage resources other than our habitual thinking and feeling apparatus when we take a psychoactive substance. My experiences, which I share with others, suggest to me or engender a vision of the future where we need to cease this distinction between the "normal" state of consciousness against an expanded or "altered state of consciousness". As I see it, humankind is progressing towards a state that will be able to describe both states as expressions of one and the same "integrated consciousness". It will then be necessary to develop a new terminology, an improved vocabulary that is better able to describe the territory.

The use of psychoactive substances and the use of the various meditation methods developed in the East flow down the same path – from existential separation into being at "one with everything". But the modern world, while enhancing unity in some ways, runs the risk of cutting us off from our deepest roots. Because we have developed as a species through evolution into a being that is capable of a high level of reflection (logos), I believe that we are beginning to suffer from the side effects of the logical mind and are feeling increasingly separated from an important version of reality that is denied us by our over developed intellects. Driven by an intrinsic search for unity, we find ourselves constructing a staggering network of mobile phones, gadgets, iCloud, Google glasses and other developing technologies. The next evolutionary step might involve losing some of our current range of perception to achieve a kind of unity where we are all identified in the Here and Now in a world mediated through web based technology.

The triad of dosage, set and setting – the controlled setting

The founder of this triad is Timothy Leary. The three terms belong together like father, mother and child; each is meaningless without the others – they complete one another, and knowledge of their substance and significance is vital to how we approach work with consciousness-expanding substances. Although much has been said and written about this, I believe it is important to discuss it again in the context of this book.

The issue of **dosage** involves considering how much of an intended substance an individual should receive. The fact that the quality of the substance has a part to play is self-evident. "As much or as little as necessary", as the saying goes. This statement might sound simple, but it is essential nevertheless. If you do a search for "MDMA dosage" on Google, you will come up with a whole series of different references. The pharmacologically active amount of MDMA (not ecstasy!) is given as 100-150mg. To characterise the client's level of experience, I use the image of the school pupil, who starts with an initial orientation day at school and undergoes a natural process of development from primary school pupil to college graduate.

I have personally administered between 80mg and 100mg to beginners to see how they react and assure them that they will remain in control at all times. Depending on the response, I have administered 110mg to 125mg to clients that I liken to "primary school pupils", observing in each case how I think they are doing in the "ascent" and "plateau" phases (I will explain these terms later). As I see it, each individual therapist approaches this issue in their own way, but there are upper and lower limits with MDMA and 2CB. In my experience, 70mg is the lower limit at which you can still detect some effect and I have never exceeded 130mg as the upper limit. I don't take any notice of the procedure suggested in the literature of setting the dosage according to body weight in kilograms, as I am personally small and light and using this rule I would not have received an effective dosage.

The effect is strongly dependent on dosage with some substances such as mushrooms, ayahuasca, LSD and mescaline. You therefore have to have a plan with these substances from the outset so that the dosage is carefully considered as part of the set. What effect is to be achieved? A low dosage of LSD takes you to completely different areas of psyche than a medium or high dose. Another aspect of the set also needs to be taken into account when selecting the dosage for these substances: what internal attitude does the person taking the substance have towards it and what previous experience do they have of it? How is the person actually doing? These parameters must be applied when determining the dosage. Particularly in the case of ayahuasca and mushrooms, the same amount has a different effect on the same person at different times. Handling them requires not only knowledge of the substance as such but also an awareness from one's own experience and above all the views of the client. If they help to select the dosage administered, there is a greater likelihood of that dosage being useful to them. The dosage chosen must have a correlation with the initial intention. It is for this reason that dosage and set cannot be separated.

The effect depends on the set. The **Set** or mindset refers to what the client brings with them: their mental state, their personality, their formative experiences, and the lens through which they experience and interpret the world. This includes their education, motivation, health, disposition towards illness and mood as well as their current state of mind and problems. The set includes everything that shapes their personality. The most important component of the set for a specific session is the question or intention they bring with them. Given that everyone brings a different set along with them, the same amount of LSD has a different effect on each individual. The set also includes the level of experience of the person who takes the substance. This does not necessarily mean just the level of experience with substances, but also the ability to remain centred, as we find with people experienced with meditation, for example. An experienced and centred person can take high doses and exhibit none of the clichéd phenomena, but will sit quietly as they go through an inner experience. On the other hand, with a low dosage and no controlled setting, an inexperienced person who is unable to remain centred may end up in one of the clichéd types of "hell" – which is all of his own internal world anyway.

The effect also depends on the setting. The term **Setting** refers to the qualities that the environment offers: the place, the layout of the place, the atmosphere, the music – in short, all of the external circumstances creating an ambience that might affect the client. The setting also includes the qualities of the therapist: their personality, cultural, emotional and social background, their ability and willingness to engage with the person and their self-awareness. The same setting will obviously affect each participant differently. This is why a caring, compassionate but nevertheless simple setting is preferable, so that any experience is not disturbed by outside influences. The room needs to be bright; a few flowers, a candle, a comfortable mattress for the client and carefully chosen music are also part and parcel of a pleasant and helpful setting. This type of setting is also called a "controlled setting". A further aspect of the setting is also whether it is an individual or group session. I worked with my clients in a group setting as I found this format to be more effective than an individual setting. I will talk about this in detail in the chapter entitled Tools.

The secure (in professional jargon: controlled) setting begins with the invitation and registration. The scheduling of time and place well in advance allows an anticipation of the sessions, which further prepares the mindset. I always follow the same procedure throughout the weekend. My preparations, getting the room ready and generating a suitable atmosphere all provide a framework carefully designed to optimise the setting. A more internal setting is provided by the ritual of forming a circle together for the opening group, the mutual agreement about confidentiality, the affirmation that we would not hurt one another and the affirmation of our individual responsibility. We take the substance together with clarity about the objective, with the correct dosage and working with care in a pleasant environment during and after the session. This is the setting that is required for a fruitful outcome.

The controlled setting, an overview

Dose
- **The right dose** of a well-known substance
- Carefully chosen by the therapist and the client

Set
- **A well prepared client**
- with an attitude of respect for the substance
- with the intention to own their process
- with the capacity and willingness to explore and experience their conscious and unconscious psychic material
- trusting the therapist
- feeling safe in the environment

Setting
- **A professional therapist** with an attitude of respect and attention towards the client and the substance
- offering an ambience in which the client can trust and surrender to the process

Everything beside that is called an "**uncontrolled setting**".

Arc of unfolding

After intake, all psycholytic substances show a similar trajectory of unfolding, which can be described as an arc with a specific choreography.

Ascent – Beginning of the effect – The inflow phase
Plateau – The phase of maximal and sustained effect
Descent – Decreasing effect – The outflow phase

The mode of action within this general arc characterises each substance and is also influenced by the above triad.

The **ascent phase** begins after a period of time specific to each substance; it lasts for different lengths of time for the various substances.

The **plateau phase** begins when the substance has unfolded its full effect. It is also marked by the characteristics of the individual substance. The actual work of the substance-assisted therapy begins in this period.

The **descent phase** is where the effect of the substance diminishes noticeably; insights are less profound, the clarity and depth of thoughts slow down and the opportunities diminish to look at secrets in hidden corners. It is as if the curtain that allowed the expanded consciousness a view over the entire stage for a moment is now slowly but surely being closed. The descent is essentially the opposite of the ascent; progression is maintained but in the reversed sequence. We can see that the head is becoming fogged by everyday concerns and that the old thought patterns are regaining the upper hand. As the heart closes up again, intense feelings fade and the old sense of the body returns. Beginners often say at this stage that it was a waste of time and that everything after the session is the same as before. This is why we need to pay particularly close attention in this phase – the curtain that was opened must not close completely, as we still have the capacity to remember. The more experienced the person is, the more they are able to keep some of the insights from a session in view. New corrective experiences, knowledge and formulated intentions also ensure that there always remains a small, permanent opening of the curtain, even after the restricted consciousness has come back into play.

I have used **MDMA, LSD and 2CB** in my therapy, plus **psilocybin** and **mescaline** on very rare occasions. These substances belong to what are called "psychedelics", substances that make people "bare the soul". The eponymous similarity of all hallucinogenic substances is the possible incidence of "hallucinations". I will discuss this definition later.

MDMA and 3,4-methylenedioxymethamphetamine

- Entactogen, empathogen and sympathogen
- Onset of the effect after 20 to 50 minutes
- Persistence of the effect for four to six hours
- Normal dosage: 125mg to 140mg (not administered by me)

Psychoactive substances are described as **entactogens** (adjective **entactogen**, "touched within", from the Greek *en* "within" and the Latin *tactus* "touched") where one's own emotions are perceived intensely under their influence. The client becomes more aware of his own psyche, providing

easier access to the unconscious. The principle representative of the entactogens, MDMA, does not belong to the group of psychedelic substances, as
it is a methamphetamine in terms of its chemical structure.

MDMA was patented in 1914. Alexander Shulgin recommended it as
an empathogen and entactogen for psychotherapy in 1960, and it was used
in numerous psychotherapy practices until it was banned in 1985. Because
MDMA became available "on the street" and became a "party drug", it lost
its quality as a valuable therapeutic substance, was classified as an intoxi-
cating drug and criminalised.

MDMA has been the subject of decades of research. It is consistently
described as highly effective and beneficial in professional literature. In
2001, the US Drug Enforcement Administration (DEA) gave conditional
authorisation for it to be used for scientific studies including clinical
research in post-traumatic stress disorder (PTSD).

There have now been a large number of research reports from the
USA, Canada, Israel, Switzerland, Australia and many other countries,
which can be viewed on the Multidisciplinary Association for Psychedelic
Studies (MAPS) website.[1]

The Effects of MDMA

MDMA increases the concentration of serotonin at the synapses in the
brain. Serotonin is an endogenous neurotransmitter that regulates mood.
The action of antidepressants is based on inhibiting the re-uptake of serotonin in the synaptic gap so that mood is improved through the increased
level of serotonin. Noradrenaline – and to a lesser extent dopamine – levels
are also raised.

The "self-reflecting I" which is the capacity to identify oneself as the
experiencing, speaking and thinking being, is maintained under the constant influence of this substance. MDMA is very easy to control; this means
that the client can steer his thoughts and focus onto certain topics if he
wishes to do so. It has no addictive potential. In simplified pharmacological terms, MDMA primarily removes anxiety. If anxiety, an obstacle to
remembering in the normal state of consciousness, no longer has a hold,
otherwise inaccessible repressed psychic material becomes available.
Under the influence of MDMA, intra-psychic stored traumatic experiences
become more tolerable so they can be more objectively observed, described
and communicated by the client. The cognitive functions – the self-
reflecting I – are sustained which allows the mature adult part of the client
to be present as an observer, alongside the part of the psyche undergoing a
regressive experience. In this way, so-called "cortical processing" occurs

---

[1]   http://www.maps.org.

that repairs the effects of previous psychological trauma. This "corrective new experience" can take place under guidance – or even alone after some practice and this in turn paves the way for integration and behavioural change.

As an empathogen, entactogen and non-specific psychic amplifier, MDMA increases the openness of human beings to their own psychological processes. It increases their willingness to engage with fellow human beings and encounter them without anxiety. With the aid of MDMA, the client can reconstruct his intra-psychic framework after exploring, identifying and integrating his trauma. This tends to lead to an entirely different emotional perspective, which allows a fundamentally altered relationship towards oneself, one's significant others, one's life history and the world around.

MDMA also seems to activate the long-term memory, so that very early events can be brought from the deep unconscious into the conscious mind. As the name suggests, as an empathogen, it also has the effect of facilitating understanding and compassion so that a completely different perspective can be brought to relationship problems. The increased clarity of the emotional state brought about by MDMA also allows the afflicted person to observe "their truth" about themselves with regard to their relationship. In addition, MDMA heightens the perception of the inner state, bringing clarity of thinking to the conscious mind and a subtler awareness of inner intentions and motivations.

What does it feel like to take MDMA?
After taking MDMA, the state of consciousness generally remains clear in terms of self-awareness and its grip on reality. The capacity for memory is not affected. You are aware of yourself, especially your body and you experience an intense connection with your own feelings. Many clients say that they were able to feel for the first time in their lives, or able to feel **again** under the influence of MDMA. Thinking is sustained, but thoughts appear to come from the deep interior. They are accompanied by a certainty that we are not used to seeing in rational/logical thinking. Thinking is highly integrated; it seems to come of itself, and has its own logic. Connections appear that you could not have seen in the everyday state of consciousness, with the result that we figure out and understand untrue or misunderstood situations from long ago and become more able to classify their deeper meanings and consequences.

Above all, knowledge is acquired at an emotional level, and, even as it emerges, there is an increased empathetic understanding of events. When used in psychotherapy, difficult and conflict-ridden subjects from early life rise up under the influence of MDMA. With MDMA it is particularly noticeable that bigger connections across various different levels of experience are intuitively understood. For example you might be able to identify an event from your own or your parents' life as a behaviour-forming aspect of your own behaviour and attribute relationship problems to this. Because several levels of consciousness are addressed at the same time, the result is a wide-ranging integration of unconscious material. All the knowledge acquired in this way is closely accompanied by the corresponding emotions. It is important to trust the process, to honour these new insights and know that the process is empathetic, benign and available for integration.

Group sessions with MDMA have the advantage that the characteristic anxieties and attitudes around relationships and the activities of daily life that are the result of a person's individual history are activated by the presence of other people. Due to the anxiety-relieving effect of the substance, the roots of this behaviour can be identified, which may lead to new corrective experiences in the context of the group. Contrary to the fear of many clients that a group session might be traumatic or chaotic, the increased mindfulness and emotional opening-up of the individual participants causes the group to become a vessel where people are loving towards each other, where individuals can discuss and share their knowledge, possibly feeling part of and supported by a group for the first time.

People who receive their information through the press and other media often have the impression that people under the influence of MDMA behave as if intoxicated by alcohol or simply dance for hours. This is not the case. No participant would feel like dancing or running around after taking MDMA in a therapeutic setting.

The dosage I administered allowed clients to control the flow of their own experiences and their reaction to such inner events independently at all times. They were always able to communicate their inner experience and remain in contact with their surroundings. The ability to control oneself is a capacity that improves continuously with increasing experience of MDMA. As a therapist, I have generally allowed clients to abandon themselves to the substance for their first experience. This enabled them to get to know the substance and find out for themselves how thoughts and feelings are perceived.

In subsequent sessions and as with a session of meditation, I would encourage them to remain in silence, "abandoning thoughts", letting go of any issues that arise and "not clinging on". When the substance achieved its full effect, I would encourage clients to address their issues in a focused way and plunge themselves deeply into self-observation, holding their intention question in a central position in their mind.

I was always available for a client if they reached a difficult inner state and indicated a need for help. Very often these issues concerned the group as a whole so that working with the individual in the presence of the group was particularly fruitful. Since very challenging experiences can also come up, it is very important to feel in a safe environment as a group. The setting is of particular importance with these more challenging experiences in order to prevent retraumatisation. The experience of uniting feelings and thoughts, facilitated by a suitable setting can lead to long-term change.

Taking MDMA also results in psychophysical relaxation and a greater need for closeness. Taking MDMA does not actually have the effect of sexual stimulation. As the research reports written by Peter Gasser also confirm, the atmosphere is desexualised, indeed Professor Passie likens it to a "post orgasmic state".

The major effect of MDMA is its role in the activation of feelings. This is why it is suitable for couples who want to identify the psychodynamics of their relationship. Thanks to the deep state of introspection facilitated by the inner peace that flows from a new-found freedom from anxiety, behaviour patterns can be analysed, emotionally understood and clarified.

If both partners are ready and in agreement, they can – also moderated by a therapist – bring a specific issue into the session. A deep understanding of the other person can be reached in this way. Shared mutual openness results in corrective new experience. The same applies to the relationship problems of parents or other people whom other participants represent for the purposes of the session. The goal in each case is the corrective new experience referred to above.

The specific effect of the substance may also result in age regression, where the client relives situations from early childhood with the intense emotions associated with them. However the I-structure and the cognitive abilities of the adult are preserved, so that it often becomes possible to process the emotional issues and move to a new found position of acceptance and resolution. There may be a profound sense of "meaningfulness" and even a knowledge that what had happened was helpful in some way, but which was hidden at the time. The nature of the setting and the integrative process is especially important here.

Not least, the influence of MDMA can lead to transpersonal experiences with philosophical or religious content. These experiences are the spiritual precursors to an understanding of the Big Whole and an acceptance of one's fate, whatever that may be. At the height of the experience, MDMA proves itself to be an entactogen in the truest sense of the word: the result is total self-acceptance, coming close to the inner core and an affirmation of what is there.

The MDMA "ascent" phase

If it were the substance itself that determined the experience, the effect of a substance would have to be the same with everyone. I would therefore like to return to the point that the nature of the experience is profoundly influenced by the triad of dosage, set and setting. MDMA obviously has the same effect on every individual in terms of biochemistry. The biochemical effect of MDMA is well understood and information on this subject is readily available, so I will not deal with this in any detail.

The effect of a substance unfolds over a certain period. Around 20 minutes pass after taking MDMA before you feel the first effects. The substance reaches full effect after about 90 minutes. Although the beginner will not know this, the effect of a substance always takes a similar trajectory. Particularly in initial sessions, they will have the impression of being submerged or carried along by a wave, possibly feeling that the substance itself is moving through the body.

With increasing practice, you develop the capacity to observe the inflow, follow the opening that appears and become aware of any resistance that arises during the ascent phase. The ascent phase varies in length depending on the level of familiarity with the substance and practice with using it. At a physical level, the effect mainly begins with a slight tingling sensation in the feet, which then travels up the legs. Then a kind of warmth is generated in the genital and pelvic region. This moves up to the abdomen and then passes through the diaphragm into the chest cavity with a greater or lesser gentleness depending on the ability to surrender. It can be physically painful to start with or you may feel slightly queasy or nauseous.

Once the substance reaches the chest cavity, many participants feel the need to breathe more deeply. You might feel that you are getting lighter and can breathe more easily. It feels as though the heart is beginning to open. This is the point where it can get difficult, as you can easily feel something like a fear of surrendering yourself. To many people, the pain when the heart opens up feels like a strong ribbon around the ribcage. As before on entering the chest cavity, it does not seem to be possible for the heart to open up properly until you are ready to accept the presence of anxiety and consent to this internal opening.

After the heart opening, the effect of the substance spreads further into the neck and throat area and then into the head. This often feels like a bright space of emptiness, filled with moving silence. You may become particularly aware of the powerful presence of physical perception at this stage. You feel consciously located in a totally relaxed body.

As the substance continues its inflow, your thoughts move away from everyday matters, the mind chatter fluttering through your head and your superficial bodily sensations. It is as though these factors are moving further and further into the background. Many clients describe the ascent as a journey leading them out of a dark valley, away from the hustle and bustle and via a steep path to a bright summit, from which you have a panoramic view on a clear day. It is difficult to reduce these experiences to language as the perceptions and sensations of this stage are expressed more metaphorically. A new kind of clarity typical of MDMA appears at this high point, enabling insights and connections to emerge with absolute certainty. When this clarity of mind is achieved you have reached the plateau.

This describes just *one* possibility of how an ascent with MDMA can be experienced. Because the advanced participant or "college student" is more open and fearless, he will no longer perceive the transitions in this form. The entire ascent can take place within him quietly as a soft continuous motion with or without thought until he reaches the emptiness of fullness at the summit. However, as I already mentioned at the start: no ascent is the same, not even with the same person, substance and surroundings.

The MDMA ascent of a "college graduate"
(The notes in brackets are explanations added to the experience report.)

Feeling of high-frequency vibrations in my head. No thoughts, my brain is empty. I am feeling this emptiness and am very alert at the same time. There are movements going on inside me, I am observing them: forces are struggling against each other inside me. (This is a typical example of how the brain provides an interpretation to explain a phenomenon and to be able to classify an observation in some way. Only mindfulness enables silence to spread).

Big bright spaces are appearing in my brain – I keep on observing these spaces. It's getting brighter and bigger and wider. (I notice that I want to interpret this right away and look for a certain terminology and feeling for it. I try to stop that.) *The space inside me is getting bigger and I notice that I have to start to move towards the heart level in order to understand what is happening on an emotional level too. I am separated from what I feel.*

The bright space is flowing through my entire body, I am guiding my mindfulness consciously towards the heart level – just guiding, with no intent. (I tell myself.) *The flow spreads over this level and further into my body. The bright space fills my pelvis, spreading out there. Whole body increasingly aroused* (as with an ascent of the kundalini) – *entire body aroused, opening up, entire body, mind joyful, activity and passivity are in balance.*

Surrendering to life, affirming life, clinging on and letting go at the same time.

The MDMA plateau phase

For me, the MDMA plateau phase does not last as long as it did in the initial years. Where it took up to five hours in the past, it now takes two-and- a-half to three-and-a-half hours before for the first signs appear of the effect wearing off.

MDMA enables total mental clarity in the plateau period. Thinking is slowed down slightly, and I can observe my own thoughts. I ask myself a question and wait for the answer. The answer rises up within me as if there was something inside me that knows the answer and speaks to me. I am able to see connections that I cannot see in the everyday state of conscious-ness and that I could not invent, either.

Messages coming from within are accompanied by such certainty that there is no room for doubt. I am even able to affirm highly unpleasant messages. This is often a first step towards integration. If I experience an opening up of my heart – which doesn't necessarily happen – I am not only able to look at connections with benevolent and affirming under-standing, but am also able to reflect on subjects fraught with anxiety and resentment.

In my opinion, it is the absence of stress and anxiety that makes the state of "love" (as it is called under the influence of MDMA) possible at all. My body is relaxed under the influence of MDMA, and what is special is that I am in conscious contact with my body, and feel that I truly inhabit it.

I observe with my mind's eye. I rest my gaze approximately 30cm in front of my body, in this way I can explore the "inside" of myself. Some people report images, others report spontaneous thoughts, but every person eventually finds their own way of expressing the process.

In this stillness the answer to my intended question forms within me.

LSD; Lysergic acid diethylamide

- Hallucinogen, psychedelic
- Occurrence of an effect after 20 to 60 minutes
- Persistence of the effect for 8 to 12 hours
- Normal dosage: between 50 and 300 micrograms – as a tab or drops

If you google "effect of LSD", you obtain a whole series of different statements. The description of the effect corresponds to the attitude to, experience or inexperience of, the substance of the person making the judgement. An ideological opponent of LSD or person unfamiliar with LSD will talk about intoxication, queasiness and vomiting, the shivers, inner turmoil, dizziness and hallucinations, a rise in blood pressure and increased breathing rate. They will warn against "consumption" and use key expressions such as "oceanic boundlessness", "dread of ego dissolution" and "flashback disorder" with varying degrees of accuracy – mostly at the lower end. People also assert that you see things and scenarios that don't really exist. The "user" can see that they are not real and that they are pseudo hallucinations. True hallucinations, where you can no longer distinguish between reality and imagination, hardly ever occur. There are many warnings about bad trips with a frightening disintegration of the self or challenging flashbacks.

On the other hand, a "soul-baring" (psychedelic) effect is also attributed to LSD, leading to a "deeper understanding of things". It is said that it can also bring out "suppressed and subconscious (meaning negative!) experiences" again. In films and videos, the experience of LSD is generally depicted in blurred, fuzzy images – in a context of rapid flashing disco lights and young people dancing in wild abandon. The soundtrack is mainly rock or heavy metal. Misrepresentations of this kind are common, and are passed on and copied; they form the basis of the widespread attitude to LSD.

The Swiss chemist Albert Hofmann, who synthesized LSD-25 for the first time while conducting research for the pharmaceutical group Sandoz and explored its effects by experimenting on himself, once said in a lecture on the subject:

"I therefore attribute the greatest significance to the shift in consciousness. I see psychedelics as catalysts: They are agents that guide our perception towards other material from our human existence, with the result that we become aware of our mental background. Psychedelic experiences in a safe setting can help to ensure that our consciousness is flooded with this feeling of connectedness and oneness with nature again.

LSD and related substances are not drugs in the usual sense, but belong to the sacred substances that have been used in a ritual setting for thousands of years. Classic psychedelics such as LSD, psilocybin and mescaline are distinguished by the fact that they are hardly toxic at all and are not potentially addictive. I am very concerned to remove psychedelics from the debate on drugs and demonstrate the immense potential that these substances have for self-awareness as an aid to therapy and for basic research.

I would like to see the creation of a modern-day Eleusis, where seekers can undergo transcendental experiences with sacred substances in a safe setting.

I am convinced that this kind of facility would help to confer a fitting position on these soul-baring substances in our society and culture." [2]

How does LSD work?

The effect of LSD **depends on the dosage**. This means that a small dosage of 25-50 micrograms will have a different effect from a high dosage of 150-200 micrograms, for example. An even higher dosage of 250 micrograms provokes another kind of experience. As a beginner on a low dosage of around 50 micrograms, I notice that something is beginning to change in my head after about 20 to 30 minutes. My thoughts start to race and I can't hold on to them. If I keep my eyes closed, internal images may appear with a wide range of subject matter: geometric figures, scenes from my life history and images that often can't be interpreted right away. With my eyes open, I get the impression that objects in the room are being slightly agitated. I don't have any specific feeling in my body with this dosage. Maybe I feel a little hotter than usual. I am able to sit, lie down or walk around. Brief thoughts pop up. If the room is quiet, my hearing is more acute than usual.

LSD works like a microscope when it comes to thought content according to Stanislav Grof. You can look deep inside yourself, identify and interpret the slightest emotion, force your way to the process of your own creation and penetrate deep into the detail of a problem. But Grof points out that LSD can also work like a telescope and lead us to the "vast open landscape" of consciousness expansion, where we are nothing but pure consciousness.

At a slightly higher dosage, a beginner will see movements in the face of an interlocutor if they look at them. I believe that perception is expanded and refined in such a way that you can see the extremely subtle muscle movements in a face as they are generated by thoughts and feelings or accompany them as might be seen under a slow motion microscope with the naked eye. This can end up giving you the impression that, as you interpret these exaggerated facial expressions, you can "read" the thoughts and state of mind of your fellow traveller without the need for words. Obviously, we perceive these movements in our everyday state of consciousness, too. The only difference is that they do not enter consciousness – whereas every individual ultimately does react to these subtle

---

[2] (Rittimatte, Sunday, 19th April 2007)

movements, believing that they do so through intuition and a particular sensitivity.

When a client regresses to an early age, you can perceive this in their facial features and in their voice, especially if they cry. You can often determine the age of this regression with some accuracy. If someone thinks of a person with immense hatred you can see the accompanying involuntary facial expression, revealing their thoughts in their face. In my training in behavioural therapy for children and adolescents, I learned to use the "true language of facial expression" as opposed to the spoken word, using a video camera to repeatedly observe a couple of important seconds in extreme slow motion. In doing this, I realised that one can experience these phenomena without a camera but under the influence of a substance.

In the normal state, the process of seeing consists of information reaching the retina through the eye in the form of light and being transmitted from there as electro-chemical impulses to the brain. "Unnecessary" optical information is already filtered out at this stage. The image on the retina is not transferred to the visual cortex in exact detail. This means that the brain does not receive a full version of our surroundings. The receptive fields of the visual cortex receive electrical impulses, from which our brain creates a totally personal, subjective picture of our surroundings. In this way, it is our experiences and memories (drawing on all the other senses) that determine the picture that our brain finally composes and presents to our conscious mind. This activation pattern in the cortex is not necessarily a reproduction of external events. When a person takes a psychoactive substance that sharpens the senses, this activates material from the unconscious and connects areas of the brain that would otherwise not be linked. It is important to emphasise at this point that a psychoactive substance does not alter the seeing or perception of things, but lifts the barrier prevailing in the normal state. Through the image that we consciously see, LSD shows us our perception of a person, at the same time showing us our appraisal of that person and our emotional connection to them.

For example, a client once told me that he perceived me as an ancient and strict old woman at first (he considered me to be strong and I was significantly older than he was). When he got to know me better and we learned to value each other, he increasingly began to perceive the face that he also saw when in the normal state. It was worth me considering how to explain the fact that I always saw my grandmother as an ancient old woman when I was a child and why she lost this ancient aspect as I grew up, and just looked old. Ultimately, the reason for this phenomenon is that our total perception is linked to memories. Recognising the known is associated with the attendant circumstances and then judged as pleasant or unpleasant. This forms the basis for action and reaction.

Perception expands under the influence of LSD, becoming more accurate, and therein lies the change. This is why "normal interpretations" no longer apply here, either. Other areas of the brain communicate with one another, so that memories are interpreted differently than when in the normal, restricted perceptive state, for example.

In my opinion, neither hallucinations nor pseudo hallucinations occur under the influence of LSD. I would therefore like to express a few thoughts on the concept of "hallucinations" at this point. For some time now, people have no longer referred to "hallucinations" but "pseudo hallucinations" in relation to psychoactive substances, which is a step forward. A hallucination is defined as "the perception of a sensation without any demonstrable stimulus". By definition, it has the nature of reality for the person who is hallucinating. After taking a substance a client is highly capable of distinguishing between internal images and the external reality presented to him. The self-reflecting I is able to understand and name this distinction consciously. The client can follow his varying sensory perceptions and interpret them meaningfully.

In my view, it is not even appropriate to speak of pseudo hallucinations. In everyday life, we often have – even though not with the intensity specific to substances and often not consciously, either – an "inner picture" of a thing, person or situation: "I can see it now", "I can still hear her saying". We are not talking about pseudo hallucinations in this type of context, either. I stated that we do not "see, hear, smell and feel" anything under the influence of a substance that has nothing to do with us as an individual. It is not the substance that creates the sensations. Every sensation is individual and personal, which is amplified by the substance and therefore has something to do with us. I can personally think of a few images that I was unable to understand when I started working with substances, which I thought were generated by the substance, and which I was unable to understand and classify meaningfully in terms of their interpretation and origin until years later. Everything that is experienced in a session with a substance has a meaningful connection with oneself, and is therefore not to be labelled as either "*halucinatio* = mindless chatter or dreaming" or false, fake or feigned "*pseudo*-halucinatio". These terms come from a context where one was not yet able to make such observations and, in terms of their psychiatric significance, they mainly indicate the importance given to psychoactive substances in traditional psychiatry.

Everything we see, we generate ourselves. It is not possible to classify most images right at the beginning of psycholytic therapy. It is therefore an advantage to describe the images in notes as well in order to be able to interpret them later. Most people also think in pictures, resulting in internal images that speak a symbolic language. How could we see something that is not within us? And additionally everything we see is only interpreted by ourselves. It takes time to be able to interpret our images as seen by our parents and grandparents. Their experiences with their associated pictures are epigenetically imprinted within us. It is always only about our own inner world welling up within us.

This observation leads us on to the term "bad trip". Even what happens in one of these trips is inherent to us. There is no such thing as a "bad trip" for someone who wishes to explore themselves in a determined manner. Described in this way, these so called "bad trips" are in fact the most important experiences anyone can have. The substance opens up our consciousness on a very deep level. Unconscious, difficult, traumatic and previously dissociated psychic material can rise to the surface with all their associated feelings. This opens up the opportunity to work through these feelings, projections, associations and events with the help of the therapist so that this crucial material can be integrated and worked through.

If the person is not aware of the therapeutic potential of these challenging experiences, they will see the material as extremely threatening, interpret it as coming from outside and try to push it away. That is why it is important for LSD to be taken in a controlled setting and for any difficult material coming up to be experienced as part of a supported and "cathartic" process. Stan Grof also gives a stern warning about stopping a "bad trip" with tranquilisers. The uncompleted, unprocessed experience would be stuck as if "frozen" inside the client and come up again when they came off of the most commonly administered tranquilisers, looking for closure. If you "helped" someone out of a "bad trip" in this way, it would be tantamount to retraumatisation. A difficult experience is essentially a good and important experience – but only if it can be worked through and properly integrated!

A challenging emotional experience – the story of N.

The author of the report is a woman born in the early 1970s. N. is very intelligent, she has a university degree, she is personable and good-looking. She lives with her son, sharing her life with her partner who gives her "the opportunity to focus on love rather than mistrust".

I met her together with the father of their son for the first time when she was pregnant and I have accompanied her through her psychological journey since then. Her boy is now fifteen years old.

Over time and in various relationships the fundamental problem emerged time and again. She had "attachment difficulties" and constantly needed evidence of security and trustworthiness in relationships. This is her story.

Through my experiences in psychotherapy using different kinds of substances, I have been able to explore the hidden layers of my own traumas at prenatal, infantile and epigenetic levels. At each of these levels, there was a disruption to the bond to my mother, father or to the Divine. Each of these disruptions was followed by a primal and profound loss of faith.

"I will start with an account of my background – this is what I knew before my perspective was changed through my therapy with substances. In infancy my birth was induced so I was not allowed to go through the normal birth process. This was not because of any medical need, but as a matter of convenience to fit in with hospital's renovation schedule. I believe that this resonates with a pattern in my life where I tend to await events – reacting rather than pro-acting. After birth I was immediately taken away from my mother, wrapped in aluminum foil and taken to a different part of the hospital to keep me "sterile". I believe that this had significant consequences in my life; if I don't receive any external input, I tend to feel lost, disorientated and disconnected with everything and everybody.

In early childhood my parents were always arguing and they separated when I was 3 years old. My mother moved back to her home country and my father disappeared from my life. As an obvious consequence, I have great difficulty having any confidence that any partner will stay with me. Any argument with my partner was followed by an intense fear that he would leave me.

From a prenatal perspective, I have had several experiences with substances where it felt that I was fighting for my life, battling against death and I realized that this actually happened in my prenatal existence. It seems to me that this was reflected in my great difficulty in maintaining an uninterrupted attachment with my partner. If I felt relaxed and connected with him for any length of time, my body started to show signs of stress, as if I was in a state of danger. I projected this on my partner. Putting this together with my separation issues, my unconscious emotional evaluation of the situation following the signs of stress within my body fostered mistrust and a negative emotional and behavioral reaction towards him. This tended to end in a symmetric escalation between him and me, since I triggered something in my partner as well.

From an epigenetic viewpoint, my father was Jewish and he left his home country when he was 18. According to him, he had a happy childhood and nothing bad happened to him because he was Jewish. My grandmother, who was catholic, was married to a Jewish man but she had to divorce him in order to save her life. He was deported to a concentration camp where he was gassed. My mother was born into the Catholic faith three years before the war ended and a few months after her father's death. She was later told that her father was a German soldier. In front of her home there was a train station where countless Jews were crowded into the trains, crying for water and most likely deported to the camps.

The consequences for my biographic life are manifold. The most obvious parallel was that my first serious partner and the father of my child is Jewish. As my grandmother and mother did before me, I too became separated from my Jewish man. The less obvious consequences can be illustrated through **one of my most difficult and intense emotional experiences.**

The intention was to see what I can do in everyday life to deal with my "state", which I felt must have its origin from an intrauterine near-death experience and other traumas. This emotional state was having a negative impact on my life, especially within my relationship. The substance was 1.8g psilocybin and 50 micrograms of LSD.

Within a few minutes a physical discomfort began, which grew stronger and stronger. I realized I was rapidly approaching a certain mental state that is very familiar to me. This state holds a strong feeling of being totally disconnected to everything and everybody. Physically it feels as though I am approaching the limits of my endurance and mentally I feel that I am going mad.

I was panicking, because I knew that the feeling was going to get worse and I didn't think that I could bear any more. I made a conscious decision to seek contact with F. and to trust that this would support the process. It was an incredible relief when she offered me to stay close to her and to be in physical contact. She held me and I held on to her. The first round was done.

As I relaxed and started to feel connected again, the bad feelings returned – even more forcefully than before. It was more than unbearable. I was struggling for breath and F. encouraged me to breathe slowly and fully. She emitted calm and peacefulness and I started to feel a little better. I was able to gradually relax again. But that suddenly drove me back to the unendurable state. I sensed I would not be able to get enough air – it felt as though I was suffocating. It felt as if it would never end, that it would be like this for eternity. This process repeated itself over and over, with its relaxation and intensification.

Sometimes I was able to think consciously and check in with the self-reflecting part of me. I told myself that when the substance started to wear off that I would be out of this state again. As soon as I had this thought, I went straight back to the unbearable sensation.

I asked the substance what I should do. "Carry on, allow it," was the reply. But at the same time it worsened. I wasn't sure if I could carry on, but I made a conscious decision to try to keep going. My chest seemed to explode. Then I developed an intense anxiety that F. might be struggling too. What if she was not feeling well, what if she left me? This put me into a state of unimaginable terror. It was pure and maddening fear. But I was able to seek contact again; I checked in with F. who she said she was doing fine. I was relieved again.

I relaxed again but once again the horror returned and it became unbearable. I couldn't get enough air into my lungs, it felt as though I needed to cough and expel something from deep inside me. That calmed me down for a few moments and I noticed that I could connect better with F. It was clear to me that this would be the way forward and there was no alternative but to go keep going through these endless loops.

I became aware of my breathing, which was very rapid. This panicked me again and I wondered if I was going to die. I was not sure if my life was really at risk or if it was simply my mental process.

When this physical and mental state was at its most intense, and I had the feeling that I was about to be shattered, I had a revelation, an epiphany. It involved "knowing" that the most Divine and the most dreadful were as one. At this point there are no poles and no dualism – there is unity. But I sensed that that my human body could not endure this. I seemed on the verge of passing out again and again.

At this stage, I felt that my body was beyond bearable physical and mental pain and in the midst of a war of evil against the Divine. This was completely out of the normal range of experience and imagination and is impossible to adequately describe in words.

It seemed to me that I did not belong at this place because humans are attached to their bodies and this war was taking place at a much higher, non-corporeal level.

I could see an ocean of souls. The souls were all in agony and fighting against death while at the same time being released through death. It was a mass of souls where individuals no longer existed, no one was connected with anyone else and there was no prospect of change.

Suddenly I was incredibly grateful to be a human being with all our potential for growth but I could still feel the agonized souls as a dark mass in my body and brain. It was still there when I opened my eyes, as if I was seeing through a dark filter. Cognitively, I knew that this sensation would get better eventually, but it felt like an eternity.

I tried to pay attention to my breathing. I came to the conclusion that as human beings we have to contact and connect with each other to feel part of the divine energy. I was so grateful that F. was still with me, offering me contact and that I was able to accept and trust it. Slowly my system began to calm down, and I became less anxious and vigilant.

During the phase that followed, I wondered if the war between evil and the Divine would ever end. It looked to me as though evil had greater power and that the Divine was defenseless. Then a light appeared which was on a superior level to everything that had been before. It was the source of the Divine. And it appeared to me that having faith and trust means that humans are essentially connected with this ultimate level of Divinity.

In the next phase I was actively working with F. and I realized that the cycles of intensity and relaxation had been a re-enactment of my struggle to be born. I had been in an intrauterine battle against death but it seemed that I had not properly arrived in the world yet as a human being. I still felt trapped in the collective of the lost and tortured souls. The intrauterine death experience appeared to have catapulted me into a space where I was still connected with the collective, and some of these sensations had been stored in my body. I felt an intense fear that powerful forces would take me back to these collective souls again. I worked with F. to stay with the precarious gift of my birth and she told me to stay in direct eye contact with her. This helped me to stay in the here and now until the fear of merging with the collective faded.

After my rebirth I felt totally disorientated, like waking after a deep sleep. It felt as though I needed guidance and needed to be told what to do for a while. Being reborn involves learning how to live in a different way; it is like learning to walk again. It took me a while to get used to the changes and integrate them into everyday life.

The substance had helped me to overcome past and collective energies but I had to process these in small steps. Human beings can only bear so much. Having faith is a precondition to breaking through".

Commentary on the story on N.

A perspective on the intrauterine disturbances: Her mother and father lived in an atmosphere of intense stress, distrusting each other and arguing constantly. It is scientifically accepted that maternal stress is biochemically transferred to the unborn and has significant impacts on the fetus. The body of the mother signals to the child in this way that the world is and will be an unsafe, dangerous place. This naturally has consequences in the child's emotional and behavioral state. This state of arousal is mediated through hormones and neurotransmitters, which biochemically affect the developing fetus and cause morphological alterations to certain brain regions. For example, the amygdala, which stores information linking events with emotions, enlarges through stress, which in turn lowers the threshold for the triggering of a stress response. This alteration of the stress response system affects an individual's ability to regulate stress. This means, that the person gets stressed easily, which in turn has consequences in practically every area of life including difficulties in interpersonal relationships.

The expressions of these phenomena are highly individual, but have behavioral consequences, which tend to be classified as neurosis, attachment disorders, developmental disorders, affect-regulation disorders and many others. Naturally these labels, which imply pathology, only manifest themselves when difficulties arise, particularly within relationships. The situation becomes more complicated, if there are differing ideas as to what "normal" behavior should be.

The other problem is that when we start to name and address the difficulties, there tends to be an assumption that the symptoms are some sort of illness or disease, which the person "has" or "suffers from".

But the fact is that the person does not *have* these symptoms, they *are* the symptoms. The fundamental cause of the symptoms has shaped the personality from such an early stage that it has *become* the personality. To talk about healing in this context, we need to find a way of accessing and working with the very roots of personality development, which requires an entirely different and deeper level of consciousness.

A perspective on the perinatal circumstances: The circumstances of her birth and the fact that her mother "left" her and "neglected" her needs as a newborn, reinforced the message that the world was indeed a dangerous and uncertain place.

The developing human animal has to rapidly find a way to handle this type of situation, which in time becomes hard wired as an unconscious action and reaction pattern. If these patterns can be brought into conscious experience, they can be worked with, conceptualized, processed and eventually resolved. But they can also be resistant to change, even after many years of psychotherapy.

Perinatal experiences of this kind result in a chronically elevated level of activation, which expresses itself as hyper vigilance in any kind of relationship. As I have indicated before, such experiences are stored at the level of body, mind and psyche and they express themselves reflexively by disturbances in trust and self esteem, with impaired ability to bond – an attachment disorder. The increased vigilance expresses the constant warning: "do not trust anybody, the world is a dangerous place and nobody is there for you". On a neurophysiological level, this evokes a constant need to control the environment; to make sure that it is safe, that she can trust and even dare to relax. Such a state of being is very tiring for a small child.

Psychologically this leads to feelings of total abandonment when an "untruth" is perceived, (the control failed, which leads to intensified control) and annihilatory anxiety with fear of death, when left alone. There may also be increased requirements for attention, reassurance and reliability, accompanied by irritability and tantrums. There is a constant background feeling of existential despair.

A perspective on the early childhood experiences: Her father left the family suddenly and vanished from her childhood. Such a family trauma would affect the developing psyche of any small child. But coming on top of intrauterine and/or perinatal trauma, there is a cumulative effect, which reinforces and solidifies the damage. One can easily understand that her system needed to develop a viable and effective way of dealing with situations perceived to be dangerous. Her difficulties with bonding and attachment, her increased need to control and her demands on her partner for complete transparency can be seen as an inevitable response to this succession of traumas.

These psychological imprints and behavioral patterns from childhood are so powerful that they persist into adult life without evolving into more mature patterns of behavior. In other contexts, especially in an intellectual environment, her adult persona functioned very well. Indeed there were aspects of her life where these patterns even conferred an advantage. Thus she developed a remarkable ability to analyze relationship constellations and she interacts with humans and horses in an extremely sensitive way. She turned these qualities into a profession by detecting and changing people's dysfunctional habits through their interaction with horses.

On a psychodynamic level she is unconsciously seeking, in all her relationships, a man representing her idealized father who would finally satisfy her desire for recognition and parental care. It was an extraordinary realization for her to see that instead she chose exactly the kind of man who re-enacts the original trauma by betraying her and leaving her. So a cycle was set up where despite her heightened attempts to control her relationships, this failure of caregiving was repeated over and over again.

A perspective on the repetitive process: Whenever she fell in love she put all her faith in the partner until she detected a "lie" or an "untruth" with her exquisitely sensitive alert system. Once she detected a lie – big or small did not make a difference – all her faith collapsed completely. Now she can see that her body started to show stress symptoms when she detected an untruth as if her life was in danger. So she unconsciously interpreted a lie to mean that there was a total and irreversible loss of connection between her partner and herself. This led her to a dissociative state where she felt great emotional pain that felt as though it would never end.

Since any lie was unconsciously associated with her previous traumas, any wrong or missing information became an existential threat and triggered mistrust. In distrusting she kept herself and the partner(s) in a permanent hyper-arousal, which was often interpreted to be a "lively relationship". The closer she felt to her partner, the more sophisticated and sensitive her system became and the more desperate her need for reassurance.

After treatment, she was not only able to understand the source of her difficulties but underwent a fundamental change in her attachment patterns so that she became more able to trust her partner and focus on signs of love rather than proof of distrust.

An overview: Stan Grof calls the birth the "gateway to spirituality and the transpersonal". An individual with a difficult, unintegrated birth process often shows symptoms that indicate that she still perceives the world from the perspective of the traumatic birth situation.

We have found that under the influence of a psychoactive substance, a person's birth process can often be relived. With proper mindset (the self reflecting I) and supportive setting this reliving allows a healing of the psychic wound and a resolution of the original trauma. The traumatic nature of the birth many years previously can be now be "digested" and metabolized. In this way it is not a repetition of the birth, but becomes a psychological "rebirth". This is what happened to N. – she had been in the second perinatal matrix (BPM 2) that Grof described as cosmic engulfment, no exit or Hell. She experienced the typical characteristics of this stage of the birth process; fear of death, fear of no return and fear of losing her mind. There was a crucial moment when she lost her connection to the Divine; I asked her to hold on to me, to leave the dark and move towards the light, breathing her way forward and through it. After that she seemed to be blank, without history for a moment, purified and liberated.

After the session there followed the work of integration as she gradually learned how to interact with the world about her in a new way and build a relationship free from her previous patterns.

Unusual effects of LSD and other substances

LSD has a reliable effect where there is a need to bring unconscious psychic material, suppressed memories, trauma and other conflict-ridden experiences out into the open. LSD activates some brain structures and deactivates others, ultimately breaking down resistance to remembering deep-seated material. It can result in age regression, where previously suppressed memories become so vivid that they seem to be happening again in the present moment. This "recapitulation" can be accompanied by powerful emotions; so the therapist needs to be in tune with the client and capable of guiding them intuitively through this experience.

Oceanic boundlessness is the term neuroscientists use to describe the state where the ego disappears completely. This extreme state is also achievable through the practice of meditation, during sleep or under anaesthetic. Oceanic boundlessness describes the pleasant, exhilarating aspect of a state that is marked by endless joy, a deep inner contentment and all-embracing love. It offers a feeling of oneness with the self and the world; a liberation from the restrictions of time and space, the sense of a higher reality and mystical or spiritual experiences.

Dread of ego dissolution describes the anxiety-ridden aspect of an expanded state of consciousness, where anxiety is triggered by the loss of the capabilities inherent in normal waking consciousness – such as self-control, power of judgement and control of reality. You may experience the feeling of being threatened and tortured, of being controlled like a puppet by someone else, or concern that you will never escape this situation. You may have a strong feeling, even a certainty, that this situation will never end – similar to Grof's description of the second perinatal matrix, characterising "no way out", total imprisonment and hopelessness. I have already described the value of the term "bad trip". Oceanic boundlessness and dread of ego dissolution are different expressions of a similar theme. Both in fact represent an ego dissolution, which can be experienced as blissful and frightening at the same time or alternate between the two.

Visionary restructuralisation is the most complex aspect of any extraordinary state of consciousness and involves the restructuring of both perception and meaning. This includes **synaesthesia** – the overlapping of the sensory systems, so sounds may be perceived as colours or visual input perceived as sounds.

I do not entirely subscribe to the usual definition of visual restructuralisation. During the course of a number of LSD sessions, I have been able to observe how the sense of hearing became extremely acute, to the point where I was able to perceive the spaces between sounds. (This is similar to the phenomenon that I have already described with regard to visual perception). If I continued to listen in a centred way but without any particular intent under the influence of a high dosage of LSD, I felt that I was able to identify the primal state or origin of a sound. This was ultimately energy vibrating like waves, which I could see and hear at the same time and – depending on the frequency (which is even common in everyday speech) – had different colours. In my opinion, this phenomenon is less about acute perception and restructuring the auditory stimuli and more about the phenomenon of acute perception, a widening of the frequency of the sense of hearing and an acoustic retardation, which, like the progressive disintegration of an image into pixels, goes back to the primitive state, which is also accessible to the other sensory channels as a kind of basic state (energy, waves).

I believe that such perceptions represent the phenomenon of "overall perception" and that they can be interpreted as a first step towards the separation of the perceiver and the object perceived – as I have suggested as a possible evolutionary development. But, it is also possible that a natural evolutionary progression from a certain uniformity to the diversification of perceptions has taken place and that, in a state of expanded consciousness, the next level can be reached, where overall perception is possible through simultaneous differentiation, involving the optical and/or the acoustic. Our current model sharply distinguishes the modes of perception – the optical and acoustic channels, for example. Our world is constantly exposing us to various waves, which we perceive as either acoustic or optical stimuli, which are portrayed by various sensors in the brain and perceived and designated as mutually independent stimuli.

I presume that LSD has a neurophysiological effect on deep areas of the brain that are responsible for "perception as such" and that these areas don't specifically need to be stimulated directly via the organ of the eye or ear. (Blind people "see" under the influence of LSD!) This would also suggest that overall perception is a primary form of perception with a low bandwidth. Evolution has presumably led to the development of multiple channels, due to the necessity for specification. By eliminating the separation between the channels of perception, the substance facilitates integrated global perception. This is my own view and naturally I am fully aware that other interpretations are possible.

Taking a substance can result in a kind of slow motion or microscopic view that allows insight into the molecular level. Because all of the senses are simultaneously opened up, more basic or primary states of each of our senses may become accessible to the same extent, so that they become merged into a non-specific global perception.

The special nature of LSD

It is essential for the therapist to have an idea about the processes occurring in the client from personal experience and to be able to be totally with them at any moment, supporting them with continuous attention and commitment. With this help – and sometimes having the benefit of their own experience – the client understands the full significance of what they have experienced by reliving the past in a regressive state. Accepting and submitting to this process on a cognitive and emotional level represents the first step of integration. Before the training to take the position of the "empathic observer" it is crucial to preserve the "self-reflecting I" and prevent retraumatisation.

Described as a side effect, the altered nature of the thought processes makes it possible to look inwards, identify, break out of deadlocked patterns of thinking and change them. This often results in a long-term change in the way in which we may see ourselves and the world around us. In this way, the earlier symptom of distress and suffering turns to some extent into a precondition for the desired change. As I have said before, sensory experiences are activated and pulled from the depths of the unconscious, and the client regains contact with their feelings, whatever they are. The relief after regaining a lost feeling in a session is enormous. A very experienced person can explore situations and connections under the influence of LSD. The acuity and wisdom of thinking, understanding and insight can sometimes be breathtaking.

With regard to my own work with LSD, I would like to give my opinion on a number of aspects from a psychotherapeutic point of view. LSD supports the psychotherapeutic process by deepening, intensifying and accelerating it. In an unspecific way, it activates the psychodynamic processes occurring in traditional therapy as well. But the access to any suppressed psychic material is much easier. Unlike with MDMA, the client experiences the memories that are triggered as experiences that are present in the moment. The main focus of the work therefore is less on the verbal expression, but more about supporting the client in a humane, warm and empathetic setting, so that they can re-experience, neutralise and integrate their process rationally and emotionally.

In those moments, physical contact can be perceived as a healing and corrective new experience. Sometimes the experience of simply being held at last – after suffering from a childhood with little or no bodily contact or touching is a profound and deeply mutative experience. If the session creates a true feeling of symbiotic oneness with the mother, in a case where a lack of attachment and bonding dates back to the neonatal period, this can lead to a dramatic improvement in their ability to form beneficial relationships. The closeness experienced in this state can fill the vacuum of early emotional deprivation.

Other emerging dynamics perhaps require the psycho-dramatic replay of the underlying conflicts. When we start this work, sometimes the breakthrough of previously suppressed material might result in an initial worsening of the client's condition, as they become more aware of the traumatic experiences that they went through and how awful things have really been. At such times, it is important to keep the dialogue going and stay available for them. Sometimes, in order to establish the step back in time during such a re-enactment, I encourage the client to repeat: "It's over and I am grown up now" over and over again.

Later on in therapy, after the client has learned to keep in balance with the substance, they can focus on specific problems and situations, getting to the bottom of them and engaging more consciously in these emotional processes. Over time, the client changes their perspective on the formative experiences of their lives. This happens too, of course, in traditional psychotherapy. In this respect, therapy is the same both with and without expanding consciousness through a psychoactive substance. The difference that all clients are unanimous about when they look back is that the emotions are deeper, "really experienced" and not just "thought", as is the case in talking therapy. Time and again, a conversation typical of psycholytic therapy has been: "We talked about this and I was aware of it when therapy started, but now I have *experienced* it".

Even if the spoken word is not to the fore at times, a verbal summary of what has happened in the session is still important at the end. An individual can use language to describe themselves and the aspects of their existence. This spoken self-reflection gives rise to an awareness of self and personal identity. Given that the client has to be made aware of everything experienced during a session so that it becomes their reality, consolidation through sharing and a set of written notes is an indispensable element of the therapy, facilitating integration.

On a physical level, LSD is less harmful than alcohol and nicotine. It does not have its own pharmacokinetic process, meaning that it does not develop any physical effects. There are no withdrawal symptoms. The processing of information in the brain seems to change, generating new capabilities to some extent. In the field of memory research, it could be said that LSD and psilocybin bring memory traces out into the light, which would otherwise be inaccessible. According to Franz Vollenweider of the University of Zurich, this is where the benefit lies in psychotherapeutic terms.

Finally, I would like to mention Dr Torsten Passie's research into personality change under the influence of LSD in a controlled setting. The core personality remains unchanged. But an intense mystical experience, the feeling of being at one with everything, for example, can shake the previously elaborated value structure from top to bottom. At least a third of people who have had this kind of experience report incredibly positive changes in their personality profile. Values change towards a less materialistic attitude, a less environment-damaging way of life and a focus on society and its basic role.

In his book entitled *LSD Psychotherapy* Stanislav Grof describes the far-reaching and positive changes towards acceptance that have been effected by giving LSD to patients with terminal illnesses with regard to disease, pain and attitude towards death. Dr Peter Gasser conducted a study published in 2014 that described similar findings.

Inflow of the substance LSD

A wide range of different reactions can be observed after taking LSD. Some clients notice the first signs after only 10 to 15 minutes, some after 30 and others after 40 minutes. The effect of LSD does not have a typical trajectory through the body as MDMA does. With some people, it travels into the head in a more or less gentle way. Others have a certain feeling of uneasiness, which expresses itself physically in a variety of ways. Some people start to feel cold, others hot – or first cold, then hot. We could produce a long list of the various reactions – including intrapersonal – during the ascent with LSD.

Every now and then, especially with a high dosage, awareness of the body loses all significance. With very high dosages I also have the sense of no longer being in my body, or my body feels light and totally free of pain. In examining over 5,000 sets of LSD session notes, Stan Grof did not find a single phenomenon that appeared every time. But he concurs that thinking processes show a noticeably altered quality.

As an experienced user and at a dosage of 150 to 200 micrograms, I notice that something starts to change after around 20 to 30 minutes. There is a slight buzzing in my head. I enter an empty space and feel like the top of my skull might be lifting a little. There are no images when my eyes are closed. It depends on the level of tranquillity that I can achieve as to how things continue. I can spend a little time inhabiting the nothingness, guiding my thoughts and focusing on subjects that I have decided on beforehand. I speak to myself internally, telling myself: focus on a thought or insight right now (how I did it exactly or what do I see exactly now...) and enter into finer and finer details. The quiet space becomes a space where I experience being in the Here and Now, experiencing healing in the widest sense.

LSD report from an experienced client

Every single LSD session was unique. I can't say for sure: this is how LSD does or doesn't work. In the beginning, I was confused or you could say that I had trouble staying with it. But it became easier and easier. I also had "hallucinations" at the start; they were images and scenes that moved and had contents. I actually thought the images were fantasies or visions. Looking back, I discovered that all of the images had significant and meaningful content as far as I was concerned. I did not understand many of these statements and information until years later.

These days, I do not see images any more when under the influence of LSD. Nothing moves like it did in the early days, either. Nor did I "see" any images under the influence of mescaline, psilocybin or ayahuasca, the content of which would not ultimately have belonged to me. I don't even consider inner images during spiritual experiences – a visual insight into the core self, for example – as a pseudo hallucination but as a logical internal translation of my thinking into a different sensory mode.

Hearing seems to be more acute under the influence of LSD. My surroundings quickly become too noisy for me and I "hear" the silence at high dosages. I have acquired the ability to listen to the silence. I am able to observe everyday life well at low dosages of 50 to 75 micrograms. It can often be a little "irritating" because it seems banal and because I can see only too clearly the degree to which I experience everyday life in a state of unawareness.

At medium dosages, I experience my feelings keenly and am particularly able to explore relationships. At high dosages, I have insights and make discoveries based on my particular objective or focus. At low and medium dosages, I can hear music as in my normal state of consciousness, and at high dosages I have been able to perceive the spaces between sounds and also experience the phenomenon of synaesthesia, "seeing" sounds, which I now simply take to be a translation.

I suffer from dyscalculia (problems with arithmetic), and saw numbers as colours as a child: the difficult number 17 was chequered in different colours and multiplying by 17 resulted in visual chaos for me. The phenomenon disappears when I am under the influence of LSD and calculations with the number 17 seem totally logical to me. I also lost the ability to perceive time correctly at high dosages. The total collapse of time and space was a spiritual experience for me, enabling me to feel myself being in the Here and Now, totally centred.

Describing my thinking under the influence of LSD seems to be the hardest thing to do. It totally depends on the dosage and other factors but, as I see it, the principle effect is the experience of and facility for centring myself. A psychiatrist or opponent of LSD would characterise the change in thought processes in pathological terms: thinking is impaired, cognitive functions diminish. It is true that, depending on the dosage, it becomes more difficult "to stick with a thought", as we know more or less (!) from everyday life. I really couldn't control the flow of thoughts at the beginning. I won't lie about that. Today, I am able to work through subjects in a totally focused way under the influence of LSD, and am always pleased with the discoveries that I make.

The plateau phase of LSD

The plateau phase with **LSD** is greatly dependent on the dosage in terms of quality and length. It is also influenced by the degree of experience of the person taking it and whether he can remain effortlessly centred. At a medium dosage, a beginner is able to follow his own inner processes himself. He can provide information and work through issues. The plateau phase is particularly fruitful if the person persists in exploring the various aspects of an issue thoroughly until all the detail has been brought to the surface. Thoughts are very clear during the plateau phase, you become more perceptive and you miss this kind of clarity when you return to the distractions of daily routine. The plateau phase can also be very tranquil, it is possible to enter a clear, empty space without any mental reaction, characterised by an absence of thought, but full awareness. The plateau phase lasts 6 to 8 hours or so at a medium dosage, and correspondingly longer at higher doses.

2CB; 4-Bromo-2.5-dimethoxyphenylethylamine

- Hallucinogen, empathogen, aphrodisiac
- Occurrence of an effect after 30 to 60 minutes
- Persistence of the effect for four to five hours
- Normal dosage: 10 to 25 mg

The effect of 2CB depends on the dosage. In the training group, Samuel Widmer described the effect of 2CB approximately as follows: "2CB gives you whatever you are ready for. If you are ready to open up your heart, it works like MDMA. If you still have psychosomatic issues, it will have an effect on your body and tell you what is going on there. It can behave like mescaline and LSD, too."

2CB reveals the structure of resistance. This characterisation is perhaps hard to understand. In the ascent phase, you often get in to a "state of confusion", which is hard to endure physically in your body and most people describe as unpleasant. You often begin to feel cold, and trying to warm yourself doesn't seem to work. If you simply remain in this confused state and don't try to fight it, a memory pops up very suddenly on most occasions, giving you a sudden insight into why you feel uneasy. You realise why you protected yourself in this way – it is mostly about memories and experiences that you would rather not have.

The ascent with 2CB

The ascent feels like a steep flight of stairs – from an emotional perspective it feels like utter confusion at first, followed by clarity. In the moment of clarity, it feels as though you haven't taken any substance at all. Your task is then to become totally still again, letting everything go. Then something like a cycle begins: you are drawn upwards like a thread into another new state of confusion, which is in turn followed by clarity. This is repeated about three or four times until you reach the plateau.

At every stage, you have a very clear perception of how the substance is taking effect: feelings of sexual arousal can appear in the pelvic area, and a slight feeling of nausea in the solar plexus, especially at the moment when you are fighting the confusion. If you are able to remain open and non-resistant, your heart may open up as with MDMA. Thinking in the plateau phase is clear in a similar way to when you take LSD, but not crystal clear as with LSD. Subjects on 2CB are not on such a high intellectual plane, relating instead to relationships and the evolution of humankind and the earth. Spiritual experiences are powerfully cognitive and emotional. I must mention that some clients can experience some low mood and irritability two or three days after taking 2CB. Where acknowledged and not acted out, this allows another opportunity to integrate these mood states as being a further manifestation of resistance.

Reports of 2CB experiences

2CB showed me different faces. The first physical signs appeared fifteen to thirty minutes after taking it. I felt a little cold to start with, sometimes slightly sick, especially when unpleasant feelings emerged and I didn't want to accept them. I experienced wonderful, gentle and friendly moments throughout the ascent phase, but also an unbearable sense of confusion and "hellish torment". In the meantime, I was reaching higher and higher levels of clarity, giving me something like hope that it would all be OK in the end. To begin with, I almost hated

2CB, saying it would bring me nothing but confusion. Later on, it almost became my favourite substance. The perception I have of my body is similar to that with MDMA.

Having received 20mg of 2CB, a client still felt no effect after 90 minutes. He sat up, complaining that I had given him a placebo. I remained calm and said: "You are right at the point of your resistance. We still don't know what against. Resistance is the ability to want to feel nothing". He just sat there. He became annoyed. I just sat there, too. After a long time, he started to give up a little, his shoulders relaxing a bit. But he also seemed to be bored. "Boredom and giving up are also part of resistance." I sat down beside him and put my hand on his knee. After a while, I looked at him and he started to look at me. We looked at each other for a long time and eventually our eyes met. He was breathing more heavily. His eyes were boring into mine. Very slowly, and hardly noticeable to him, he began to feel that he could perceive his own body. He could feel his heart beating, his breath flowing in and out, until he finally became sad. After crying for a long time, he reached a state of deep love and gratitude.

The plateau phase with 2CB is also marked by intense clarity of thinking and feeling. You could describe it as a mixture of the plateau phases of LSD and MDMA, with a little hint of mescaline, which is mainly expressed in visual terms, as if you can truly see in three dimensions, or that the leaves on the plant are constantly moving ever so slightly. The plateau phase with 2CB is brief, lasting about two to two-and-a-half hours at a normal dosage of 15mg.

Entheogens: psilocybin, mescaline and ayahuasca

Wikipedia definition: a psychedelic substance (from the Greek *psyche*, "soul" and *delos* "manifest, open") is one that helps to "bare the soul". Taking these substances results in an expansion of consciousness, providing the opportunity for self-awareness, introspection and other experiences, including the spiritual dimension. A spiritual experience of the unity of all things is described as **entheogenic** (from the Greek *en* "in", *theos* "god", and *genesthai* "effect").

Psilocybin, psilocin

- **Mushrooms,** indole, tryptamine
- Hallucinogen, entheogen
- Occurrence of an effect after 10, 20 or 60 minutes or so depending on psilocin content

- Persistence of the effect for about four to eight hours
- Normal dosage: 2 to 4g of a powdered mushroom

There are over 200 different types of mushroom. The effective amount of a substance varies greatly across the different types. You therefore need to be fully aware of which mushroom you will be taking. As we hardly ever took psilocybin, I will only be discussing it briefly in general terms.

Specific effect of psilocybin

The effect of the mushroom depends on the dosage. Mainly physical sensations occur at a low dosage of 0.5-1.0g: you are flooded with warmth and there is mostly an intensification of the basic feeling you came to the session with: if you go into the session relaxed and with happy expectations, the sense of relaxation increases, but if you go in rather anxious, then that anxiety increases. You get an answer to the question posed but you should be aware that a low dosage will not result in any particularly profound insights. The session is brief and you go back to feeling normal again after about three hours and with no subsequent fluctuations.

Higher dosages of around 1.5-2.5g increase the body sensations. I personally feel as if the mushroom is taking possession of me, my body and spirit – like mycelium penetrating all of my cells. Colours seem more intense and thoughts flow more freely than with LSD – they are not so bright and sharp, but still very clear.

At a higher dosage of up to 4g, the effects described are stronger. Insights are mostly deeply meaningful, reaching metaphysical dimensions. If you do not fight against the fear of dying, you reach a state that you recognise as being the real life.

I can only take medium dosages, as I am small and highly sensitive. But even here I reach places that other people need much higher dosages to reach. In general, my experience with teacher plants shows me that the dosage given has to be adjusted to the specific person. 1.8g is enough for me to have spiritual experiences, whereas some clients need dosages of up to 5g in order to have the same experiences.

Along with ayahuasca, the mushroom is one of the "*teacher plants*". This is also the reason why I haven't used the substance very often in a therapeutic setting. Ideally, a mushroom should be taken in a circle ritual at night. Before you take it – as with other substances, too – you state your wish or intention clearly. When the substance has taken full effect, you can start to ask the mushroom questions. You receive verbal or non-verbal answers in the form of images or symbols. The answers are often not what you expected and you don't understand them immediately when they come. It is important to let the mushroom take the lead, particularly during the ascent phase, but also during the plateau phase. If you do not do this and start wanting to control the session, you feel slightly dizzy, fuzzy headed and muddled.

As I have already indicated, the details of the answers to questions posed are often unexpected, including "lessons" and occasionally have something severe and implacable about them in the sense of "take me seriously". You can talk to and discuss things with the mushroom as if in a dialogue. The mushroom is quick to show its humorous side, and sometimes you find what you see and hear extremely comical and funny. If a participant starts laughing in a mushroom session, the entire group usually starts laughing too, and it is hard to restore peace and order to the session.

Communication is not so important in the plateau phase because everybody speaks to the mushroom on his own behalf and goes through his own experience. As with other substances, we worked together in our setting, which evolved as our experience increased – it is a "teaching plant", after all. Regressing to experiences in one's personal history enables a very vivid reliving of the original situation, accompanied by the associated feelings. The feelings tend to be very strong, overwhelming and truthful. Aligned with a high level of emotionality, this targeted re-experiencing has a cathartic effect, in most cases leaving the client highly relieved, but also exhausted and in a wonderful state of relaxation and gratitude.

An early mushroom experience

Talked about mushrooms a lot on the evening before the session, lots of things were explained to me. A restless night ... my inner self was very resistant the next morning, refusing to go through the experience. Just thinking about taking the stuff filled me with a powerful sense of resistance. I had to force myself, the smell was vile. I shuddered when I thought about what could happen. Drinking what looked to me like an "old thing from out of the ground", this dirty, awful-tasting thing was supposed to make me open up? Supposed to make me see? I was supposed to trust it? I didn't want anything to do with it, I wanted to leave and not put myself through it. I stayed. My teacher noticed my demeanour just before I took it and put me safely between two experienced people. I decided to muster the courage and lie down. I am very impatient, and also someone who is easily distracted by noise and "happenings", especially if the idea is to keep quiet and watch. It suited me that, as I saw it, the mushroom "arrived" in my body in a different way from other substances. It didn't arrive physically for me at all, I just felt increasingly unwell. I had no pain in my body. No tingling, breaking out in a sweat or feeling cold, as has been described. I thought that nothing was happening. I just thought that I didn't feel well and ought to leave.

After spending a while in tranquillity, I realised that I was at the centre of "myself". I didn't look, but was in the middle of two currents circulating in opposing directions. Lots of currents and tributaries running parallel, a bit like the street layout of New York City, with narrower and narrower streets. It was very dark inside me and all I could see was these currents, almost with directional arrows and two-colour tracks – one red and the other blue. My teacher sat me up and asked me where I was; I described my picture to her. I was gradually "caving in"; I didn't feel well, I was kind of stunned, something was wrong with me, I was "on the ropes", and there was not much left holding me up.

My teacher laid me in the lap of someone experienced, their arms around me. They held me, and my teacher asked me to give a better description of the state I was in. I couldn't speak any more. My teacher looked deeply into my eyes but stayed at a distance and didn't come near. I could not reach her, and she didn't offer me her hand or touch me. She left me to continue reliving my own experience "more deeply". She watched me, gave me and my experience some more time and then started to speak to me softly. I could only nod or shake my head in answer. No other language was available to me. My teacher seemed to realise that I was still in my mother's womb. Yes, that's what it felt like; when she asked me if I could move, I couldn't do that, either. I just felt awful and had pains in my head. She explained to me that I was still at an extremely early embryonic stage and that it looked as if I had been exposed to poison in the womb. She put me in the embryo position, put a cover over me and put her arms and legs around me. As she spoke words to me that I no longer remember, I slowly felt better and realised I was exhausted from fighting the nausea.

The air was fresher now and the struggle slowly came to an end. I noticed that I was really feeling better and the teacher laid me in the arms of the experienced person again. They held me and looked into my eyes. I found this really difficult but she kept encouraging me to stay in contact and breathe. Everything slowly started to feel better and my body stabilised a little over time. I stayed in the person's arms a while and all I had to do was allow myself to be held and watch. I did this for as long as it took to feel big and grown up again. A few days later, I confronted my mother, asking her if she had consumed high-proof alcohol and nicotine during her pregnancy, and she confirmed that she had.

Harman alkaloids and DMT: ayahuasca

- Occurrence of an effect after a few to 60 minutes
- Persistence of the effect for around 6 hours
- Normal dosage: depends on the strength of the extract and needs to be decided by the leader with the individual client.

In my experience, ayahuasca is the most powerful and effective of all of the substances. Experiences are similar to those with mushrooms but much stronger, and often accompanied by intense physical reactions. I have never administered ayahuasca myself. However, because I have made important progress with the help of this plant medicine, I would like to include it in my account.

Combinations of substances

Eventually as I felt more secure in administering and dosing the substances, I started to combine them.

In this way the special quality of one substance was combined with the quality of the other. LSD added to MDMA takes some of the "maybe too sweet and simple " of the MDMA away and allows a combination of the crystal clear mind with the heart-opening.

MDMA added to LSD, softens a difficult experience and leads to an integrative and agreeable cooperation between the substances.

With beginners I always started out with MDMA. In a second or third session I added about 50 micrograms of LSD. This main effect of the LSD in this small dose was to prolong the process – to obtain an appreciable effect it needs up to 100 micrograms. Another aspect of adding LSD to MDMA is to reduce the tendency to get too used to the beautiful feelings on MDMA alone, thus avoiding looking at difficult issues. It is a method of gently penetrating resistance.

In more advanced practice, we would take both substances at the same time. We varied the dosages and we experimented with the time space between the intakes. The selection of the first and the second (once in a while the third) substance depended on the issues pointed out by the intention questions on Friday evening. Where we wished to overcome powerful resistance, I would give 2CB and afterwards LSD or MDMA to soften the descent and provide a gentler experience. Adding a substance to 2CB also lengthened the process. LSD also extends the length of the psilocybin effects, giving them together changed the experience into a combination between teacher plant and LSD in a specific way – the insights become extremely clear while the intelligent guiding of the plant remained.

It is important to know which substances should not be combined: MDMA should not be taken together with psilocybin.

The issue of self-intake

The issue of "self-intake by therapists" is highly controversial. In the book entitled *Therapy with psychoactive substances: practice and criticism of psychotherapy with LSD, psilocybin and MDMA,*[3] the chapter headed "Self-intake by therapists" contains the phrase "The safety aspect comes before intensive support".

What does this sentence mean? First of all the focus is directed at "drugs" and their presumed effects. "Inexperienced experts" go by their own prejudices – very different to personal experience – when judging the state in which they assume you must be when "tripping". They obviously believe that the whole thing must be an unsafe affair. You detect from their warnings that they hold the – probably commonly touted – idea that people totter about in an intoxicated state without any control of their senses. They warn against this type of danger, admonishing that the therapist would not be able to react in case of an emergency. Ideas of this kind are totally false. Your consciousness remains clear if you take MDMA, for example. The ability to interact and openness towards others are intensified, anxiety considerably reduced, feelings are experienced more powerfully, aggression is diminished, you become more aware of unconscious memories and you achieve emotional peace.

These authors referred to above prioritise the safety aspect. The second part of the phrase "The safety aspect comes before intensive support" is an implicit acknowledgement that the therapist's self-intake allows a more intensive support for clients through increased empathy. What would be the point if empathy were greatly increased in the client but not the therapist? They make only one brief mention here of the fact that the health risks are close to zero.

I never took anything myself when I started individual sessions. When I began my group work, I would try to lead a group after they had taken a substance. I would play the background music and take care of the setting but I would often hear the complaint: "You have no idea where I am at the

3   Edited by Henrik Jungaberle, Peter Gasser, Jan Weinhold and Rolf Verres,

moment." So I started to take a half dosage. When I did this, I found that my clients felt much more understood and empathised with in their substance induced state. I continued to practise maintaining a balance until I reached the point where I perceived normal and expanded consciousness as almost the same state – with the difference that I was able to observe and think with much greater acuity. Eventually I found that staying "in tune" became effortless.

During psycholytic training, where some of the authors referred to above acted as assistants and trained together with Samuel Widmer, it was a given that everybody in the room would take something so that they would all experience the same vibrations. Apart from the fact that this is the way I learned, the main reason for self-administering is to be in tune with the client and, in simple terms, be there for them where they need me to be. I can only achieve this if they and I meet in the same house, on the same floor, in the same room and at the very same point. A therapist cannot understand the inner sensitivity, location and condition of a client in a state of expanded consciousness if they are in a normal everyday state of consciousness themselves. When any traumatising "event back then" took place, caregivers were absent for the most part or unable to pick up on the child's emotions, let alone help the child to cope with such emotions. If I am not in tune with the client as they re-live the event in the session with me now, if I am not in the place where the event took place and don't meet them at the difficult point, I am abandoning both the child from back then and the adult of today in the therapeutic situation. This would be tantamount to retraumatisation.

By taking the same substance, I can get close to the event, vibrating with it, feeling it and enduring it with the client. But even though I am experiencing it too, I still don't sink into my own feelings. I remain discrete during the ascent, most importantly keeping quiet. I accompany, support and encourage the client during the plateau phase, staying by their side. They feel safe and held by this. A surgeon's scalpel cannot operate by itself. It becomes an extension of the surgeon's hand as he works. The same goes for my "tools". I ultimately become a tool myself, applying myself at any particular moment when required. The basic requirement for this is that you have to be in a similar state of consciousness. If a client needs to lie in my arms, they become my child. I am not the therapist acting is if I were the mother. In my book, this would also be just like the trauma all over again. Something flows from mother to child and child to mother, and healing occurs when this flow can take place in a session.

Everyone familiar with psychotherapy in the widest sense agrees that a therapist must have sufficient self-experience to draw upon. This also applies to psycholytic therapy in particular. When experiencing it for themselves, the therapist is no longer a therapist but experiences everything that their future clients will also go through. All they can do is deal with themselves. They have to process the same problems, go over the same stumbling blocks and above all follow the same path from "beginner to school leaver" (a developmental path that I will discuss later). You cannot opt out, evade or cheat in psycholytic therapy.

In my opinion, the amount of self-experience needs to be more than just sufficient. It is common knowledge in therapeutic circles that a client can only progress in their process as far as the therapist has progressed himself. A mountain guide cannot lead a walker through territory that they have not explored personally. It is highly likely that both of them would be exposed to danger. As I mentioned before, the "danger" with LSD for example is that you can end up in a situation where you come up against the darkest aspects of yourself that you have previously pushed away. If these shadows are not acknowledged as one's own and if they are projected outwards in a session, the client can become afraid of what they see in their interlocutor, calling it a "bad trip". Experiencing this oneself and recognising its value is a fundamental component of the therapeutic knowledge required in order to support the client in a similar situation and assist them with the integration of the experience. Extensive self-experience is also one of the requirements for being able to recognise any real dangers that might be lurking. This might be feelings of power that the therapist might develop in response to the client's admiration. Unrecognised projections by the therapist onto the client due to their own badly processed abnormal neurotic attitudes are also dangerous.

There are countless groups doing underground work with psychoactive substances in our society. For anyone interested in this, an important requirement before working with a group should be to find out how much self-experience (not trips!) the facilitators have had, and how and if they are able to deal with "bad trips". It is an unfortunate fact that even people who are officially allowed to work with these substances hardly dare to reveal publicly how much self-experience they actually have. So as not to put themselves or others in danger, all they are able to say is that they have acquired their self-experience within the context of medical studies. The reason for this is that these substances are illegal. Whereas opportunities to obtain personal experience in a legal setting are extremely rare and nobody is seriously convinced, this could be enough to acquire sound knowledge for working with substances while giving enough support to difficult clients in a research context.

Integration

In the *Song of Songs*, the significant words after each thought are "… and have not love", meaning that everything previously achieved would be worthless without it. It is just the same with the phenomenon of integration: everything experienced, acknowledged, understood and processed in therapy is worthless if it is not integrated. Without integration, experiences remain as a static quality, symptom or pattern, separated off from the individual.

Integration brings the insights that have been achieved in the expanded state of consciousness back home into everyday life. Integration begins as the therapeutic process starts, as an affirmation of a state of distress and a need for fundamental change. It supports the continuation of the process, with discrete and separate aspects of the psyche being repeatedly acknowledged, accepted and affirmed as "one's own". These split off aspects come from processed memories, painful suffering and loss, anxiety – and much else besides. Eventually these disowned aspects of the personality can be incorporated, transforming into authentic parts of their personality. The most important place where integration needs to occur is the daily routine of normal everyday life.

Through the medium of personal insights and managed interventions, we were able to achieve integration in the context of the setting developed in my guided groups. Because the "self-reflecting I" was maintained at adult level, it was possible to achieve "corrective new experiences" based on emotional and empathic support from the group or myself. The state of openness allowed emotional sensations to emerge, whether or not they were felt or perceived at the time. By reliving these feelings in this kind of setting, expressing their emotions, totally giving themselves up to the event one more time and accepting the support now available, the client allows a corrective new experience.

This is not a case of changing or negating the event that occurred at an earlier stage but, through the expansion of consciousness, much more a case of re-discovering feelings still present, which could not be seen back at the time of the traumatic situation and therefore failed to enter consciousness. This is why the expression "corrective new experience" needs to be supplemented with "extended experience of self-awareness" and an "incorporation of the circumstances at the time and the acknowledgement of how other people involved were affected by the event". To put it succinctly, the spectrum of past experience is extended and transferred to a more comprehensive conscious experience of memory. A real experience from way back in the past can be relived under the influence of a psychoactive substance exactly as if it were happening again, but this time with the result that the memories that were suppressed then are now accepted and integrated.

For example, a man who did not mourn as a 15-year-old boy when his father died suddenly was able to rediscover the deep pain and unfelt love and mourn his father 40 years after his death. He was able to identify the consequences of inexperienced grief, which felt like a major developmental step forward for him. He was also able to feel his mother's grief and recognise the effects that the sudden death had left behind on the whole family.

The integration of knowledge acquired under the influence of a psychoactive substance into everyday life takes time and can require repeated re-experiencing of the past trauma. The setting that we developed in our groups was optimised to fully support the integrative task.

The intention expressed on the evening before the session signals the first stage of the process of integration. This intention shows that the client is ready to engage with their process and their issue. It makes it possible to take up the issue during the sessions and confront it if necessary.

The details of the experience, leading to acceptance and processing of those details during the session itself, is the second stage of integration. Because it becomes possible to transform the existing content of perception and feeling into the content of current consciousness and at the same time understand that what was experienced as traumatising belongs to a remembered past, it can be possible for a trauma to be stored as "over" during the sessions and the client can "arrive" safely in the Here and Now.

The third stage of integration is the sharing session on the Sunday morning. What has been experienced is communicated in the round in the sense of a meta-communication process. This stage addresses the experience in the context of the issues that each person has brought to therapy and the next stages are worked out. Gestalt therapy elements and behavioural therapy interventions are sometimes necessary in order to transform what has been experienced into something tangible that the client can use. The role of the group as mirror and witness is particularly important at this juncture.

The fourth stage of integration involves writing a set of notes. These enable the client to go over the experience again in their home environment. Beginners often record the music played at a session while they are doing this task, so that they can enter the general mood of the experience again. The details of the session and the sharing of work are brought back into mind and reflected upon.

For the therapist, the notes are records of the content of the session and how that content was understood and integrated. For us, writing notes was the "ticket" to the next session. These notes often indicated the central issue and focus of the next therapy session. The notes also helped to identify developmental progress and possibly unrecognised resistance. A "traditional" therapy session sometimes helped process material between psycholytic sessions but was rarely required by clients who were further on in the programme. This therapy session generally discussed the details of the psycholytic session again, exploring the material, the possible lessons, the impact and how it may have affected them and their relationships since.

A further interim stage of integration may be required if there is a recurrence or reliving of the emotional experience of the session a few days afterwards. This may involve powerful feelings of anxiety, rage, and shame to name a few. These feelings often have an intensity and severity that have not been experienced before. It may feel as though the floodgates have opened. I often heard beginners say: "Now I'm right back where I was before" and "But it's no use". When this happened, I used the four-stage method:

1. Acknowledge that I am back in the feeling
2. Name the feeling
3. Own the feeling "This is my feeling of .... It belongs to me. I am merely observing what is going on inside me"
4. Try not to react to the feeling, but turn your attention to an activity in the Here and Now.

The key to managing this phenomenon of emotional re-experiencing is to stop the identification with the feeling and move to a position of observation and acknowledgement, while also taking responsibility for it as an internal process. As with the formation of a pattern of behaviour, emotional identification with the distressing feeling seems to intensify a neurotic or dysfunctional attitude and can be retraumatising. Some clients can have mood swings after a session, which a number of authors describe as "depressive mood swings after the event". This is why I have always been available for my clients at all times. If such mood swings are also accepted as being part and parcel of the unfolding process and observed, the challenging mood state generally resolves.

In most cases, however, normal everyday reality – the fifth stage of integration – is the most important arena for on-going reflection and gradual integration. Continuing reflection on the insights of the session, modified interactions and emotional responses in the outside world, increasing trust and confidence in the process all reinforce the integrative process. This maintains the patterns of long-term change. Integration into everyday life is the decisive stage of integration. Insights are useless in the end if they are not reflected in behaviour and our relationships with the world and other people.

The power and capacity to integrate experiences completely into everyday life require more than simple psychotherapy. Spiritual experiences – in the widest sense – gaining wisdom with regard to life, death, love and existence – experiences with a philosophical and religious impact, and deep human encounters, lead to an entirely different perspective. As a result of this attitudinal change and on the basis of this wisdom, the person continues to develop as part of an on-going, organic and evolving process. The symptoms that used to cause distress have resolved.

CHAPTER 6

The Arcs and Tools of Psycholytic Psychotherapy

Chapter six provides an overview of the different "arcs", where the overall therapy process constitutes the main arc. The process is illustrated with examples from clinical practice.

I describe the two sub-arcs, the first sub-arc comprises the external structure of a weekend. We return to the intention question and continue to the second sub-arc – the formal process of a session.

The six therapeutic tools are introduced.

The concepts necessary for understanding the details of the individual procedure of a session are clarified:

- **The function of symptoms**
- **Key assumptions regarding the client's intention**
- **Corrective new experiences**
- **The iterative integration process**

It will become evident that, as we look back and describe the event after a psycholytic therapy session, that a certain shape appears that was not obvious during the session itself.

Processes occurred as described. Any attempt to compress the complexity of the simultaneous processes into the single dimension of language would require a new type of book, where several parallel pages could demonstrate the phenomenon of simultaneity. In describing the process of a session or an intervention, the real-life experience during a session loses some colour and complexity through the act of attempting to capture it through the written word. This kind of description tends to be unavoidably rigid and one-dimensional.

To make matters even more complicated, every session worked differently, even if they followed a similar sequence. Something new developed with every new experience, or something that was already known developed further. This is why everything that has happened over the years in my psycholytic therapy work needs to be seen as a continuous process. Even when I used the same methods, I never did exactly the same thing. My approach was increasingly adapted to the situation at the time, and the tools became a natural component of my own therapeutic approach. While participants were in the process of change, I felt that my skills were growing, and as the process took new turns with the passage of time, the "tools" were honed, in turn exerting an influence on the transformation of the participants and myself. This was also helped by the fact that the group stayed together relatively constantly and I didn't have to keep starting "from the beginning" again. Naturally, the fundamental principle of looking, listening, observing and resonating was the basis for everything.

Any attempt to illustrate this complex process can only give an image that is approximate to the truth. An image of a mountain is not the mountain itself. Any picture that the reader might have in their inner eye is a photograph; it captures a moment, it has a rigidity and perhaps it is only in black and white and shades of grey. The more accurate the description, the more we lose the actual vibrancy of what has happened.

In order to manage this complexity, I am compelled to provide explanations at various points, which may sometimes feel redundant.

The first sub-arc: the external structure of a weekend

Friday evening – The intention question

We worked in a weekend setting from Friday evening to Sunday afternoon in my own home. In the early days I sent invitations to the sessions by post, then we switched to email contact as Internet use became more widespread. The recommendation was to take part in a session every two months, but the frequency increased as time went on. Participation was arranged with me as required.

As early as the Wednesday before, I would start to get the house ready for people to stay the night, go shopping and do the cooking and baking. Over time, the preparations and framework became a ritual, meal times included. I put mats I had acquired down on the floor in the work room, decorating it with a few candles and a bouquet of flowers. The music was prepared and I had read the notes from the previous session. The weekend started officially at 7 pm.

Most of the people present had been to therapy with me in the period between the sessions. There was a good atmosphere, and the participants were pleased to meet again, having lots to tell each other. We started the weekend by sharing an evening meal. All the participants would sit down on the floor cushions in the work room at 8 pm on the dot. Everyone reported briefly on what had happened in terms of their process since the last session, how they were doing and, most importantly, what their intention was for the next day's session.

The intention question generally came as a continuation of the process that had started at the previous session, or developed in their therapy session. We worked very hard on the intention question, fine-tuning it so that the subject could be identified as accurately as possible. I decided on the substance and set the dose based on the issues that came up during this discussion. The more experienced the clients were, the more they took the opportunity to make suggestions for the choice of substance and dosage.

The discussion ended at between 10 and 10:30 and we all went off to bed.

The second sub-arc: the formal procedure for a session

Saturday – Preparation, administering and ascent

We had a meagre breakfast of bread, jam and tea between 7:30 and 8 on the Saturday morning.

I withdrew into my office, where I weighed out the substances with someone supervising me. It was always important for somebody else to keep an eye on the scales. I put the weighed amount of powder into the little beaker with the person's name on it. I also prepared the second substance so that I would not have to weigh the powder or cut the LSD under the influence of the first substance.

While this was going on the participants set themselves up in the work room. I preferred beginners to stay close to me so that I could assist them quickly if necessary without disturbing the others. The very experienced ones sat in armchairs in the corners of the room and could also help if necessary. It was my role to decide where people would lie down and next to whom. We sat down together in a circle at 9 am, concentrating in silence. We held hands and all took the substance at the same time after making our open mutual promise of confidentiality.

This was followed by the ascent phase of approximately 90 minutes, accompanied by music in the introspective setting, which requires everyone to lie down on their mat with their eyes closed, not moving or speaking if at all possible, but focusing their attention inwards. If involuntary movements started up, especially if at the beginning, I would sit down next to the participant and allow these to happen gently until they passed of their own accord.

The plateau phase

When we had reached the plateau – the full effect phase, we sat up and remained silent for a while. Then the "expression-orientated" and "process-oriented" phases began. Expression-oriented means the essence of whatever was experienced in tranquillity had to be expressed in words. This approach meant that material was taken to a meta-level and brought into consciousness through verbal expression. All participants sat upright in the circle with their eyes open or closed, listening to what people said and adding things or nodding.

After a while, I would ask who wanted to do some work. Whoever spoke up took their turn. But I would occasionally name a participant too, especially if I could see that the subject to be addressed would be hard to open up. The substance exercises its most powerful effect at the start of the plateau phase, and the ability to embark on an inner search and overcome any remaining resistance is maximal at its zenith.

Work is process-oriented. Processing work is based on the conviction that the solution to problems lies in the symptom itself. The aim is therefore to go through the experience (the problem, hurt or whatever emerges) consciously and subjectively once again in a protected setting. The client is able to enter the directly (re-)liveable mental process, absorbing it cognitively and particularly emotionally with all of the associated attendant symptoms and without having to fend it off. They are also able to understand and describe it at the same time. By going into precise detail, the meaning of the reaction to past situations returns to an understanding and empathic mindset so that its effect can be deciphered and processed in terms of its meaning for the client's life.

In purely practical terms, I proceed as follows (I am writing in the present tense here in order to emphasise the immediacy of what happens). When we reach the plateau, I ask everyone to sit up. We centre ourselves and make conscious contact with our inner self. This happens with everyone concentrating on their sit bones for a moment, thus becoming present within their bodies. Where exactly am I now? Do I have a reference point that I can focus on in this inner place? To a certain extent – am I in touch with myself? This doesn't always happen, or to everyone, either. I then ask who doesn't feel centred, or I ask who would like to do some work. I then begin to work with that person in most cases.

I then look at the client directly as we make conscious contact with each other. I ask them what internal space they are at. I get them to continue describing what they feel there, how they feel there, or whether they can see, smell or hear anything. It may be that they are unable to answer some of these questions. I explore where they feel the feeling they are talking about in their body. This is my way of checking if they have a reference point for the feeling or even for themselves. Often, it isn't possible to give one specific place in the body. Then I know that it must be about an event where the link between the cerebrum and the anchoring of the feeling associated with the event in the body has been lost. I take in the answers and wait with empathy until I reach approximately the same energetic place within me.

I ask more questions, allowing the client (and myself) to get closer and closer to the feeling or perception, as if they might be zooming in on a detailed internal view of this one moment. I ask how it really, really feels, how they are clinging on to what they perceive and what else they are aware of. If they can still speak (!), I get them to tell me what thoughts are coming into their head or what they remember, encouraging them to continue experiencing this acutely. I repeat most of the phrases in a familiar tone to reassure myself that we are in close empathetic contact.

Because of all the work already done on all the details of their personal history and family history, I usually know almost as much about the person doing the work as they do themselves. I remember what has happened in previous sessions and about interventions and (previous) results that we have achieved with them. When in a state of expanded consciousness, my thinking is like a networking system. I am able to go into a state of resonance with the client, perceiving moods and states of being. In the moment of going into resonance with the client, all of their personal details are present as a whole on the meta-level referred to earlier, facilitating the associative understanding and giving the emerging material a context.

When in resonance I can put myself in the position of what it must have been like for the client back then, but I don't allow myself to be overcome by emotions. I express their emotions, "normalising" them by nodding in agreement and saying something like "That's right, that's part of it, I understand, it's alright", and I mirror their thoughts and feelings until we find a place where they feel completely at one with their feelings. This is similar to the process of leading a child who is scared of water gently into the water, holding their hand until they start to swim on their own. If the client engages in the process, it continues on its own after a while, and emotions begin to emerge.

I encourage the client to look further and stay with it, letting them know that I am right by their side, that they are not alone and that they have already overcome and been through everything that is happening. This moment of the process happens as if in slow motion. I endure with the client the thing that was unendurable in the past, forming the basis for dissociation or the state of being frozen with terror. It is endured through contact – gestures, posture, words, touch, being there, silence or a piece of music. Whatever is right and appropriate is determined by the moment. Held in secure contact, the client is aware of their senses. This enables their unconscious to let the overwhelming emotion burst through cathartically, releasing the feelings frozen within the body and mind when they could not be expressed, because they had got stuck. This moment of resonant contact often results in a release of emotion with crying, sobbing and trembling.

The client lets in the longed-for healing experience of letting himself be held by his father or mother. This new experience always requires physical contact – the connection between feelings, the body and the cerebrum has now been corrected to a certain extent, resulting in a corrective new experience. This approach has developed over many years of experience within and outside my psycholytic therapy. It is an approach that evolved organically to fit our needs – that does not mean that it is the only way to do this work. I would not want to make sweeping statements such as "The work is right that way" or "This is how it's done".

As far as possible, all participants watched what was happening as we worked. We often touched on an issue that affected everyone. A similar internal process took place in several people in the room at the same time. All participants took their turn – many of them entering their processes several times during the day. This continued until they all felt that they were "through" with their issues.

In most cases, the descent had already begun during this time. Everybody lay down on his or her mat again for the descent. If more issues came up in the room during this time they were identified. Then everybody sat down and we would set to work again.

The descent phase

There were different types of descent phase. If there was no intensive work required in this phase, I played *"non-resistance-music"* – emotionally evocative music. Most of the participants didn't like this music as it is intended to release resistance, the challenge is to not act out the resistance. I went on to play personally chosen songs and pieces during the descent phase. This sometimes triggered a process again, which we then worked on too.

Towards the end of the descent phase, my husband, who always took part in the sessions, went into the kitchen with a helper and prepared the evening meal. If everyone reported that they had now "landed" again, I declared the session officially over and we left the room.

Therapeutic tools

I. The therapist

The most important and primary tool for any therapy is the actual therapist – by making themselves available and being a constant empathetic presence. I have talked about my self-image as a therapist in both forms of therapy, where personal commitment in terms of psycholytic therapy work was much more intense than in the traditional form of therapy. In the previous chapter, I described how I worked in a psycholytic session.

My approach to a session in the early days was not as a therapist. Given that the request to hold sessions came to me from other people, I simply created the same relatively strictly regulated setting that I had learned in my training with Samuel Widmer. There was never any dispute with him over authority (either then or now), but the setting gradually evolved, becoming more liberal and flexible.

I did not actually start seeing the work as *mine* until after my first experiences with ayahuasca in Brazil in 2001, when Mother Aya told me to "Bake your own bread". Then I used a sequence from constellation work during a session – more by trial and error – and the other tools began to take their place alongside this technique, facilitating other therapeutic approaches. As the tools developed, the setting that I hade learned and borrowed from Samuel Widmer evolved with some of my modifications based upon my own trainings and experience. I believe that my own special contribution is the tool of "resonance contact". This is also present in traditional therapy, but its impact is not so great.

II. The substances

The substances are the second tool. I have talked about them and their function in the previous chapter.

III. Modified family constellation work

The roots of family constellation work, the third therapeutic tool, lie in systemic, psychoanalytical, psychodynamic and body-oriented procedures. Constellation work is a transpersonal method that makes it possible to acquire insights and solutions for familial entangled dynamics and problems that are not easy to resolve under normal circumstances. By setting up the protagonists, the inner images of the person to be set up are relocated externally and made visible. This can be about intimate personal relationships and entanglements in the family, their effects on individuals and personal or transgenerational trauma.

Deeply embedded inherited experiences often have their origins many generations back in the past, and are often connected with the fate of an ethnic group or nation (such as war), being part of a collective memory. The most important tool in constellation work is "representative perception", which is known to be a basic human capability. This enables you to reproduce the experiences of other people within yourself, without receiving any information about the circumstances or person beforehand. During this procedure, where you physically, emotionally and mentally "step into the other person's shoes" to a certain extent, information seems to be drawn from a kind of "morphogenetic field", taking account of the fact that everything is connected with everything by the underlying energy fields.

To reveal these hidden dynamics, the protagonists express their individual experiences until a coherent image of the relationships within the system has developed.

This process is usually accompanied by the emergence of strong emotions and deep feelings. The aim of this type of work is to make peace with the past, affirm it and accept it – however it might have been. This becomes possible because a deep empathetic understanding is achieved between the people involved, and this makes it possible to accept past traumas on a deep psychological level. It is also important to forego something consciously, as might be required following the early loss of a father or where a mother's love has been lacking. It is also about respect and appreciation of one's forebears.

We set things up in a "modified" way in our setting: we did without the initial image with the spatial representation of "standing by each other". We also dispensed with the pictorial representation of the developmental process that generally appears through movements and shifts within the space. The formation of hypotheses was also excluded by the external image. Because we found ourselves in an expanded and highly sensitive state of consciousness, the protagonists were able to enter the role of "representative perceiver" directly. Particularly at the beginning, we only ever looked at specific aspects of a relationship – between a mother and son, for example. The person affected did not choose his own representative, but still sensed his own issue within himself from the beginning.

The participants sat (rather than stood) opposite each other as the work was being done. They then simply looked at each other, feeling and perceiving the atmosphere and what was going on inside. Then they each expressed how they were doing and feeling. A dialogue would then often begin. I would sometimes moderate the dialogues between participants, offering them words and phrases that they could repeat as affirmation. We identified this as the current state of the dynamic using understanding and descriptive phrases. The recognition of this early reality often resulted in a long-desired embrace of overwhelming closeness, enabling respect and love to be expressed. Often it felt as though a profound and honest dialogue between the two characters was taking place for the first time.

These processes reached depths that I believe would have been very difficult, if not impossible, to access in a normal state of consciousness.

This seemed entirely due to the specific effects of psychoactive substances, which strengthened the capacity for empathy and improved the ability to think in a connected way. This type of corrective experience had a major impact on the lives of many of my clients.

IV. Live-Body-Work

Theoretical principles

A human being is created by the fusion of the female egg and a male sperm. The organism that results from this fusion develops according to a specific and immanent order. Each individual organ differentiates itself at a specific point in time and space. If this order is disturbed, depending on the moment and severity of the disturbance, this can result in either an abortion or, with less severe disturbances, any number of different malformations affecting body and brain.

We can assume that there is a kind of order in other fields of development that also has a certain range of tolerance for variations. We could also use the terms balance and homeostasis. In physiological terms, after the impact of a stressor i.e. an impact causing a departure from the baseline state, the organism always strives to go back to its initial state; this is an auto-regulation mechanism that we call homestasis.

If biochemical disturbances occur in very early pregnancy (medication, extreme emotional or physical stress in the mother) and the embryo survives, depending on the severity of the disturbance, it might return to the normal baseline state once the stress has passed. But sometimes the normal homeostatic mechanisms fail and the disturbance lives on in the person, perhaps with an increased sensitivity of stress responses – without them being aware of it. This sensitivity tends to have a presence in what we call the "implicit memory at physical level". These stress responses become readily triggered by certain stimuli, resulting in reflex behaviour. This tends to cause high level of tension even when there are no obvious stressors. This results in a state of constant vigilance, increased irritability, sensitivity and the inability to relax.

There are some interfaces in the development of an individual where biochemical activities, neuronal anchoring and the retention of emotions seem to merge. The embryo's system "classifies" every major neuronal or hormonal deviation from homeostasis as life-threatening and, depending on the stage of the pregnancy, stores it as an implicit sensorial memory in the thalamus and later in the hippocampus as a result of trauma in later life. Storage only occurs at the physical level at the beginning of pregnancy. Sensory experiences and reflex responses occur more frequently as neuronal development sets in and progresses. Every experience is recorded, embedded in the overall system as an early impression with all of the associated parameters and stored as such at the same time. As I have already mentioned, this procedure does not occur within the realm of the conscious mind and remains in the deep unconscious.

Disturbances occurring during this time caused by extreme stress suffered by the mother – such as violence or threat to survival – have a profound effect on the developing organism and affects the future pattern of response to stimuli in such a way that there is a reflex and sometimes disproportionate reaction to similar stimuli in later life – stimuli to which people not affected in this way do not react at all, or only very mildly. This disturbance is hardwired and remains constant within the individual. These patterns of responses at the interface of the biochemical and neuronal impact are deep within the unconscious. They cannot be suppressed and they are not usually acknowledged or labelled as such by the individual. In certain situations, the individual notices the disturbances in their feelings, others recognise them in behaviour, relationship patterns and other factors. Such developmental traumas lead to psychological stress in its widest sense, and sometimes lead a person to therapy.

This baseline state of stress response activity is deeply embedded in humans. It is present as knowledge in the cells – bringing us to the succinct but essential phrase: the body knows and remembers everything. What is felt as a disturbance in the earliest imprinting of the individual determines the pattern of perception and the subsequent patterns for interacting with the outside world. During the early years, new events and experiences graft themselves onto the already pre-imprinted unit of body, brain and psyche.

We were able to explore these patterns of perception in slow motion in our work with psychoactive substances. Interestingly, we gained insights into the perception process as also described by neuroscientists; immediately after the external sensory stimulus has been transformed into something heard, seen or physically felt, we go into interpretation mode. This interpretation is already dependent upon stored past experience. It then passes through a similarly embedded response experience (was it good or bad to react in such and such a way?) or a kind of weighing-up process to arrive at an actual reaction, which is then externally visible as behaviour. The very first experience leads to a concept and an initial interpretation that is dependent upon the degree of well-being or discomfort – i.e. on the extent of the deviation from the neutral zero line (I feel good. I don't feel good. I feel really bad. I feel a threat to my survival) – and the possibility of regulating back to homeostasis.

Some of my clients explored their own typical dysfunctional response patterns using this procedure. We ascertained that disturbances appear in the same way in all people and that individuals definitely apply their perception in the light of the disturbance in their own way but, in principle, still in the same way in reactions and therefore relationships.

Live-Body-Work as a tool

The term Live-Body-Work, the fourth therapeutic tool, did not exist when I started my psycholytic work. It only developed through minutely detailed descriptions of what my clients and I practised during the years when we were working together undisturbed. "Live" stands for direct, immediate, vivid, "body" for the physical and "work" for the body work we do and its effects. It is not meant to denote "direct body work" on its own, but going through the phenomena embodying the psychic process. My own experiences of "body work" at Todtmoos Rütte and "specific body work" from Holotropic Breathwork have influenced the Work. In bodywork, the body is seen as a manifestation of our being in terms of what has made us what we are. With specific body work as developed by Stanislav and Christina Grof, existing sensations are supported and intensified in order to release tensions and the feelings they conceal. In this way, the tool of Live-Body-Work essentially facilitates the integration of information stored in the organism and the material from various stress-ridden and traumatic events. In the beginning, clients sometimes spontaneously started to relive a state experienced as traumatic. I already knew of this phenomenon and its symptoms from Holotropic Breathwork, and was able to act in an unspecific but appropriate way in each situation.

As I have stressed many times before, it is in the nature of psychoactive substances to bring traumatising events into consciousness. It often took several sessions to obtain a significant insight into and clear picture of this type of event. At times, it only resulted in vague feelings, and pictures without feelings that provided a helpful pointer in the right direction. In our Live-Body-Work, we allow the traumatic event the opportunity, and the time, to manifest itself as if it were just happening again. The thinking behind this approach is to connect the client to the feelings that were within him before the onset of the fragmentation and dissociation, the expression of which is "frozen". As the client re-experiences his immediate anxiety, his helplessness and inability to defend himself, escape or go on the attack, by being able to relive and express these feelings as feelings belonging to him within his body in a protected setting, *"re-membering"* takes place in the true sense of the word, being a "re-connection with oneself". The most fundamentally important thing with this work is that the client knows that they are being held in a totally safe environment, so that re-traumatisation is avoided. Because he remains in contact with me through his adult part (the so-called self-reflecting I) for the entire process, he is able to tell the difference between the past and present at all times.

The real contact work consists of me holding the client, looking at him and talking to him, ensuring that he is really present with his self-reflecting I at all times. But it is not just about the holding. If a spontaneous event does not occur, we (re)stage the process so that the client regresses to the situation concerned. I then pursue the process: I press, pull and hold him very firmly – depending on the past situation and what is required to move forward. We always remain in contact through listening as this happens. If necessary, group members provide support when I ask for it. The process generally works cathartically, ending with the client coming into the Here and Now with absolute clarity.

Integration consists of the emotional and cognitive realisation that the moment of the event has passed, and is evidenced by the fact that thinking about the event can happen without emotion.

V. The group

The development of the group into a tool

As with the other elements of substance-based psychotherapy, the "group" tool has evolved over the course of time. The original individual setting with "stranded" meditation students became a little group: we sat together with a calendar at the end of the weekend and decided on the next meeting. There was no interaction during the session itself, and the sharing session didn't produce any group dynamics. This particular constellation was in fact all about a small number of people, who were definitely doing the same thing in the same space, but who otherwise had nothing to do with each other. As a number of people achieved self-awareness, they came to represent a group when they knew each other, and especially when they went through a group experience. They participated as competent co-therapists during the Friday night and sharing sessions.

When a difficulty emerged during the session, I began to go over to where the client was sitting and talk to them softly. This was then addressed as a topic in the subsequent sharing session. I began to guide participants when appropriate towards certain issues – such as their childhood relationship with their mother or father and other issues. This introduced a certain sense of togetherness into the room, but often it did not seem helpful as some of the participants had already worked on the issue or found themselves in an altogether different inner place. I therefore distanced myself from this approach.

At some point it became clear that I needed "support" with challenging issues, whether with approach or just "being there". I asked individual participants to sit up, give a hand and then lie back down again. I then introduced the procedure of everyone sitting up briefly to talk about how they were doing and if there was anything to report. A very brief discussion ensued, after which everyone lay down again to pursue their own processes - in silence if possible. But emotionally moving moments always led to disturbances in the room, causing some participants to sit up more. During intensive processes, this led me to ask all participants to sit up and remain quiet and present. This was when we started to shape the final setting as a group. Sitting up in silence and then sharing information connected us at the level of the heart.

As the "process-oriented, expression-oriented" setting emerged – working with individuals in the presence of the group – participants started to feel like members of a group. We practised talking about ourselves "in the moment" and giving each other feedback from this position. Aided by the specific effect of the substances, the path towards a trusting atmosphere and natural openness was a lot easier than in traditional groups. I was continually amazed at the sensitivity with which even difficult relationship issues could be addressed, and how the capacity for addressing and resolving problems and conflict grew as a result. The overall ability to communicate was also improved, especially since the two connected states of anxiety and aggression were significantly reduced, or even totally absent, under the influence of MDMA. This transitioned quite naturally into "substance-free" communication. Without having to be introduced specifically, the group operated as an image of the family, and some people became projection screens for each other, providing the opportunity to relive and integrate childhood relationship experiences and associated feelings.

The open and totally authentic observations made about behaviour and events during our work were experienced as consistently enriching and nurturing the process. The size of the group had increased to an average of 16-18 people by this time – sometimes there were more participants, but hardly ever fewer. I obviously also received feedback and criticism, too. But there was nothing of the group dynamic that I had experienced and feared in the encounter groups during the period of my own training experience. Over time, I would ask towards the end of the session whether anyone had something else they wanted to say about the issue or if we had forgotten to look at something. Nevertheless my position was always clearly that of the leader.

Obviously, I also had to "intervene" sometimes to restore peace to the working environment. The atmosphere was lively from time to time, but never undisciplined. Modified constellation work resulted in a special understanding developing between group members. In making themselves available to each other as representative figures, they gained an insight into the other person's system. It was not without moments of humour when someone said "I'm your mother, tell me what's the matter with you!" while they were working, sitting down in front of the person and carrying on with their work.

For most participants the group turned into a source of encounter and comprehension – a kind of "representation of the world". Behaviour patterns from everyday contexts were reconstituted in the group network, undergoing change over time. If necessary, participants gave each other the nurturing gift of touch without any further demands, relationship-wise. The integration of experiences into everyday life was made considerably easier by mutual interaction and communication.

The group as tool

Through regular work in a group setting, the group itself became an important fifth therapeutic tool in addition to the setting, Live-Body-Work, physical contact and group discussions. Each participant entered the group vessel with their own problems, but we also addressed a series of general issues together: often involving making peace with our parents and our place in the family system. Every one of us confronted our areas of shadow, exposing our projections and the way in which they affected our behaviour. We focused on spiritual issues during the session, acquiring shared insights into the existential state of being and a higher order and sharing philosophical and theological issues. We shared our developing insights and experience with regard to epigenetic phenomena and transgenerational trauma, recognising common features that we could formulate as general theses. We explored perception through the medium of perception.

Over and over again and with increasing intensity, we encountered each other at a deep human level, experiencing our shared humanity. We were in a dynamic involving a transition from "therapy completed" to "further spiritual development". The point at which this can happen is reached when the network of relationships of each individual with other group members is at a level where there are no more major issues to work through. This means that the problems that the individual has with himself in the basic father-mother-child story and relationship structures are clarified and largely resolved in the context of the relationships between group members. At this mature stage in the group process a cognitive process occurs within the whole group based on the cooperative interconnectedness of the group members. When our work together finally ended, the group had reached a point of synergistic interaction where we could be in silence and simply ascend together in a state of shared consciousness.

The meaning that we had for each other changed again with this development, although I was always the person who accompanied the therapeutic processes, managed the setting and retained authority. We came together on our path as humans in friendship and respect, feeling connected to each other. It sounds as though it was easy and happened naturally, but there were some very awkward sessions for both therapist and clients. Relationships and situations had to be clarified over and over again. Everybody in the room had to learn to deal occasionally with honest feedback that sometimes felt like the criticism. Questions and comments like: "What do you think you're doing?", "Why did you deceive yourself like that?" and "That does not sound authentic!" were commonplace. This explains why I had told the clients beforehand that the process would be no picnic. I wasn't spared these questions as group leader, either.

I say this to demonstrate that we didn't always go through therapy and life together "problem- and conflict-free". It was evident in everyday life that we obviously aren't completely enlightened and that there is still plenty of "room for improvement". But how we resolve our problems and treat each other is definitely marked by shared experiences.

VI. Music

The tool of music was also part of the development process, and this required much trial, error and practice to get it right. The use of music as a therapeutic tool was somewhat lacking in the training with Samuel Widmer. Samuel let us bring our favourite pieces of music with us and inspected them closely. A few participants were allowed to lead a small part of the session with their music, and the group was asked to give feedback. I grew up in a context where you had to listen to anything other than classical music in secret; the Beatles and swing music were taboo. I did not trust myself to use music to reveal something about myself. But in time a new world of music opened up for me in the sessions with Samuel.

According to Samuel: "You just have to listen to the pieces of music with your heart." This was hard for me to do. I tried to find out the titles of the pieces I heard but Samuel didn't like this and my plan made me feel like a thief. I recognised a few of the pieces for the heart-opening phase as it had been used in Holotropic Breathwork sessions. The music for Breathwork has a specific arc that powerfully shapes the process. I was able to ask other participants about the singers and composers of some of the pieces of music. I started an intensive search and spent hours in CD stores. I kept on listening to see if I was able to listen with my heart. I looked for pieces that sounded similar to the music in the session and began to watch out for the moment when I had a certain feeling of love or my heart opening up. When I found pieces that Samuel had played, I bought them and listened to them over and over again. I trained my perception of the feelings evoked by this music like a muscle.

When I found pieces that touched my heart I would buy them. I made quite a few bad purchases. So I just played the pieces I knew with my individual clients to start with and kept a list of the pieces I had played for each person. It is important not to play pieces twice, otherwise the feeling that dominated the first time it was played comes back again immediately. I listened very carefully when I attended other encounter groups and asked about the music. As I had to play new pieces of music for each session of Holotropic Breathwork, I was spending almost all of the money I earned through breathing work on music – almost 600 francs per weekend on CDs. There was often only one piece on the CD that I could use.

When I started with the psycholytic therapy I had a small portable compact device that I put in the centre of the room, piling the CDs up next to it. When I went on to work with my first groups, a simpler system was required. I bought a portable rack in which the CDs could sit one behind the other so that I could easily see the titles. I made a note of the CD tracks on a sticker so that I didn't have to search for them in the session. I prepared for sessions in minute detail: I pictured the various phases and thought about the kind of issues that might come up for individual clients. I looked for music with the relevant words. I put all of the CDs in a sequence, which I learned by heart.

The next stage in the development involved burning the tracks onto a CD in a certain sequence. But I always kept individual CDs to hand, too. With the advent of iTunes, I gradually started to take my laptop into sessions in 2004/5. I also gingerly started to buy single tracks on iTunes. Over time, experience had deepened and widened my knowledge of music – I had learned "to listen with my heart". I had also found my own style and had the confidence to play some challenging instrumental music to my clients. We moved to our current house in 2004, where I had a music system with speakers on the ceiling, giving the music a more intense effect.

Why include music in a psycholytic session?
Music has a special effect on people. It seems to work on different levels of the brain, giving direct access to the emotions. The reason and language of the left brain can be switched off.

The ability to hear comes early: at the 18th week of pregnancy the baby can hear the mother's heartbeat and internal sounds, can hear muffled sounds from outside and perceive the rhythm of the mother's heart, voice and movement. In this way, it begins to interpret acoustic signals – noises and sounds – from the external environment. This is a major factor in assessing the possible danger of situations in later life. All mothers speak to their baby in an onomatopoeic way, communicating with it through sounds rather than words. The brain links sounds coming one after the other to a melody. This kind of "melody", and ultimately all sequences of noise and sound, are stored in the amygdala, along with a certain vibrational energy and all of the other simultaneously triggered sensory impressions. There are links between the amygdala, which is also involved in long-term memory, and the limbic system – the site of emotional evaluation.

The convergence of many pieces of cognitive information means that listening to music can bring back emotional memories from the combination of all sensory impressions in a matter of seconds. A kind of exchange of information occurs within different areas of the brain (amygdala, hippocampus and prefrontal cortex), assessing whether information is already known or new, or whether known information has to be stored again because the content has changed. Auditory memory is therefore an essential component of overall memory function, and is primarily for orientation within the environment.

A number of different objectives are pursued through the use of music. As described earlier, music releases suppressed emotions both consciously and unconsciously. Without the mediation of language, it penetrates deep into the psyche. The feelings that emerge can be worked through by (re) living them intensely. In this way, anxiety, rage but above all grief and many other feelings can be felt authentically (again) for the first time. Music brings unconscious memories to light, engaging the psycholytic process.

Music supports and guides the choreographic arc of the effect of the substance to the same extent – ascent, summit, plateau phase and descent. Such music is important in that it subtly supports the process in terms of style, rhythm, tempo and volume, enabling the highest degree of openness and clarity of view. An important aspect is also whether the music has words, is vocal but without understandable lyrics or is purely instrumental. In making the choice, further differentiation is required due to the varying specific effects of the substances. The choice of music for an MDMA session will differ distinctly from the one prepared for an LSD session.

Music also acts as a climbing rope, which the client can cling on to at difficult points of the process. If they feel stuck or lost, they can "cling on" to the notes and the melody, enabling the process to continue. However much a piece of music may release certain general feelings, it is still possible for an individual reaction to be totally different. For example, if one female client of mine heard solemn religious music, she had a memory of being sexually assaulted by a man of the cloth, triggering a massive outburst of rage.

The choice of music is also influenced by the developmental process of the participants. A "primary school pupil" needs simpler, less challenging music than a college student; the more advanced and centred the client, the less music is required. My own development and the reactions and feedback from clients have played an important part in changing the music selection. Whereas I favoured similar pieces of music at the very beginning of my work that mainly differed in tempo and volume, I dared to choose individual pieces that seemed to be right for the individual mood as I became more experienced. We used a very wide range of music by the time my work ended and I felt that I had developed an intuitive ability to play just the right music at just the right time.

To sum it all up, you could say that the choice of music needs to be determined primarily by the substance chosen and the point at which it is to take effect. The participants' level of experience and the decision as to whether the session is aimed at being therapeutic or contemplative and spiritual are secondary factors.

The last LSD session that I guided started with a ritual introductory piece entitled "Calling all Angels". 20 minutes after intake I marked the beginning of the ascent with the piece entitled "Ambient" from the CD *Dance of the Heart Voyagers* by Byron Metcalf and Mark Seelig. About 40 minutes after intake – I followed the effect of the substance within myself and noticed a quiet unrest in the room – I played Paul Giger's *Chartre*, "Cript 1+2". Through its dissonances, indeterminate rhythm and absence of melodic elements, the piece engendered a certain sense of unease, seeming to amplify the palpable mood in the room, thus providing assistance to the process.

The next piece, which I played 65 minutes later, was called "Violina (the Last embrace)" by Lisa Gerard from *The Mirror Pool.* This piece was still dissonant, but interspersed with a continuous series of liberating harmonies and melodious elements. It then becomes orchestral; after a while you hear a voice and can't really tell if it is a man or a woman. It is not really possible to distinguish the lyric – but they sound like a dialogue. The piece ends as a voice fades away, leaving the form "open".

I led the transition to the next level with the piece entitled *"Ombre ma fu"* by Thomas Otten from *Close to Silence*. The piece is based on a stable 4/4 rhythm. A man's voice sings a slow, moving melody in a subtle vibrato, but which is moved on by the underlying beat. A choir sings interposed in the background, giving the piece a sacred feel. This was the final piece before the summit. After this, I kept the room quiet for at least 15 minutes.

At the summit of this session I played "Octaves of Light" by Deborah van Dyke from *Crystal Voices*. I was able to play this because there was complete silence in the room.

You can obviously make a completely different choice of music for any occasion. When using music as a therapeutic tool in this way, it is important to stress that I am only talking about my own personal choices and my own model of work.

The function of the symptom

The symptom, which the client describes as his "problem", which causes suffering and leads to psychotherapy, is the outward manifestation of an unresolved inner conflict. This conflict has its origin in traumatic events that are no longer accessible to the conscious mind and which therefore cannot be described in words. The symptoms are an expression of unconscious psychic material or trauma and indicate the nature of the underlying emotions connected to the trauma.

The re-emergence of traumatic material in the everyday consciousness is unconsciously hindered by the process of suppression, as the brain, not having a consciousness of its own, cannot tell the difference between the traumatic situation itself and the associated emotions from the past. This mechanism protects the client from the potentially dangerous situation, attempting to maintain a "healthy mental state" to some extent but, by doing so, it generates the symptom and its attendant circumstances. This affects the person's personality, in that the unconscious constantly tries to resolve the conflict through repetition, thus perpetuating and intensifying the symptom while giving the semblance of a quasi-stable situation. It is vital for the original traumatic event to be integrated in order for this cycle to be broken.

The conflict needs to be separated from the accompanying emotions so that the detail of the trauma is allowed to re-emerge. The traumatic event can then be viewed and understood in a new way. The client in therapy can then affirm and acknowledge the fact that the symptom has enabled him to survive. The solution is therefore "hidden" in the symptom itself, and must somehow be rendered in a new form so that it can be re-interpreted. This is the central issue, the recurring theme and the ultimate goal of the therapeutic process: the identification of the conflict expressed through the symptom and its transformation into a genuine personality trait, whereby the symptom becomes meaningless and disappears. Based on the dynamic described here, it is not simply a "problem" that I am working on.

The clearer the demarcation of the central melody of the issue, the less the symptoms need to appear. They are no longer necessary. As the issue is approached on the inner pathway and the aspects of the trauma resolved, the symptom-forming conflict is "demystified", thus losing its influence. The symptom loses its meaning through the process of integration.

The client is able to express this with a simple phrase at the end: "That is how it was. I affirm my story. It was painful, and now it is past. I can think and talk about it without feelings or emotions anymore." If the affirmation "It is what it is; it was what it was" is made, everything becomes normal, everything belongs and resolves itself. I call the following state "natural responsibility". It is the opposite of the kind of responsibility that I take upon myself and that sometimes weighs like a burden on my shoulders. Natural responsibility *per se* is no longer perceptible and is a further stage of integration leading to "This is who I am".

The importance of the expressed intention

Just as therapy can only be successful if it has a clearly defined job to do, each individual session – in both the traditional and the psycholytic setting – is more likely to produce a result if an intention has been formulated. This work with the intention question was a powerful factor with each person in therapy. The intention question evolved as the therapeutic process progressed. When therapy began, the central issue had usually not emerged, but when this central issue had been clarified, the intention questions became more specific and presented themselves more easily.

As I have described, the client formulated the intention question for the session on the Friday evening. In my remarks on "dosage, set and setting," I outlined the huge importance of expressing an intention for the specific effect of a substance under the section entitled "Set". Through conscious intent, our inner awareness focuses on an unconscious level, where the "need" or issue lies. This can only really happen with the knowledge that, if the setting affords the stress-free time and space for it to do so, the unconscious allows the very issues to emerge that have created the symptom. This means that the intention question together with the specific effect of the substance and the suitable setting will carry the client through the process in the direction of eliminating the symptom.

For this reason on the Saturday morning, I advised my clients to let go of the expressed intention and not to focus on it or any other issue during the ascent phase, but to open themselves up consciously to "everything that came up". I even advised them not to react to anything that came up in the first hour and a half. We then worked with the material that had emerged in the plateau phase.

The corrective new experience

A session can result in a wide range of different experiences. A psychic experience is a coherent unit that represents the storing of an event, the emotions associated with that event and its anchoring in the body. The term "corrective new experience" means that a new experience can take place that is able to supplant an old pattern of thought and feeling. "I acknowledge that my mother loved me" is a redemptive, liberating experience, promoting future relationships for a client who had problematic issues with his mother. His mother is probably already deceased so the issue cannot be worked out with her and the whole problematic issue lies dormant in his unconscious so that it is no longer accessible. The emotionally corrective experience creates an entirely new reference point for the mother and any associations with her.

I am talking about something more fundamental and superordinate in the context of trauma. In my view, the best formulation for this is *re-membering* – "bringing all members back to their rightful place". It is not a question of acquiring a new reference point after a trauma, but of knowing who I am and that I and all of my components are present and correct again, undamaged. These new reference points and *re-membering* (after *dis-memberment*!) appear for the first time in the session, but have to be consolidated and practised in everyday life. They must somehow be tested cognitively and emotionally over and over again as support until they become automatic.

Mystical experiences have a particularly high impact in generating corrective new experiences. Experiences of mercy or gratitude that cannot be expressed in words effect lasting changes.

The iterative integration process

Iteration is the act of repeating a process with the aim of achieving a desired goal, target or result. An illustration of the integration process shows how repeating a procedure in this way ensures that, after the integration of an emerging issue, the next intention question takes a direction that brings central issues further into consciousness allowing symptom resolution. I am seeking to illustrate how we avoided working on the symptom directly but allowed the healing to occur in the arc of the therapeutic process.

In most cases, what happens in the sessions does not lead directly to a final or conclusive answer to the question and the intention expressed the evening before. Often, they seem to have no connection with the main issue or goal of the therapy. But we can look back and establish that the knowledge, insights and experiences from a session guide the inner eye towards the next intention question. The sharing and written notes that come after the session, the next session, practising integration in everyday life and the client's gradually evolving awareness, also work alongside this.

The central issue or recurring theme (leitmotiv) becomes visible over time and after a certain number of sessions. The fact that the central issue produces the intentions, how it does this and the way in which it guides the process only gradually becomes apparent. Ultimately, these aspects all affect and react with each other. The method was oriented towards a process – the motor that drives inner development forward to a certain extent. The developmental path from intention question 1 to intention question 2 is not a linear one. It is more like a circular movement; every sequence of steps paves the way, opening up the process-orientated basis for a new path. Such iteration is embodied in the realisation that the path is the destination.

The new question is worked on in the same way in each case, so that the inner dynamic and central issue must be kept in view on the path leading from the defined starting point to the end state. In concrete terms, this means that we need to check over and over again whether we are keeping to the issue during therapy or whether we have somehow been sidetracked. As unconscious psychic material appears and becomes integrated in sessions, and as the central issue becomes ever clearer, it follows that symptoms lose their function and dissolve.

An ascent with MDMA

It is 9.00 on Saturday morning.

Everyone takes their place on their cushion. We form a circle together in silence. We hold hands.

Me: "I promise not to divulge the location or names of the people present or the medication. I promise not to harm myself or others in any way during or after this experience. I promise that I will come out of this experience healthier (more *cured*) and wiser. I take personal responsibility for what I do here."

I call each participant by name, asking: "XXX, do you agree to this?" They answer loud and clear: "I agree to this."

I hand out the beakers or capsules. We close our eyes and hold the medication in our hands for a moment.

"Have a good journey." We all drink from our beakers or take the capsule at the same time. Then there is one more opportunity to visit the toilet.

Everyone lies down quietly in their positions with their eyes closed. The idea now is to lie still without moving if possible and without talking. I sit down in my armchair, from where I can see the whole room, and play the introductory song *Calling all Angels* sung by Jane Siberry from the film *Until the End of the World.* I now close my eyes and focus my attention inwards to observe the effect of the substance as it spreads through by body.

After about twenty minutes, I notice the first signs of an effect – a slight tingling sensation. To support the process, I play a rhythmic piece of music lasting 10 to 13 minutes (such as Byron Metcalf, *Dreamtime Alchemy* or *Dream Tracker*). The rhythm and the darkness of the music feeds into the pelvic area.

Ten minutes later:

"Maybe my heart is beating a little faster. It's passing through."

"Now make a conscious effort to let go of all problems and questions and your intention and allow the substance to spread out inside you.

"Take gentle, regular breaths." – "Try not to make a noise. Keep quite still."

Silence

"Thoughts come and go like clouds in the sky – look at them. Don't react to them – let everything be, say yes to anything that comes up for you."

There shouldn't be a rigid silence, and everything should slowly fall silent instead.

Silence.

Occasionally I look at the participants lying with their eyes closed.

I follow where the effect of the substance is located in my body. The subtle and often barely perceptible tingling in my legs has gone. It now feels like a warm liquid is gently flowing into my pelvis, which opens up.

45-50 minutes have now passed since we took the substance.

I play a second piece of music. There is no regular beat anymore. A melody with a medium pitch and "allegretto" tempo, with dissonances that mildly irritate and slightly brighter in pitch than the previous piece (such as *Kerala Dream* by Kraig Kohland, Terje Rypdal pieces played softly for advanced participants)

Silence.

"Keep letting it all go. Just observe. Whatever comes along – perceive it and let it go. We will remember everything. Don't cling to anything. Only observe. Absolutely no reaction."

Silence.

"Say yes to the substance. – I surrender. – Please and thank you."

My pelvis is open. The effect of the substance will now wander through the diaphragm area in order to reach the chest cavity. Often, you can sense a gentle groaning coming from the chest cavity at this moment. The associated issue here is giving permission, giving up the power, letting things be. This stage of the substance's effect is easy if I can affirm the event within my body. The chest cavity starts to open up, breathing becomes a little deeper and a feeling of expansion emerges. If I am anxious or resisting, I might feel nauseous at this point. A struggle is being played out between my unconscious and conscious side, and can be felt in the body.

"Please breathe gently." – "I say yes."

I support this transition with a slow, solemn, melodically harmonious piece of music with a medium pitch, ideally purely instrumental. (Lisa Gerard, *Valley of the Moon, The Silver Tree*)

My heart hurts a little, as if it is expanding.

Silence.

The silence oscillates now more than before, vibrating slightly. The pain passes and the heart dilates – a relieving sense of certainty rises within me. My breathing is deeper again.

We have now been "on our journey" for around an hour and ten minutes. I play a piece of music with harmonies overlaid by a slow melody (instrument or voice – Anoushka Shankar, *Rise*)

Silence.

"And keep letting go of all thoughts. Let your breath flow deeply and gently. Let it all be. Simply affirm."

All is quiet in the room now. Almost as if we are at prayer.

One hour and 25 minutes have passed.

I play a short piece with a slow tempo and higher pitch – melodious, underlaid by gentle harmonies (Lex van Someren, *Calma e tranqulidade II, Intro*)

Silence.

"Once again: say yes and let it happen."

If everything becomes really quiet inside and I stay in observer mode. The substance seems to flow like warm liquid from my heart to the throat area and into my head. Any kind of resistance results in swallowing or a mild feeling of nausea. The path is always made easier when my heart opens up.

I whisper: "It's all about affirmation."

The warm liquid turns into a bright light in my head – Tranquillity, Vastness, Now and Forever, for which there can only be one word: Love.

I carefully fade in the sound of Tibetan singing bowls, no words, but sustained notes and sounds, which help to further expand the range of consciousness.

When the music has died away, the room remains silent for a while. Everyone is deep within themselves.

After this period – around 90 to 100 minutes have passed – I feel a sense of total clarity within me. I do not feel the effect of any substance, I feel very alive, very alert and deeply sentient. I have no thoughts or images in my head; there is just silence and vastness. Sometimes a phrase or word comes to me as if from within. I experience these words, phrases and statements as being appropriate, correct and coherent. They become guiding principles and maxims for my life and the session, such as "Gratitude is a special form of love" and "There is meaning to everything that happens to you". I sometimes feel blessed and in a state of grace. Heart energy has transformed itself into the energy of realisation. For me, this state means that I have reached the peak.

I watch what happens in the room. I am able to feel the type of energy in the room in this state.

"We have reached the peak."

After 10 to 15 minutes or so of introspective silence: "I would like to ask you to sit up for the next piece."

I play a "peak song" with lyrics, for the beginners it may be Kirtana, *Meet me*, for the advanced a classical piece, such as Double Concerto C-minor, by J.S. Bach, 2nd Movement. The music brings us together, intensifying the profound feeling that we share connectedness and love.

Working on the plateau

Example 1: Working with modified constellation work

The issue that comes up for O. is the "power struggle" with her ten-year-old son, S. O. takes her own role and chooses a man in the room to be her son, S. I ask her what the issue is. As she goes about her daily routine, O. senses over and over again that her son feels nothing for her. They sit opposite each other and look each other in the eye. We wait.

O.: "S., I am very proud of you. I love you very much and you mean a lot to me. It pains me that you don't feel anything for me."

S.: "You don't feel anything for me, Mum."

Me to O.: "What happens in you when he says that? And when you look at him now?"

O.: "I see his father. He is the spitting image of him. And I feel such rage when he behaves just like him. His father deceived me and left me."

Me: "And what is happening inside you now?"

O.: "I don't want S. to be like that."

S.: "I can see that."

O. looks steadily at S.

Me: "Tell him: 'S., you are allowed to become like your father'."

O.: "This is really hard for me. There's a lot of resistance. It annoys me. Now I'm sad."

Me: "Don't give up. Give yourself time."

A long silence. Mother and son look at each other.
Me to O.: "Say: 'You can be like your father'."
O. says to S.: "You can be like your father."
S.: "I don't believe you."
I ask someone to be the father. The father and O. are now looking at each other. This lasts for a long time again. The room is in total silence. An internal process is occurring in O. and nobody talks about it.
Me to O.: "Say: 'S., you can be like your father'."
S. moves right up close to O. and lays his head in her lap. O. is very moved, strokes S.; he snuggles up contentedly.

Afterwards, when we asked the person standing in for S's father what had happened for him, he said that he had felt a rapport and understanding between himself and O. that had never been there before.

We have sometimes been able to uncover traumatic events in a family's history in several sequences in this way, which subsequently enabled us to identify similarities between current and past behaviour, thus helping to explain the current behaviour. In O.'s case, the behaviour towards S.'s father was concealing traumatising experiences of being abandoned by her own father, which then became a long-term issue.

Due to the known specific effects of the psychoactive substances and through the increased ability to empathise and the improved capacity for networked thinking, setting-oriented processes were able to dig much deeper than is ever possible in the normal state of consciousness. This kind of corrective new experience had a powerful effect on the lives of many clients.

Example 2: Live-Body-Work

In order to prevent re-traumatisation, it is absolutely essential with this work for the client to know that they are being held in a totally safe environment. By remaining in contact with me throughout the entire course of our work through their adult part ("the self-reflecting I"), they are able to distinguish between the present and the past at all times. I would like to give an example of this:

A middle-aged lady was suffering from breathlessness and fear of suffocation. During a session with MDMA she identified the connection between her problems and her brother's attempt to stifle her with a cushion when she was about two years old. A number of sessions after this realisation, she expressed the intention to go through the trauma again. She wanted to look her fear "in the eye". We discussed the procedure: we would take LSD this time, and we assured her that she would be would be safe and held. We set the scene after she took the substance. She lay down on a mattress and slowly went back to the evening when she lay in bed as a little girl. When she arrived there, I remained in eye contact with her and the rational "Can you hear me?". A group member pressed a small cushion over her nose and mouth. I maintained eye contact. When she started to drift away I called her back: "Can you hear me? Look at me!" She assented by looking and nodding her head. After a while she began to fight back – he kept pressing the cushion over her nose and mouth. I put my arm around the woman, remained in eye contact with her and slowly encouraged her, as if in slow motion, to carry on and enter into every feeling that emerged: "You are safe, you are alive, it is only a memory, go on in ..."

A lot of time went by before she seemed to feel anything. Then she started to fight back hard, kicking her legs and trying to tear the cushion away. She shoved the brother away with her arms and legs, finally beginning to shout loudly, gasping for air. I held her, telling her to breathe: "Breathe, deeply, deeply, come, look at me. Can you see me? You are here with us in this room, look at me, what colour are my eyes? It's over, it's over."

During this sequence, I was able to catch the moment when she had left her body back then, consumed by the fear of death. When she started to shout and fight back, she was re-connecting automatically with herself and her true feelings in that moment in the past. Our eye contact and my voice kept her in the Here and Now. The safe place and friends surrounding her made it possible to go back through the hell and reach present reality again.

With Live-Body-Work, which focuses on the interface between the state of intactness and the trauma, we cut the link between the inner feeling and the inner event again. I consider that this leads to subtle changes in the wiring of the brain; you could call it neuro-psychotherapy. In the group, witnessing experiences like this help everyone involved to deal with such situations safely. On the one hand, the participants needed courage to be able to surrender to the process. On the other hand, they needed to be able to stay in contact with the therapist with the help of the self-reflecting I – even in difficult processes, which can sometimes require a relatively high dosage. A relationship of trust between client and therapist remains vital to success.

CHAPTER 7

Stages of the psycholytic therapy

Chapter seven describes the procedure prior to starting psycho-lytic psychotherapy; the introduction to the work, the selection and briefing of clients.

I introduce the targeted skills requiring intensive practice for this work.

We revisit the non-performance-oriented model of "From beginner to school leaver" under the heading of "Stages of the psycholytic therapy" illustrated with examples.

Introduction to the "work"

I had developed the setting for my psycholytic therapy work by about the end of 2004, and I stayed with it in this format to the end. The participants were now exclusively my own clients. The clients whom I informed about and then invited to the sessions had already been to conventional therapy sessions with me several times at least, and often for a number of years. My decision to suggest the psycholytic method to a client was mainly based on the observation that current therapy and other methods such as Holo-tropic Breathwork weren't making progress or effecting change in terms of symptoms or state of mental health. Based on the symptoms presented, I sometimes suspected a dissociated traumatic event, meaning that I would recommend further work through consciousness expansion very soon after therapy began. If I felt a real need to trace the background of a client's symptoms, I asked them whether I might talk to them about my "other tool" (working with substances).

Selecting clients – briefing and contraindications

I now had firm selection criteria for clients who might be considered for psycholytic therapy.

- Did they have any previous experience of therapy?
- How great was their motivation for working on their issue and staying with it?
- Had they also tried this with Holotropic Breathwork?
- Had I been able to exclude a psychiatric diagnosis, such as borderline personality disorder or a severe case of weak ego-strength?
- Were they physically healthy, especially with regard to blood pressure and asthma? Were they taking medications, particularly antidepressants?
- Would they engage with me as a therapist – It wasn't going to be a picnic!
- Were their support systems built in such a way that they could endure being destabilised for a while, too?
- What was their social milieu like?
- What would their partner say about psycholytic therapy?
- Could the partner be included or not?
- Were they prepared to enter into a confidentiality pact with me?
- Were they disciplined enough not to talk to acquaintances about the "work"?
- Did they have sufficient capacity for taking personal responsibility and self-reflection, meaning that they would not blame the substance or me as a therapist for any disappointment?

But the most important question of all was: "Do I trust this person?" Because it was illegal, my clients ultimately held the fate of substance therapy in their hands. This made the question a very important one. Strictly speaking, it could not be answered beforehand anyway. Once I had answered this question to my satisfaction, there came the delicate point when I had to ask the client up front not to disclose anything about what I was about to tell them. "If what I am about to tell you is not for you, please keep what I tell you to yourself. Can you promise me that?"

I would then talk about psychoactive substances and consciousness expansion in general terms. They almost always fired back the immediate question: "Do you mean LSD?" Most of them had heard about it, and some had tried "drugs" once. In the beginning I had a little brochure called "MDMA" that I would lend to people. As Internet use spread – I didn't begin to use it intensely myself until 2003 – clients would do their own research, which led to longer decision-making processes and preliminary discussions. Years later, the website of the Multidisciplinary Association for Psychedelic Studies (www.maps.org) was the best source of information that I could offer. There were also clients who simply said: "If you are recommending it to me, then I will do it. I trust you. I really don't want to know too much about it."

The briefing about the effects, side effects and contraindications of substances changed over the years in line with the current state of knowledge in each case. Little was known about contraindications or health risks at the time when the first psychonauts were experimenting with substances. There was hardly any reliable information available, and you had to rely on hearsay to a great extent. Whenever I experienced anything new, I would just observe until I could assess whether to even talk about the issue. I was already observing in normal therapy sessions whether the client had health problems or was taking medication or exhibited other contraindications.

After the appropriate introduction, I would leave it up to the client until the next regular session. If the client decided to do a trial with a psychoactive substance, we had a "beginner's session" – a session in an individual setting where MDMA was administered – apart from a few exceptional cases. Every experience with a substance – not just the first – is different, and is highly individual. I will now describe the "guidelines" that I had extracted from the advanced phase of my earlier psycholytic therapy work.

Learning objectives for effective psycholytic therapy

You need to practise and develop a number of skills in order to work with a substance safely:

- The ability to simply observe without any kind of evaluation
- Listening and hearing
- Not reacting
- Silence – not in the sense of keeping quiet, but of achieving peace
- Seeing with the heart
- Being in the moment
- Establishing and maintaining the "self-reflecting I" – the "empathetic, benevolent observer"
- Self-guidance

From "beginner" to "school leaver"

"Taking a psychoactive substance" in a therapeutic setting is fundamentally different from recreational use or "tripping". Having an inner experience with a psychoactive substance with the aim of self-discovery is not an innate ability; it has to be learned, and above all practised. You have to have the determination to enter the process of self-discovery and a willingness to both impose self-discipline and allow yourself to be guided.

This type of emotional and psychological development in my method of psycholytic psychotherapy was likened by the group to the progression from starting school to that of school leaver. But the same thing applies here as everywhere else in life; we all know that the actual learning phase doesn't begin until, often at the point when we have accumulated the greatest amount of knowledge, we complete our studies and start applying this knowledge in everyday life. And we all know that knowledge can only become wisdom by using it and fully living our lives.

The first session
Here are two examples of experiences during a beginner's session:

I.
I'm on a roller coaster again, which I know well from Holotropic Breathwork. I feel like I'm speeding up, down and up again through the air, constantly picking up speed. It's not a feeling of anxiety, but rather of thrilling intensity and a noticeable opposition – increasingly centred – like swirling waters, ending up in a single stream.

The cramps are slowly disappearing ...

... My head is thrown back, shaking back and forth ...

I look closer: suddenly, everything disappears into a giant terrifying black hole. Black as pitch. I'm seized by panic and anxiety.

I babble: I don't want to die (I nearly died from an illness as a child).

... I come to the crystal-clear realisation that everything is resolving itself, and that my quest for meaning will be met if I let go of all my wishes, interests and ambitions. I understand spontaneously some of what I read and what I never understood before ... Everything is clear for a moment. Minutes later, these light-rays of realisation have disappeared.

II.
... Something is wrapping itself around me, passing through me and carrying me up into a bright, illuminated room on a plateau. But as soon as we get there and I expand myself through my breathing, it recedes ...

... Music passes through my entire body as a soft, vertical process of opening up. As if taking off a coat, I step out of my body and take my path. ...

... In the 3rd phase I pass though bright, expansive, delicate spaces. No questions emerge, no expressions or images for me to follow. Time and thought are lost, I'm just... "This is love!" comes the intermittent realisation.

The "beginner's session" is for initial contact and impressions. Ideally, this first encounter with a consciousness-expanding substance can be used to eliminate concerns and received ideas about "drugs", or at least show them in a different light. But the client might come to the conclusion that they don't actually want to work on themselves in this intense way. Or maybe they felt nothing and therefore believe that this form of therapy isn't suited to them. They have to make a decision; do they want to take the psycholytic path with my support – or do they prefer not to? Both decisions have far-reaching consequences.

The problem is that yes, we can say that there will be inevitable consequences, but we can't be specific or say what exactly they will be. The path may be stony but we have no way of knowing beforehand what theses stones are like, how big they are or where they might be lying on the path. As with any effective therapy, the "psycholytic path" always brings changes affecting the individual's entire biosphere as their ways of seeing and thinking are extended into new and different dimensions. Their social relationships will inevitably change with the passage of time.

As part of this change, old friends of the client may disappear and new friendships will be made. The same thing can also happen with so-called "enemies". Maybe they will no longer be able or want to stay in their job. Maybe they will realise that their relationship is no longer right for them and that they do not want to remain in it. If the client gives space to what they experience, their entire approach to these experiences will undergo a basic change.

We cannot predict the extent of the impact of these factors in advance. Nor is it possible to predict what might "escape" the client if they decide not to include working with psychoactive substances in their box of self-awareness tools. Only the issue of illegality is resolved by deciding against such work.

There is often something a little overwhelming about the beginner's session, which, as I have mentioned, was always conducted with MDMA. The experience of sensing something, feeling love, recognising a little bit of themselves and knowing that they are being held securely in the setting provided has certainly made 95% of clients want to "carry on" after this session. A small number of people felt nothing at all, except maybe a lift in their mood. In hindsight, these cases mostly involved a very serious trauma, and I had to assume that the resistance to trusting the substance and myself was just too great.

In this kind of situation, some clients have tried a second time, which has resulted in a slight change – they felt a little better in themselves, and a very subtle change towards a less anxious state of being could be observed in their everyday life. In turn, this made some of the clients decide to continue with the adventure of exploring their unconscious. Very few clients, maybe two or three people from my entire client base, decided to give up at the beginner's session. This was mainly down to a consideration for the people around them and the illegal nature of the work.

Sometimes after the session, some clients experienced a period of about ten days when feelings of openness and love returned, while others had emotional mood swings ranging from total certainty to serious doubts about crucial life decisions. In all of these cases it was important for me to tell the beginners not to make or implement any life-changing decisions during the first four weeks after the session, such as quitting their job, leaving their partner or bequeathing their house. I sometimes described the process to them as follows: "Imagine your inner self as a glass of water, in which you can see various layers of sand from the outside. These layers represent the different feelings that have been laid down in your life as a hard layer made up of different colours. When we are in a session, it is as if we are stirring the contents of the glass with a stick, making the sand swirl around in the water. During the period following the session the sand will settle back down again, but in a new order. In fact, some clients said they felt different after about four weeks – mostly for the better, perhaps "a bit clearer" or "at last, I can feel something".

Here are two examples of after-effects in a beginner:

The next few days throw me into a real maelstrom. Inside, I remain indifferent and distanced. I don't feel bad but I am a little "absent-minded". I find it really hard to keep a handle on things.

Over the next period of days I keep entering a state of openness, and the feeling of openness and connectedness re-establishes itself. Unfortunately, my heart closes up again but I now know that I am capable of love.

Anyone wanting to continue went from being a beginner to a "primary school pupil".

The primary school pupil

In the following sessions, which now take place in a group, the client learns how, "to be with a substance". They familiarise themselves with the fact that the effect of the substances follows a choreographic arc; on taking the substance, the ascent phase begins and the effect of the substance spreads throughout the system. They receive the following instructions and learn to remain totally silent after taking the substance:

"Whatever thoughts, feelings, realizations or ideas might come to you: observe them as they come. Let them pass by like clouds in the sky. Don't cling to anything. Be with what is."

In most cases, the client is unable to follow the instructions, remaining stuck in thoughts and ideas about how to solve problems, meaning that they often feel confused and remember little afterwards of what they experienced in the session.

"Breathe deeply. Relax your body. Surrender to the substance. Say yes to whatever comes along."

"Observe everything, don't engage in or react to anything."

Using these simple repeated phrases and accompanied by specially selected pieces of music, I lead the participants through the various phases of the ascent, which lasts for around 90 minutes. Then comes the plateau phase. This is the period when the substance has reached its full effect. This phase lasts for different periods of time and can be prolonged through silence. It can last two, four or perhaps five hours.

The primary school pupil will not yet have reached a state of totally clear expanded consciousness on the plateau. They still mostly feel "I'm on it". With increased practice, they will learn to guide their own process, ask themselves questions and focus on a specific issue for themselves. Or simply just be. They learn to make contact with others in this state, to communicate in a new and open way and to work on an issue with the therapist. In order to be able to do this, they need to practise the basic skills of non-intentional, non-reactive listening and observation and being present in the Here and Now.

At this stage, the goal is to really feel at peace and stay centred, although for many this goal is still some way away. Centring is required so that the client learns to be in contact with the "self-reflecting I". The self-reflecting I includes the ability of a human being to observe himself, establish a reference point within himself and the body and to maintain this point consciously. On perceiving it, he is able to say: "I am the person now taking part in a session."

The idea is then to merely observe thoughts and feelings in an empathic manner, which means practising introspection without self-criticism. By observing without judging, it is possible to identify inner movements and begin to describe them. Mindfulness in the Buddhist sense and being in the Here and Now is the primary discipline to learn during this phase.

Why is this important?

Consider the scenario that occurs if we were to simply go "on a trip" and take the substance without this self-reflecting I. We are likely to find ourselves "surfing around" in feelings, regressive states, wonderful or anxiety-inducing feelings, but we are merely skipping along the surface of our unconscious minds, which can lead to re-traumatisation in the worst-case scenario. The integration of any previously unconscious psychic material that might emerge requires presence and conscious processing. In the case of a traumatic experience for example, the traumatising event must be consciously reconnected with the associated feeling and experienced once again and then imprinted and acknowledged as something that is now "past".

If the self-reflecting I is not "present", and the observer is therefore somehow switched off, it is impossible to maintain this connection and process the trauma to the point of resolution, thus the trauma is merely repeated. It has to be possible to record the realisations and feelings that emerge during the session and the accompanying interactive work both cognitively and emotionally. This ensures that the resulting resolution can become a lasting "corrective new experience".

The primary school pupil will get to know the various substances during the sessions and obtain an initial impression of how to handle them. They are not yet able to perceive the dramaturgical curve of the various substances. During the ascent phase, they are not yet able to clearly identify the "location" in their system where the substance is making itself felt. They might feel a little uncertain in the plateau phase.

The task of the primary school pupil is to observe the inner process at this stage – to listen to and watch what is going on inside. This is the creation of the "inner observer". During this exercise, the individual is repeatedly struck by the way in which the critical and censoring mind comments, evaluates and interprets findings, images and insights. Gradually he develops some familiarity with the manner in which this happens. The primary school pupil first has to notice the point when he slips back into interpretation mode – be it positive or negative. He will have to observe the observer. Any evaluation hinders the cognitive process.

How can we achieve this non-evaluating state of awareness? The path to the inner observer is the path of judgement-free affirmation of what is and how it is. This is easy to write and read – but the path is difficult and requires a lot of practice. Over the course of time, this results in an attitude of increasingly consistent inner affirmation of what is. The "inner observer" becomes the "empathic observer". Empathic because he only notices and identifies what he sees – without judgement. Over time, he will evolve through this into the "empathetic benevolent observer". The very choice of words for describing experiences already constitutes an evaluation. For example, the empathetic observer may say: "I can see that I am evaluating and I affirm that I am doing it." This is how we begin to tread the path towards self-awareness.

Biographical material often comes up during sessions at primary school level. This results in age regression and the re-living of earlier experiences. Because the latter occurs in the present, these experiences appear as new to the brain. With the help of the self-reflecting adult I and with the support of the therapist, these experiences need to be understood cognitively and emotionally as events and memories that belong firmly in the past. If this happens, the first step is achieved towards integrating a problem within the session itself.

In order for integration to happen, it is vital for the traumatic emotional event to be relived and re-experienced. Experience is defined here as the cognitive understanding of a memory that is coupled with the feeling triggered by the original experience back in the moment. This means that simply talking about a trauma or reading self-help books in an attempt to resolve the after-effects of difficult life events is a pointless exercise.

At the initial biographical material stage, one of the main aims is for the child to focus on the parents emotionally and accept them. The reason for this is that the first relationship any human being has is with their mother and father, and any other relationship will repeat the essential elements of this initial form of relationship. Attachment patterns – which start to take shape from the beginning of pregnancy – are revealed through the exploration of the parent-child relationship.

In order to be able to resolve relationship issues, the nuances of this stage have to be addressed in increasing detail. This covers biographical, systemic and cellular levels, and can enter the spiritual dimension in some cases. Because realisations are made slowly and not always in a logically conclusive sequence, and because interpretation is not always successful, where possible, the primary school pupil should not make any decisions that might throw their daily routines and life into disarray. The primary school pupil is advised to take this precaution, but it is obviously left to them to decide.

For the most part, experiences in this phase have a strong emotional hue, and an almost euphoric enthusiasm for the work often sets in. In this period, transference onto the therapist often takes the form of the client believing that they have now finally met the right person in their life. The therapist is required to take a clear stance here, as there is a danger of the therapist being over idealised at this point. The individual therapist must be clear about the role they want to assume in relation to the client, and the issue needs to be discussed. There is sometimes also a kind of dependency on the therapist – as seen in traditional psychotherapy – which is in the nature of things. Resolving this dependency requires the client to move into a more independent adult position, and is part of the aim of therapy. However, the rules of traditional therapy cannot be carried over to psycholytic therapy directly.

After the plateau phase the descent phase starts. Old thoughts, feelings and situations slowly start to reappear for the primary school pupil during this period, even though they are not yet totally clear. Consciousness restricts itself to normal consciousness again. The descent phase needs to be used to recapitulate the session experience, recollect and try to carry any realisations over to the level of normal consciousness.

It is not advisable to give the primary school pupil the same substance such as MDMA several times in succession. The unconscious learns quickly to build up the usual resistance. By giving different substances, we move closer to the core psychological material by a range of means, avoiding the habituation effect. This doesn't apply to the primary school pupil alone, but I have found that the reaction to a substance is greatly dependent upon anyone's personal state of development. If he experiences an opening up of the heart at this stage just by using MDMA, he will achieve the same state with any substance and at a lower dose at a later stage.

Mystical and breakthrough experiences are possible at any time – they **always** have a healing effect. They widen the world view, lead to a reconnection (*re-ligio*) with that which is bigger than we are and focus our attention onto what is essential.

The primary school period can last up to 25 sessions before moving to the "secondary school" stage.

Examples of experiences at primary school level:

I.

The memory is very patchy at the moment. I can still remember lots of noises and you telling me lots of times not to move. Then we sat together again as two groups of men and women. I sat next to M. and then between the people in the front. I know that I would have liked to join in the conversation but could tell that I would only have been able to contribute expressions and rudimentary memories of the time with my partner to the conversation. I didn't have any experience so I just sat quietly. I can still hear your words clearly: "Move away from all feelings, move away from yourself." I still have no idea what it means and I still can't identify the various opening up points.

II.

It all went really fast to begin with and my situation became very clear to me: I saw that all of my behaviour and words are resistance: resistance in avoiding feelings that I do not yet have or want to accept. In a nutshell, I spent the whole session circling a feeling like a cat on a hot tin roof. The good thing was that this concentration had a certain cen-tring effect, and was somehow a leitmotiv (recurrent theme) for me, keeping me from dropping out. "Patience" was another leitmotiv. I have a tendency to do things too quickly. When we first got together, it was helpful when Y. acknowledged me with a nod, and he often kept me in order. For the first time, I had the feeling that I wasn't totally weird. Physical symptoms this time included a strange compulsion to yawn, which I am familiar with from long meditation sessions.

III.
A pleasant tingling in my hips made me think that I was also feeling the so-called ascent physically. Then I went through periods of bore-dom and impatience to relieve the pressure on my bladder. I did hear someone visit the toilet but wasn't able to make up my mind whether it was serious or if I was just imagining it. So I went on for ages with the pressure on my bladder, I ultimately emptied, proving that I was not imagining it. Then you played music. I felt as if my heart was going to open up. Tears came into my eyes instead and I had a strong feeling of hopelessness linked to the idea of everything being meaningless. I wanted to stop myself crying but didn't manage it and then you asked me to sit up next to you.

The secondary school pupil

The secondary school pupil starts to learn how to distinguish between the phases of effectiveness of the various substances on the body, the brain and the feelings. As MDMA starts to take effect, there is a slight tingling in the feet. When MDMA has been taken, its effect can be observed as a physical sensation. You can feel the "substance" pushing itself up and up through the genitals into the abdomen like a roadway, opening up as it goes, through the diaphragm into the heart chamber and then through the throat into the head area. If we use the model of the chakras, the ascent is experienced as if all of the chakras were opening up, one after the other. The points of transition from one level to the next are often still unpleasant for the secondary school pupil. They feel like they have to fight resistance. This is an expression of their fear of surrender and opening up. This is the point when the state of their heart and mind is revealed.

Two stages are especially characteristic of MDMA in the opening up phase; in addition to a safe setting, they specifically demand a firm inten-tion to engage in the process. Stage one is the transition from the abdomen to the heart chamber, the step towards opening up the heart. This requires emotional and physical surrender and an inner acceptance of everything that comes along, so that what is defined as love is ultimately allowed to be. This demands the courage to discover new things and maybe also some unpleasant things within oneself. The secondary school pupil still fears this surrender – fear of opening up their heart and the concomitant state of connectedness. The second difficult step is from the heart chamber to the area of expression – the throat. Allowing the state of openness, expressing oneself verbally, is the next, often frightening stage. But sometimes the secondary school pupil is already able to let the effect rise into the crown chakra. At this stage of the experience, this state is felt as overwhelming.

The secondary school pupil begins to be able to distinguish between the different types of substance, familiarising himself with their characteristics. In most cases, they develop a preference and certain respect for one substance or another. For example, the secondary school pupil often describes 2-CB, which reveals the structure of resistance, as being difficult in the ascent phase, as it reveals all the turmoil of everyday life in this phase and the dark sides of the personality in the plateau phase. LSD is still a colourful and animated experience for the secondary school pupil, although he often finds it hard to stay balanced and achieve peace.

For a while, the secondary school pupil can follow and work on the intention that he introduced in the Friday evening discussion and took with him into the session by himself. He learns how to guide the process briefly himself, go with an intention in the session, ask himself questions and wait for the answers. To put it succinctly; through listening and watching, he starts to take up the position of the inner observer. But he is still emotionally irritable. His consciousness becomes clearer during the plateau phase. The secondary school pupil sees his realisations and scattered spiritual and peak experiences already appearing as a kind of "enlightenment" and often has a premature tendency to see the issue as closed.

He continues to deal with issues from his past history but his experiences are less about age regression than before. He recognises the systemic family pattern now; he begins to appreciate his parents as people who evolved according to their fate and he understands them from a more empathetic standpoint. This phase lasts for a long time – generally around 20 sessions. The main issue starts to appear with increasing clarity for the secondary school pupil and it emerges as different variants with different substances, so that he sometimes feels like he is going round in a circle.

As with the primary school pupil, the secondary school pupil keeps having realisations of a general and spiritual kind. He also notices that his interest becomes more focused on his relationship patterns and everyday behaviour. He recognises himself in others and has an increasing understanding of the essence of projection. He begins to deal with his resistance, realising that this gives him access to feelings that he didn't have before and / or experiences feelings again when he had stopped feeling them. He comes into conscious contact with his unconscious.

Although this description of the secondary school phase is only brief, it is actually the longest and most demanding part of the work. The essentials – handling the substances, staying with tranquillity and maintaining the physical and inner balance – are to be learned in this phase. To illustrate this, here are a few brief extracts from statements made by secondary school pupils:

I.

Stopping thoughts coming up is going well today; am able to remain longer and longer in this state each time. My intentions appear, I send them up and meet them there again ...

II.

The substance is so sweet and delicate today that I set myself in motion. It feels like I am far out there really quickly but every little sound sends me speeding back. I move directly towards tranquillity and clarity.

III.

I slowly felt the effect of the substance and it was a very physical experience. My feet felt cold and I felt tension everywhere in my lower legs and feet. At the same time, I felt this "barrier" under my ribcage. I quickly realised that this corresponded with my state of control and experienced this as a reflection of what this domination was doing in my body. The barrier pressing under my ribcage seemed to form an hermetic seal, preventing the flow from passing from my abdomen up into my chest. I focused on the control and hermetic seal; I acknowledged it, recognising that its "good work" was about protecting me. I then went back into the empty space, where I was able to park my thoughts and surrender to the substance. The barrier disappeared. A feeling of pain and profound grief came from deep within my abdomen. It got stronger and stronger as it travelled upwards, spreading out. It took hold of my chest cavity. As the last of the control moved to my jaw, my teeth started to chatter and tears ran down from my eyes. The painful grief for my lost twin brother that had been dammed up for so long was able to flow freely at last.

IV.

I'm already there in the first part. I don't feel well. I find it hard to hold myself together and feel rather lost. F. works with me first. I perceive it and know what it was about but it didn't leave any traces behind. I need to look it in the eye and accept the chaos within me, taking it to myself. It is the same place I have often been to. I say "I don't understand" and the answer is "There is nothing to understand".

It was all about the Holocaust, which I still don't understand. I remember it and my visit to Yad Vashem at the same time. I see the atrocity before me again: 6 million people murdered, and I don't understand what led to it happening. I see the disbelief of the Jewish people, I am bewildered; I enter a dark space and cry until someone picks me up. I look at C. and see the huge pain in myself and everyone else and see the results. All I can do is scream. Everything is in flames.

The transition to school leaver

The secondary school pupil has mastered the range of the different substances. With his body totally relaxed and in a state of alert mindfulness, he is able to perceive the substances spreading through his body and observe his consciousness expanding. He is able to perceive the way in which he perceives things. He is able to listen, watch and be present. His mind clear, he is able to "listen as if with the heart" and "see with the heart". The inner observer has become the "benevolent empathetic observer" who is able to take this attitude away with him and engage with his fellow human beings.

The secondary school pupil is able to spend time in the state of observer – in tranquillity and without any reaction to thoughts or feelings. He is able to perceive all kinds of realisations and sensations without reacting to them. The longer he remains in the process, quiet and unreacting, the more effective the substance – although he has the same dosage as the primary school pupil, perhaps even a lower dosage. He is more frequently able to employ his "empathetic observer" in everyday life. He has learned not to avoid unpleasant feelings anymore but to "let them be". This marks the beginning of the integration of the inner stance into everyday life.

As the client has corrective insights and new emotional experiences in the sessions, embedding these insights through serving as protagonist in constellation work, he is also able to approach problems arising in normal life in a different way. Individual situations are discussed and reflected upon in follow-up therapy sessions.

Spiritual experiences often emerge in this phase, too. They have nothing to do with the frequency of the sessions. Just for an instant, spiritual experiences give the secondary school pupil knowledge of the Whole, the Higher Order and the sense of guaranteed safety. The basic messages from these experiences are similar to the findings from Eastern wisdom traditions. He begins to perceive them as a natural part of his life. However difficult it is to define the essence of a spiritual experience, it is these very experiences that take them to the core of their inner being. The death of the ego and experiences of God also belong into this category.

In clear correlation with the frequency of the sessions and intensity of the work, levels of realisation alter over the course of the psycholytic process. This produces profound insights, sometimes with a collectively spiritual hue. Events that have already been worked through can be understood in a new way, perhaps even integrating them in the next dimension and understanding their underlying purpose.

It is interesting that the discoveries that continue to be made about the client's past life go back to earlier and earlier times as work progresses. In these particular areas of consciousness expansion, many clients have been able to realise that they perceived external events from their mother's womb, and that they have shaped their entire system of perception in later life on the basis of this perception. A number of clients have experienced the moment of their conception, many of them realising how their attachment to their mother was damaged at a very early juncture by her rejection of the pregnancy.

At this level, for example, work with a client who was born by Caesarean section when his mother was fleeing a hail of bombs led to a dramatic re-experiencing of the event. He had already contracted the fear of death from his mother back then, and found himself back in the same situation in the session. He didn't want to be born at all or even live. This was also his approach to everyday life. Plagued by severe bouts of depression, he resorted to numbing himself in all sorts of ways as soon as things got tough. He could and would not cross this threshold in the session. Meditation became the best escape but was not helpful in processing his trauma and alleviating his symptoms. A client whose mother had suffered violence when pregnant with her was also able to attribute many of her perceptions and fears to these early experiences.

The secondary school pupil has fewer and fewer "experiences" during sessions; he sees hardly any images anymore, not even with LSD. A session might open nothing to him other than tranquil space or perhaps a realisation might occur within him and form itself into the next important phase of maturation. This is the point of transition to school leaver. Two school leaver examples:

I.

... I am grabbed without pity and it will not let go. There is no escape. I'm in the concentration camp looking at the horror. It hits me with an impact that I have never seen before. It is now triggered by the lady next to me.

There are sounds of death throes, which I am forced to watch. Any attempt to shut it out fails. This is my helplessness and rage. I notice that I don't know where I begin or end. Their death throes affect me as if they were part of me, but it still makes me rage. I feel helplessness at not being able to do anything.

And I feel really awful too. Everything is one soul, clinging together. It is horrific. I see the prevailing restlessness. Everything pales at the pain, the struggle with death. I am seeing things through a very challenging perspective. In the second part I wonder what you are supposed to do after such an experience. How do you go back to normality? This time, I see the side that says nothing, blocks the ears and averts the eyes. It is totally unbearable. You shut yourself off from it in order to survive. I see all of the energy hidden in this form of processing in both a direct and indirect way.

Yad Vashem is full of it and I am also part of it.

Comment: in this form it would not have been possible for a beginner or secondary school pupil to have this kind of experience from this reflective standpoint while describing and identifying their own inner processes at the same time. Working through the client's identification with the concentration camp victims was an extremely demanding task.

II.

Client W. has the intention of grieving over the victims in her family as a mourner. She has formed a picture of the Holocaust as part of further education. We meet as a group of four. We work with psilocybin at night. She asks to be shown the inexpressible in such a way that it can be then expressed. We record the session on tape.

We sit in a circle. We centre ourselves. I begin really gently with a piece by Byron Metcalf, but stop it when the mourning begins. The sounds that we then hear for a full hour make us listeners sense the horror in our bodies. W. looks like a corpse at one point and there is a distinct smell of decay at another point. We experience the fear, pain, horror, terror, rage, despair, hatred, pleading, revenge, resignation, rebellion, acceptance and death.

The space I was in was unbelievable. Pure horror and terror. No images. I personally knew exactly where I was. A very powerful physical experience. It came from within. I am glad I got the proper help. It was hard for me to know when I had had enough. My feelings were mainly about my grandfather, my father's father.

There is a fluid transition from secondary school pupil to school leaver. Because of the betrayal, which I talk about later, my therapeutic research expedition with substances, which started as conventional psychotherapy, was cut short. This is why I was only able to observe the beginning of the process, which I call "school leaver".

The secondary school pupil has gone through many (40 or more) sessions under increasingly even conditions, with clear guidance and instruction. He is centred, both in sessions and normal everyday life. Life history and systemic entanglements have been processed and grief, pain and dissociation phenomena integrated. He has been able to transition his mystical experiences into everyday wisdom and enjoy projection-free relationships to a considerable degree.

The school leaver

When the substance has taken full effect, the school leaver is clear and in physical and inner balance. Looking at him, you would not be able to tell that he has taken a substance.

The school leaver is able to engage in the process so deeply that he can identify "disturbances" at a biochemical level. This may be an illness or consumption of medication by the mother in early pregnancy; a disturbance that had an impact even before the brain developed at the physical level of the embryo. He is able to see how this event might have created a "life or death" situation and a fight for survival. This sort of realisation was no accidental result. It came from the perception and observation of certain unpleasant feelings or typical reactions to everyday circumstances.

The school leaver can go into the session with the intention of fathoming out the origin and cause of this indefinable, conceptually unclear state of affairs. If he wishes, he can take the substance and work on issues alone.

Just as life is in constant flux, working with psycho-integrative substances is also a continuous learning process. The school leaver moves on from secondary school to continue learning throughout life. He is the same as the person who took the substance on beginners' day, but with an extended consciousness in the normal state.

CHAPTER 8

Stations of the Learning Process in Psycholytic Therapy

This chapter outlines the characteristics of the therapeutic process and the learning that typically occurs during a course of therapy.

The "stations" of the process are described and we explore the limitations of psycholytic psychotherapy.

Stations of the learning process

The individual stations of the process occurred in a range of different sequences. If the pieces of the mosaic are assembled, the lessons derived from the process ultimately help the search for identity, bringing the client towards the answer to the question that underlies all other questions: "Who am I?"

The typical stations of the psycholytic learning process are:

- The main therapy issue
- Personal history, focusing on parents, family of origin issues and personality development
- The phenomena of psychosomatics
- Epigenetics – the field of transgenerational trauma and the collective experience
- The intrauterine and perinatal period and early impact of biochemical influences at cell level, impact of metabolic disorders in the mother, birth trauma, development of belief systems and behaviour patterns, appearance of initial attachment disorders *in utero*
- Everyday and practical issues
- Spiritual experiences

Although each individual works through these stations in their own distinct way, the lessons from each person's experience had direct relevance

– and learning potential – for the other participants. It was particularly noticeable that these lessons reached deeper into the psyche during the sessions involving consciousness expansion with its fine-tuning of perception. Sometimes the view to the interior seemed like looking through a microscope. Details were seen with extreme acuity and accuracy, and then had to be integrated into the overall picture. The process often began with an issue that reappeared at another level in later sessions in a new and deeper guise, and could be looked at again with a different perspective. In retrospect, the process exhibited the basic alchemical principles of separation, purification and conjunction.

We all went through an intensive learning process before we were able to identify and classify these stations and understand their significance. We did this learning together in the state of expanded consciousness. In order to do this, we practised observation, particularly of our perceptions. This seemed to be the same with everybody. Material was described in different ways in the instant of the reaction to the perception; the interpretation of the phenomenon varied according to the nature of the initial perception. On realising this, we always explored perception up to the point before interpretation, finding that this was the most informative area. This revealed the following:

Certain initial influences via the mother – either intrauterine or later purely environmental – seem to be condensed into core belief systems that determines the way that the individual seeks to manage their life. These basic belief systems become the lens – or pair of spectacles as we termed it – which become imprinted into the individual as a reference point. So the world may be seen as a dangerous place after an attempted abortion, for example. The deeper and further we penetrated the prenatal period with our observation and perception, the more clearly we could see where our feelings, reactions and actions originated. We understood that the mother-child bond begins at the moment of procreation. A mother's reaction to pregnancy defines the quality of that bond. The pain expressed in "My mother didn't want me" becomes a bridge between biochemistry and psychology and manifests in daily life by the quality of the relationship between the two.

We were also able to look at the impact of traumatic experiences of parents and grandparents in expanded consciousness, and we also understood their attitudes and actions by taking account of their difficult destiny on an emotional empathetic level. Through them, we understood our own actions and reactions, some of which we hadn't understood ourselves until that point. This was the epigenetics station. Due to the totally heterogeneous composition of the group, cultural and ethnic issues emerged on an individual and a collective level; such as the Nazi era, the roots and consequences of war, expulsion, rape, torture and hunger. We came to recognise both victim and perpetrator as being indistinguishable within ourselves.

We learned to observe physical phenomena and not react *to them*, or *as a result of them*, enabling us to perceive what lay behind these phenomena. When we also managed to observe what lay hidden behind without reacting, we reached a point where the inner motion became perceptible at a physical and psychic level. We found that an inner motion is the source of emotion (*ex-motio*, "from motion"). We saw that we identify the interpretation of this inner motion as feeling. We had to demonstrate to ourselves over and over again how differently we use such identifications and that, for this reason, we must always remain aware that we can only communicate such concepts from the point of view of our own subjectivity.

A number of issues emerged from these stations, and we explored them in more detail within group discussions. What began as psychological issues turned into general philosophical learning. The wider and deeper our cognitive faculty became, the more these lessons evolved into attitudes to daily life, becoming an integral component of the personality. There was a striking similarity with the wisdom of the Far East.

Individual participants kept having moving spiritual experiences. When we were able to access peaceful spaces, this peace was felt as a healing factor and resulted in a range of effects, including complete serenity and tolerance.

The main therapy issue

The main therapy issue can come from any area of life. It is to be regarded as a symptom; an inner psychic conflict, which ultimately manifests itself and is then resolved.

Even a couple-related issue is primarily a symptom. Greatly simplified, it consists of an unrecognised entanglement of two systems. Here, conflict and conflict patterns result from an attempt to resolve the entanglement. Conflict can also result from an attempt by one or both parties to take the lead and start addressing some of the fundamental issues.

Example of a core therapy issue

V. had gone into body therapy because he had felt for a long time that he was searching for a (his) second male half. His wife had recently suffered a spontaneous abortion of twins. He wasn't particularly pleased when his wife became pregnant again.

The intention question was why he had fought for so long against his wife's desire to have a child and why he wasn't able to be happy about the new pregnancy.

MDMA, and later LSD

After a while, it feels like some of my innards are moving upwards, it is a pain, an emotional pain. The pain becomes physical and lodges itself in my solar plexus; it constricts and gives me a sharp pain as I breathe. I abandon the pain and go into my open heart. From there, it flows high up into my head. Something starts to form before my eyes. I see an embryo. I can feel the pain in my solar plexus again. I look at the embryo again and suddenly it's crystal clear: my twin brother. I am consumed by great joy at this totally unexpected encounter. I tell myself: "I simply can't believe it, it's completely crazy." I unite with my brother and we leave my body together to move freely about the universe in our protective sphere. We are both dancing in our sphere as it floats along. We move freely about the universe in our sphere. We touch and hug one another, whooping and laughing together, and it's a wonderful feeling.

Suddenly, I see the ultrasound photo of our twins that my wife lost. And suddenly I understand everything: my extreme joy and curiosity over the twins and my enormous grief over losing them. I now return to my body with my twin brother, the joy disappears again and turns into pain. I have finally found my twin brother and know that now is the time to say goodbye to him. I see that I have to let him leave my body. Pain and grief spread upwards through my chest and into my throat. I have to let him go as if in stages. I can hardly breathe and it feels like a massive cramp. We hug for the last time and I let him go. I realise that I now have to live my own life without my brother and am finally allowed to live, and that he will now live his own life without me and go his own way.

I have a series of sudden revelations in my head one after another – a real series of insights. Now I see why I have resisted children/fatherhood for so long; my search and longing for my second male half becomes meaningful and I understand why the second pregnancy was not the same source of joy and euphoria as the first. I now sense how much I am looking forward to our son. I am gaining a son through the departure of my twin brother.

Personal history – psychosomatics

Everyone brings his or her own subjective material to the personal history station, and this is both a highly individual and collective experience at one and the same time. Experiences involving the mother or father shape most personal memories of the past. The focus is mainly on the feeling of not having been loved, noticed or wanted. Motherly love, attachment, relationship and self-perception are therefore usually the major issues. I will therefore give you an example of a guided MDMA session with exercises.

At the summit – the point of greatest emotional openness, I ask everyone to sit up.

"We go to mother. We stand before her and look at her."

"Move away from everything that she "did" to you as you perceive it. Move about in the state of: "I am your daughter", "I am your son".

Is there a reference point for this inside me? Where do I feel this point?... Can I look at my mother from the heart? ... Do I have to maybe let the other feelings (annoyance, rage, grief) in again and "let them be, let them go?" ... "Maybe I have to realise that she is the one who gave birth to me and brought me up?"... "Mother (dear mum), you gave birth to me" ..."Say it with love" ... "It is time to become really small" ... Can I maybe only now see that I have put myself above you (out of pure love and care)? That I have felt like the adult?

I leave a lot of time between statements for people to think back, and wait a long time for everyone to nod and I can assume that everyone can perceive himself as the child of this mother and is with me on the issue.

"We connect with our mother by opening our hearts up wide and letting our breath flow softly." Then everyone stays with their own process of exploration.

After a period of peace, we all followed the same train of thought together:

Every child loves his mother– I love you, mum – this is a trivial phrase.

We now perceive the feeling of connection. This is love here. I play an appropriate piece of music at this point.

After a further period of peace, I begin a kind of "lecture". I explain the mother-child relationship, guiding them into different brief experiential exercises. I sum up the whole exercise here:

As very small children, we find ourselves in a state of absolute symbiosis with the mother. We are conditioned by and in relation to each other and our mutual dependency. We experience this oneness with the mother and her attention as being, life and love without naming it as such.

Love is not a feeling – love is a state. This state comes from the bond and is the bond itself. The child only lives and stays alive because of this state of love. The mother looks at him from this state; her smile gives vibrancy to the infant, which he registers and picks up as the vibrancy of life. This gives him his first unconscious perception of himself as a vibrant, energetic being. He then vibrates with energy at the same frequency as his mother, resonates to a similar biochemical and psycho-physical state as her and he experiences this as life. This is the origin of the main statement of the mother-child relationship – I am (like) you. This is no intellectual statement; it describes state-related processes.

Becoming one's own person through the development of perception, becoming oneself, occurs over various stages through contact with the mother. The inability to differentiate between mother and self can be described as the "I-I" state. The next step towards the perception of the self is always in relation to the mother, "I–not-I" – as the first recognition of the differentiation between mother and self. This engenders a first idea of I-me or the self. The next step, which looks like a defiant phase from the outside, leads to the development of "I–you", where the mother is experienced as a separate person (the child cries when she moves away from him), but where she still does not represent another in the sense of a "you". Mother and child are simply not in complete symbiosis, as they were in the beginning. In favourable circumstances, triangulation occurs with the father, and with it brings contact with the world outside the mother-child dyad. If, for any number of different reasons, the end of symbiosis and beginning of triangulation cannot happen in the proper way, self-disorders appear in different forms in later life. For these people, it becomes much harder to answer the principal question in life of "Who am I?"– with all the consequences that this brings.

Individuals go through various mental and emotional stages on their own over the course of the exercise, experiencing the effect that statements such as "I am your child" and "I look at you, you look at me" have on them and what changes within them. After this, the question of "Who am I?" could generally be answered for the first time, if not conclusively.

We followed the same exercises in relation to the father, ensuring that the "parents" issue was integrated and that the self was able to return to an appropriate relationship pattern as a child to its parents.

Parents and family

Memorable childhood experiences can emerge at any stage during psycholytic psychotherapy. Sometimes they emerge during the early sessions and sometimes in the later sessions. If a person already has traumatic memories, these can be seen in a new light under the impact of a substance. The empathogenic effect of the substance facilitates an emotional understanding of the self, the situation and the other participants, making it possible to achieve inner peace with the material from one's personal history. This inner calmness makes it possible to explore the experience in a future session in order to more fully process and resolve that material. How did the person perceive and interpret the particular event as a small child? What emotions did he feel and what consequences did he decide upon at an unconscious internal psychic level? These emotional events had consequences that now determine his perception, behaviour and relationships. Traumatising experiences are also part of this context. The point at which they emerge in therapy depends on the child's age when traumatised, the type of subjective evaluation and degree of suppression. But the impact of the experience – following integration – on all levels of experience also needs to be explored and altered.

Example: inner peace
I suddenly felt his (the father's) love really powerfully. I thanked him deeply: "Thank you, dear father, you were so good to me, too, and you did your best." This was a big liberation, without any grief. There was a lot of love. I had the feeling: it is done with now, there is nothing else standing in my way, I can leave things as they are. Thanks.

Example: patterns
Not taking myself seriously enough became my issue: I have failed to take myself seriously on so many occasions. And I usually didn't care, as I knew what my real qualities were. [At another level, this led to a kind of arrogance towards other people.] *But I owe it to myself to make sure that I am taken seriously in future. I recognised the origin of this behaviour in the false accusations made by my mother; I made the conscious decision not to dispute these even as a small child, as I had the secret satisfaction of knowing better ...*

But I was still astonished to hear my mother say that she would have known full well if she had wrongly accused me!

In due course, our task consisted of locating the reference point for "taking oneself seriously". This started with looking at the mother and father and taking one's rightful place: "I am the child here, you are my parents, I am your son." And accepting the statement: "We are your parents and you are our son."

Whenever a distressing childhood event emerges that assumed frightening dimensions for the child at the time, it shows under the influence of the substance as a visceral re-experiencing in the moment, and not just a simple memory. The ability to articulate and stay in contact with the group and the therapist remains intact. When this happens, I use words and touch to guide them through the systematic re-experiencing process:

Example: when a situation experienced as being difficult became an everyday sensation

"I feel so weird, I just don't know what the matter with me is."

"What is it exactly?"

"My heart is knocking in my chest. My head feels so dizzy and vague."

"Where are you? Shut your eyes and look around."

"It's dark, I can't see anything. I think I'm in my room."

"What can you hear?"

Long silence. Then: "I can hear my mother screaming. They're arguing."

"How old are you?"

"Little."

"Are you able to talk yet?"

"Yes."

"What's happening?"

"The door is banging."

"Do you want to come into my arms?"

He crawls over to me.

"Lean on me."

He is very stiff and doesn't really dare to lean against me. He seems to be on the alert. We stay like this for a while.

"This is how you feel if there is conflict in your relationships today, isn't it?"

He nods.

(This is how I bring his adult ego and the parallels with his everyday life into the conscious mind. I come back to it later in the sharing session.)

I hold him quietly in my arms for a while, and then let out a slow, regular deep breath, staying with him internally. After a while, he lies down with his head in my lap. He starts to cry, sobbing and shivering. I continue holding him: "That's right – that's what total abandonment and helplessness feel like."

(I provide him with terms that he couldn't have at the time, and names that he wasn't able to learn for his feelings.)

He nods – can't speak for a moment. The sobbing stops after a while and the tension in his body recedes.

"Take a deep breath, it's over. It was just a memory. Now you can relax. You can allow yourself to. You are safe now, grown up."

I stroke him with my hands along the length of his body. We look into each other's eyes until we really make contact. He finally stands up, wipes his nose and breathes through it deeply.

"Are you OK?"

"Yes."

I leave him a little longer and then put his mother down in front of him and ask him: tell her "Mum, all the fighting worried me to death."

I can see that something is still stirring in him. I put the father next to the mother.

"Look at each other for a moment."

Mother to father: "I'm furious with you"

Father: "I'm even more furious with you."

I leave them looking at each other for a long time.

Father, tell your son: "It's our argument, we will sort it out between us – it has nothing to do with you."

Mother, tell your son: "It's OK for you to stay with your father. It really is OK."

M. looks relieved. He needs some time.

"Where would you like to sit now?"

"With my big brother."

"OK, who will be the big brother?"

He sits down next to his big brother. He remains sitting there, leaning against him. I look at him again after a while and he says that he is in a state of balance.

After the session, M's next task was to notice various everyday moods, especially feeling weird, and to remember that this is because he was in a state of recollection. The next task was to make a conscious decision about what he wanted to do next.

Psychosomatics

When under a high dosage of LSD, I could see that my mother's words "Your father is dead" chopped through my brain like an axe when I heard them, and I perceived the same wounding blow in my heart. Both wounds were the same in length, about 15cm, and had penetrated about 3cm deep into the tissue. I had a pain in the top left side of my skull and the same pain in the top left area of my heart. But I felt no grief!

Under the influence of ayahuasca many years later in Brazil, I had the same almost unbearable pain in my heart and cried for a long time in a "heart-rending" fashion. The endless grief over my father's early death was finally allowed to flow and take its rightful place.

On another occasion, I was threatened by a patient's partner. I was really scared. At the next session I had the repeated experience that this fear was being expressed by thoughts racing around in my head, totally confusing me. The fear disappeared completely a few minutes later. My head was clear, I had all the symptoms of a heart attack – chest pain, breathlessness and sweating. I managed to go deliberately from one state to another a few times. This is when I became aware of the true extent of psychosomatics for the first time.

Through this and other experiences, I saw the unbreakable link between body, mind and spirit. All three are always affected at the same time when we experience or feel anything – it seems to be necessary for the organism to be able to express itself in any available form.

Epigenetics – transgenerational trauma and ancestors

From diet to traumatising experiences in the individual, information about these events is stored biochemically in the cells and in neurons within the cortex. I suggest that these physical templates of emotional events are inherited alongside genetic and epigenetic characteristics. Descendants react on the basis of these, but are unable to decode inherited reactions because they are no longer connected to the event themselves, and nor can they bring it into consciousness. In this way, we go through the reactions of our ancestors.

Clients always worked intensively on the life circumstances of their parents and grandparents in sessions, and almost always discovered that, alongside their ancestors' reactions, they also carried their feelings within them. In this way, we experienced the phenomenon of epigenetics at a psychosomatic level. Nearly all clients looked into their family history during therapy, not only finding themselves reconciled with their parents and grandparents on an inner level, but also asking them about their experiences of the war where this was possible. Located as it is on the border between biochemistry and psychology, the importance of epigenetics probably lies in adapting people to individual environmental conditions.

Transgenerational trauma, especially the effects of the Second World War, was always an issue because of the heterogeneous composition of the group. Epigenetically acquired collective guilt, Jewishness, Germanness, perpetrator-victim roles and individual and collective responsibility were some of the issues for the group. Without intending to sound immodest, regardless of the side on which our parents and grandparents stood, we all met and connected as human beings.

Example 1: biographical and epigenetic (ayahuasca)

I am getting that fear that I know so well. I can see it. The living dead, clinging to me. I see myself in my room as a little girl. I've known these shadows since I was little. They were always around back then. I can see myself standing in bed, crying. I'm standing in the corner and feel like I can never lie down again. I am caged behind bars. My father comes to release me from the nightmare. He carries me into my parents' bedroom and I am allowed to sleep between my parents. There is no father around to save me now. Experiencing this dissociation, I always see myself as a little girl. I'm looking for a safe place to be now, and suddenly I am surrounded by love and everything changes.

I can see the unsaved souls, the living dead ... The souls are saved now, they are welcome in my house.

Example 2: epigenetic

*... I suddenly realised that I am the child of displaced persons. (This distinction was very important to my parents. They are not refugees, but displaced persons!) I too feel constantly displaced **and** in flight! And I never really dared to make any kind of contact before. I have always felt that I don't belong.*

The client started to process the fate of his entire family with this experience. This was followed by a series of experiences where he was able to expose and work through his family's epigenetic inheritance.

Example 3: epigenetic

I saw how children get things from their parents, even though the parents really don't want them to. The parents really don't want their children to take on bad stuff. But there in front of the parents' very eyes the children have already taken it on and are not little any more. I can see that I did this and that the next generation has already taken it on, too. Now I can let it go, it doesn't make sense wanting to keep hold of it any more – and it has already been handed on. I accept that this is how identity is created. I'm specifically looking at it from my side now: it happened even before my parents realised it.

I need to go into my mother's rage in my therapy work, it is my rage, too. A rage that doesn't give itself any outlet, but eats away at everything. I feel like I could burst. I go after my mother when the third stage of the music comes: I see my massive love for her, which became evident as I was sorting out her estate over the last few months. I find a way to her through my love. I encounter my mother on a totally different level from the one where I always looked for her. If I can describe in this way, I have always looked for her on my "level", and now found her on a totally different level. This level feels quite foreign to me. But I can find my father on my level.

Example 4: transgenerational trauma

... Then I had to realise: I feel alone and uprooted. I slip into my mother's life: her father was murdered when she was sixteen, then the rape, and especially being expelled from her homeland. She had to leave everything she owned behind. Lots of dead and half-decayed bodies along the way. They were only allowed to keep the clothes they stood up in. Reception camp, fever, separated from all of her family and left to fend for herself. After experiencing all of that, she tried to make contact again – she actually found her mother and sister again in Saxony. Then she found work with a farmer; the main thing was that she had something to eat.

She had to leave everything again when she married, as she followed my father to the Ruhr region when he fled there to escape the Soviet uranium mines. The city was totally destroyed, living in the most terrible conditions. She never played as a child. She is frightened in an alien, hostile world. She has no link with friends, homeland or family.

You come to me F. and ask: everything OK?

Right at that moment I realise that I am a new-born baby. I am completely cut off from everything and have no chance unless I stay totally with my mum. I open up to her completely, sucking everything of her into myself with the mother's milk. I sense that my mother is totally over-burdened, which I am so familiar with myself. I try to block out how my mother managed it and keep it at bay through hard work. And, like her, I am extremely disappointed when other people focus on quite different things ...

I also ingested the bitterness with my mother's milk. And the grief.

Early impacts: bonding patterns, from belief systems to behavioural patterns

Continuing the process, we located nearly all of the origins (place and time, time and place) of the psychological and physical "problems of relevance" in a state of expanded consciousness, where emerging biochemical and neuronal phenomena are indistinguishable from one another. Initial impressions become a reaction reflex at this point, which is in turn coupled with an emotional reflex. If the stimulus for an initial impression is unpleasant, and if the stress cannot be regulated physiologically back into the comfort zone, a long-term "disorder" develops. This disorder generally takes the form of a chronically elevated stress level, which the organism comes to accept as normal and which is manifested as a hereditary defect.

This produces a cognitive template, a way of interpreting the world, a version of reality that subsumes body, mind and spirit. Unfortunately, such concepts and belief systems are often harmful and self-sabotaging. These patterns are organised at a cellular level but cannot be eliminated there. It is therefore necessary to go through a new cognitive and emotional experience via consciousness-expanding therapy work. But the sequence of the initial experience needs to be reversed – the cognitive recognition of the pattern comes first, followed by the (new) emotional integration. Then the new experience has to be integrated to such an extent that it can take the place of the old experience. This is the essence of the "corrective new experience" that I have discussed earlier.

The origin of patterns in the embryonic and foetal phases

Processes in the developing embryo have an entirely biochemical basis in very early pregnancy before organ differentiation has occurred, and these are stored by the infant organism at a cellular level. In this way, every physical or psychic state experienced by the mother becomes deeply embedded in the hardware, meaning that it is no longer possible to distinguish clearly between the two levels at this initial cellular level.

At this early stage of development any powerful feeling totally dominates sensory experience and becomes embodied. You have no fear – you *are fear*, you consist of fear. These feeling states are responsible for our primordial perception, interpretation of the environment and for reactions to stimuli. These impressions are "remembered" in the cells. The memory is perceived unconsciously through an emotional reflex, with the result that the organism activates the stress response as a reaction to certain situations in a way that is not under conscious control. For example a fall in blood sugar level in the body may be triggered by external perceptions that are unconsciously assessed as threatening. We might just wince, or we might panic.

The initial neuronal connections mediating between biochemistry and the formation of neuronal structures are responsible for the overall organism's reflexive reaction to any change to the neutral baseline state – the normal state that ensures life, that reacts and that is always striving to maintain homeostasis. As a kind of feedback mechanism, the action is stored again in the neurons with each return to homeostasis, embedding it deeper within a network. In this way it becomes hard-wired.

Regression to the physical level is required in order to reach such early material unavailable to the memory. This involves conducting processes at cellular or biochemical level or at the border between biochemistry and psychology. Everything that happens in this period of life is pre-linguistic in nature – which is why perceptions need to be translated into the individual's own language.

As revealed by the client in the following example, behavioural patterns generated by very early disturbances, are only too readily "psychologised", meaning that they are interpreted as a neurotic disorder in the sense of self-destructive behaviour or loaded with other typical attributes from the psychology repertoire.

The developing unborn child experiences the world via his mother's womb. He is connected to the mother's overall system as if he forms a *single* organism with her. He experiences the events to which the mother reacts in the form of biochemical information. In terms of tactile and acoustic stimuli, there is still no link to the brain – such stimuli are received and stored at a physical level. The slightest biochemical deviations from the norm (such as undiagnosed diabetes in pregnancy) are a threat to the physical existence of the progeny and stored biochemically as being life-threatening. These events can be exhibited through panic attacks, for example. This happens in a totally unspecific way, but as a response that can be triggered over and over again. Even attempted abortions fall into this category, as do food poisoning and the mother taking certain medications.

These situations will be perceived or re-experienced later on in a person's life through a certain feeling, which they often try to name as the brain develops (a "weird feeling", maybe), and they usually try to get rid of the feeling or free themselves of it in some way.

Example 1: patterns generated by trauma in very early pregnancy – biochemical-psychic traumatisation

A client noticed that he kept experiencing an unpleasant physical state when in the middle of his daily routines, but which he kept on inducing. He would drink a few strong espressos and smoke a cigar. The disgusting taste connected him with a general feeling of unease in his everyday life.

He entered this state, which was so familiar to him, in a number of sessions. He would start to feel sick before experiencing something like a feeling of annihilation, which had the outward appearance of a circulatory collapse. But he was still able to communicate information at every point, linking these feelings with the espresso and cigar ritual. He decided to get to the root of the phenomenon.

We discussed the procedure beforehand, agreeing that we would place a certain energy point in the sole of his foot with an acupuncture needle if he drifted off, and that we would guide the process with him from the out-side so that he wouldn't be put in any danger.

This type of conscious exploration required a high level of experience from participants. This includes the ability to keep the self-reflecting I available at all times, even with high dosages of LSD – which is the sub-stance of choice in such cases. Courage, the intention of surrendering to the process completely and mutual trust are vital to this kind of process. We discussed his decision to go into deep regression, and he took a dosage of around 400 micrograms of LSD in a very small group setting.

He laid himself down and slowly put himself into the pre-birth state at his own pace. I maintained contact with him through talking to him softly, light touch and a simulated womb. After a while he fell silent, went pale, looked like he was going to faint and went limp. We held him, providing him with physical contact, feeling his pulse and keep-ing the needle ready in case he went limp again and we needed to revive him by applying the needle as agreed. I kept asking him to give us a sign of life: "Can you hear me?" He nodded almost imperceptibly and looked like he was zoning out, his breathing became flatter, and he was hardly breathing at all by the end. We left him in this state for a very short time – maybe 20 seconds. I then called him back with energy in my voice: "Breathe, take a deep breath!" We fanned him with fresh air. When he got back some of his colour, we gave him a sip of water and some glucose. He came slowly back into the room until he was totally with us again. He was then able to tell us:

He had entered a state where he could no longer keep a grip on things. He felt that he was drifting off into a state of disintegration, as if his senses were fading; he used the term dying to describe it. It was already clear to him in this state that he had experienced and survived the threat of abortion. He also had access – although brief – to exter-nal reality when in this state.

The blast of fresh air, telling him to breathe, the rapid supply of car-bohydrate and eye contact made him give a sign that he had survived and was still alive. The next part of the work consisted of directing the perception towards feeling the whole body and coming back to the Here and Now.

The result of these findings is that the primordial perception (stress stimu-lus) and primordial response pattern (stress response) are biochemically "hard-wired" at cellular level through the extreme irritation of the cell metabolism. (It is as if they are written to "CD-ROMs") – these store the saved data without any new input and cannot be changed or deleted. This means that exercises for long-term change as part of behavioural therapy cannot take effect, as the "programme" for this pattern seems to be hard-wired at a cellular level. This is why this type of pattern cannot even be understood or resolved at a psychological level.

My client deliberately induced his unpleasant state again and again and moved gradually towards a resolution of this very early trauma and its continuing effects in his adult life.

Example 2: patterns generated by influences during pregnancy and birth

After a series of sessions, a young lady with panic attacks was able to engage in the process so profoundly that she could perceive the threat to her life posed to her by her mother's undiagnosed diabetes during pregnancy. She was able to make an inner connection between her panic attacks, her own hypoglycae-mia and the associated feeling of not being in control anymore and of dying.

Substance: 100 micrograms of LSD
Suddenly, it was as if I was zoning out and I felt like I was fainting. I couldn't understand what was going on around me anymore and could only see F. as if through a veil. She came right up close to my face and I heard her shout "Breathe, take a deep breath" as if from a great distance. I took a couple of breaths and then all the strength went out of me. She held me in her arms. "Come on, breathe!" I struggled. "B., you are here in my arms. You are a little girl and you are breathing. You are alive." She fanned me with air, stroked my face and spoke softly to me. I struggled to breathe. Suddenly, I noticed that I didn't have to struggle anymore – my breathing came easily. I was suddenly OK, back in the room and in the present.

We had the strong feeling that this experience had to be about the moment of my birth, and I was given the task of finding out what my birth had been like. I learned the following things: I weighed around 5kg at birth. My face was so swollen that my grandmother thought I didn't have any eyes. I was put straight onto a respirator for a while because I was obviously "unconscious". The high body weight and water retention lead to the reliable conclusion that my mother had undiagnosed diabetes during pregnancy, which is also accompanied by a rise in blood sugar, meaning that normal or low blood sugar in the new-born baby initially has to be classified as life-threatening.

The same client a few years later: belief system
I had stated my intention of finding out why I always fell into the same pattern: whenever things got tough in my life, whether in exams or situations where I should have fought hard and particularly acted

quickly and with focus, I usually gave up right away or just before, having little or no confidence in myself. My teachers and parents therefore said I was lazy and complacent. They couldn't understand why I held myself back, even complaining about my behaviour: "It's a shame – she's so intelligent."

Substance: 150 micrograms of LSD

I entered a state during the session that I knew every well from these situations: it was as if I was paralysed, totally lacking in energy, I felt huge pressure in my stomach and had no idea what was wrong with me. Another part of me noticed that things were getting difficult and that I had to zone out and give up. I became restless and uneasy, but only felt this peripherally. Although I didn't know what it was, I was sure that I couldn't do it. I went even more limp. People knew about my medical history regarding my birth.

F. now realised that it had to be about the birth, put me in the embryo position and put a blanket over me. I felt pressure from outside, as if the womb was contracting. I also felt stronger pressure on my head. F. asked if I could hear her. I could hear her. The pressure on my whole body and head is getting stronger. I realised that I needed to start moving. "Use your energy – forwards, push!" I started to struggle. I wanted to get out of there.

Bit by bit, I consciously pushed myself through the "birth canal". I could hardly bear it. I managed to fight my way out. I was out. "Breathe!" – I took a breath. I was breathing and totally present in my body, feeling it for the first time.

The biggest thing for me was that I had to fight and managed it on my own. This part of me had been missing until then. I had now rediscovered my focused strength, which I was unable to perceive consciously at my birth and which I could now employ.

How did the experience affect my life? This complex dynamic that had been unconsciously affecting my behaviour and response to difficult situations until then had now been resolved. Now I also study at the university in addition to looking after the children and doing the housework. I would never have come so far without this experience. I now know and am confident that I can manage difficult situations, even if they are stressful and protracted. I am not frightened by challenges anymore.

Example 3: recognising the pattern of a belief system

I have been through various intrauterine experiences under the influence of nearly every available substance, the first times with M. and L.

I was unable to classify the issue or situation in cognitive terms at the time. I felt it as a physical threat, suffered anxiety but no panic and, as this was happening in the initial sessions, I had no insight from the point of view of an observer (this would only develop with practice and experience during sessions).

F. supported me through the sessions, taking me almost to a meta level. She did this through questions like "Where are you now?" – "What do you perceive?" – "Give in to physical sensation".

I now had a deep desire to put myself in the embryo position. F. supported this process by covering my body with a blanket and apply- ing physical pressure around me. This position triggered an intense feeling of a threat to my existence, which I had the urge to get away from as quickly as possible. Had I been alone, I would have done the same thing and sorted myself out again. But I stayed with the process, breathing deeply and allowing my body to go through the existential crisis. I experienced the process as life-threatening and would have liked to do everything I could to defend myself in such a predicament, but my physical response was far too weak. From outside myself, I heard F. say that I needed to focus on my breathing until the imag- ined but nevertheless perceived threat to my life was past. Because it exposed the meta level, I succeeded in staying with the process and experiencing cognitively the slow departure of the threat to my life and the realisation that I had "come through" it.

I felt immense relief when I "was through it", as the threat was no longer before me, but behind me. At the same time, I realised that my previously unconscious "normal" attitude to life was and is that of facing a life-threatening situation at all times. A conscious physical sensation emerged in the final phase of each session. I realised that my body is normally in an unconscious state of inner tension – similar to a continuous vibration or, as before, "a hissing television screen" with no reception.

Example 4 (another client)

In one of the first sessions with mushrooms, the feeling of a threat to my life was even stronger and more physical than at other times and I felt as if I was in the middle of a life-and-death struggle. A force seemed to pull from below and I knew that it was "lethal". A viscous liquid was surrounding me and I could hardly move. I felt like I couldn't breathe. And this came in waves. Before the process ended I heard a humming from my colleagues, which felt as a healing sound. My body and spirit could be at peace. When I had come through the process I realised that there was a collective force between them and

me, which was encompassed by a Greater Whole (spiritual realisation). *It felt like a natural connectedness that is felt as both in the Now
and everlasting.*

   *And I was very relieved when I was through it this time, too. After
this session, the process in each subsequent intrauterine experience
was coupled with the cognitive awareness that the threat to my life
"would pass at some point". I sort of practised going to the meta level
in sessions and not reacting quite so much to the stimulus of the life-
threatening feeling.*

   *I discovered in subsequent sessions that, along with at least two
other events, this intrauterine experience had imprinted another "normal" feeling in me: the feeling of being cut off from everything and
everyone, in turn serving to strengthen my existential fears. I had
the realisation that, together with my birth, being separated from my
mother for over 24 hours right after the birth and the loss of my father
at the age of about three, the intrauterine experience had etched itself
deeply as a feeling of powerlessness, disconnectedness and "not existing" – severing symbiosis in each case. I saw these events as the principal cause of my problems and my need for control in my relationships with partners.*

The way these patterns are created is similar to the previous stage. The difference is that the brain has started to function, and initial information - obviously not classifiable in a linguistic or conceptual way – is perceived and
then interpreted by the mother's biochemical systems and stored in a kind
of "early warning system" as a reflex. This early warning system then determines perception, its interpretation and modes of reaction throughout the
whole of later life. Internal and external input feeding into this early warning system are scattered throughout the perception apparatus. The individual
generally experiences this as a disturbance. He reacts in such a way that the
mind is unable to extrapolate logically. Neither he nor the environment can
give the event meaning or name it, as the chain of succession has not reached
as far as his consciousness. This can express itself in the form of bouts of
bad temper triggered by trifling matters, but also in the firm conviction that
one is only able to engage in totally manageable situations. You could say
that these disturbances in the system somehow determine the entire system
of perception. This can mean that a person's basic characteristics represent a
logical consequence of their perception. "I am my perception."

Example 5
*I noticed there was a moment when I was incredibly happy. This must
have been the moment of conception. Then I experienced an external*

change of state a few weeks later. Energy-wise: it was if my mother realised that she was pregnant.

I was really struck by a feeling of happiness – I had never experienced anything like it before. Wow, it was wonderful. My one aim is to rid myself of all the clutter and achieve that state again: feeling happy without any particular reason – being happy.

And I was also struck by the abrupt change – I keep seeing this in my life, too.

The parents had made love and conceived a child. Then the woman realised she was pregnant. She was very shocked as the couple were not married, and pregnancy outside marriage was still a source of shame in the Eastern Block back in the fifties. But the couple quickly got married. The interpretation and basic feeling of the man produced by this union was: "I am not wanted." This leads to self-doubt, feelings of inferiority and feeling unwanted. Stanislav Grof describes the initial feeling of happiness as "amniotic unity" – and the abrupt end of this state as "falling from Paradise", a premonitory disappointment and primordial mistrust of the mother – all of this leads to an attachment disorder.

Later, I didn't really want to come out. It was dark in there, and it felt incredibly pleasant. Security and protection – I had to leave that situation and I didn't want to.

I was obviously soon given away – as a general rule, both parents had to go out to work in the Eastern Block.

Obviously, the person who had just been created didn't think these thoughts in this way. It is clear from this example that what was experienced at cell level back then needed to be translated into language – consciously expressed – in the state of expanded consciousness. This illustrates how perception, states, feelings and attitudes to life are biochemical in origin. They determine the quality of the bonds that we make and our everyday relationships. Who would ever imagine that these would turn out to be the underlying issues when a couple goes into therapy because their relationship is in crisis?

Group issues

These issues arose because the material from the experiences of nearly every client still also affected the group in some context or other. The fact that we were working with so many issues like this deepened our insight into the "similarity in diversity" of human existence, bringing us closer together on a human level.

Some of the important issues were:

- Perception itself and the subjectivity of perception
- Love in all its various manifestations and the lack of love
- Responsibility towards the self, others and the world
- The relationship and engagement with the self
- War in all its various manifestations; violence
- Peace
- Being – existence – suchness
- Life itself; death and dying

The way in which the issues came up naturally varied a lot. On the one hand, it depended on the point reached in the therapy – whether the participant was a beginner or experienced. On the other hand, the emerging themes were also dependent on the type of subject being addressed.

Aesthetic experiences such as joy and serenity had a similar quality to the genre of superficial films that you might enjoy watching for relaxation – a little dreamlike. Emotions arising from all kinds of events can seem like an abstract realisation or be highly dynamic – as if the event were actually happening. The issues referred to above were often thrown up when the latter emerged. When the issues came up, we explored and reflected on them seated in a circle. This amplification by the group helped us to understand the deeper import of the experiences and led to a number of valuable insights.

Critical appraisal and the limitations of therapy

I have often made the personal observation: to be held securely by your mother at last, and feeling free from a constant sense of threat, is a kind of deliverance. But, because the sense of threat is physically embedded in every cell, it is indissoluble if viewed from a rational standpoint. The extent to which the process can lead to any deep healing remains to be seen. Personally, I believe that the most deeply embedded influences take effect in a serious situation – as a reaction that ensured survival "back then". Thus, a person does not *have* the experience, but *is* the experience and embodies it. Corrective new experiences might, can and will certainly help in ordinary everyday life. But I would dare to say that everything that we manage to change in a person's system through behavioural and other therapies, including psycholytic, only *reduces* the problem, and certainly doesn't *resolve* it altogether. A fixed reaction to an initial disturbance remains like a hereditary defect in the system of the individual.

A further critical observation as to the limits of feasibility: the system that is the human being is a closed one. This is where the initial effect was registered. The system is unable to function outside itself – in other words: there is nothing beyond the self. Even with the best command of the role of observer, any perception can only be experienced in relation to personal "self-reference". This means that you are always the prisoner of your own perception, only seeing the world from this context.

I believe that it is vital for us to acknowledge these patterns and influences. On closer inspection, we see that it is precisely these factors that are responsible for relationship constellations. The vast majority of people act from their conscious sense of responsibility or waking consciousness. Metaphorically speaking, a whole army of personal approaches secretly controls what we think of our fellow human beings, how we behave and react towards them – especially our partners! As Irvin D. Yalom once said: "The better we know ourselves, the better our lives will be."

CHAPTER 9

Processes

It is my intention in this chapter to illustrate the evolving process of mutative change in psycholytic psychotherapy in greater detail by examining how the processes of two people developed over time.
   I also discuss materiel from an ayahuasca session in Brazil.

The story of Y.

Couple Kl. came to me in the autumn of 200X. During their first and only couple session, after they described the problem to me, I advised both partners to explore their backgrounds in detail in order to identify their own patterns and use this as a basis for analysing what they described as the desolate state of their marriage. I was quick to recommend this, as I was familiar with the political situation in the Eastern Block during the husband's childhood and youth and it seemed that the family's flight to Switzerland was due to the difficult living conditions there. The wife was unable to make this step and wanted nothing to do with me or the systemic approach. I therefore referred them to a couple therapist I knew for further couple therapy.

Mr Y. Kl. stayed in therapy with me. We did intensive talking therapy with a high frequency of sessions. We initially used the sessions to discuss his personal history and relationship with his parents and sister. We worked out the family history with the help of a family tree and Kl. proved to be very conscientious about investigating his family background. I repeatedly asked him about any similarities between his behaviour and that of his father's ancestors, but we found no resonance.

I perceived Kl. as being extremely controlled, disciplined, eager for knowledge and highly motivated to find out about himself in order to "get on". On my advice, he went through personality training, which involved finding out about himself and his patterns and indeed he was able to make some changes. He made a collection of statements during this period, recording them meticulously: "If you want to achieve anything, you have to be ready to die". Our therapy sessions always ran along the same lines: we talked and he recounted aspects of his history, I asked questions and he answered them. I tried to guide him towards emotional memories but this triggered no feelings for him; he simply wasn't able to feel his emotions. Even the fact that his wife had been living with another man for a year and that she insulted and humiliated him in front of their sons didn't even seem to ruffle his feathers.

He sometimes had explosive fits of rage, however. He took part in a number of family constellations and this is where the first signs appeared that he could be emotionally moved and touched inside. He remained deeply ambivalent with regard to his marriage. He compiled the qualities of a good marriage in lists and was always trying to talk to his wife. However, the material in our therapy sessions had become boring and repetitive – we were going round in circles. But he still came to sessions once a week at 8am. I finally suggested the "special" therapy work to him. He immediately said yes.

2006, 1st set of case notes: MDMA

Intention question: Am I sure deep down that a fresh start with my wife is possible?

Three women appear: my first long-term partner, my current wife and my recent new relationship. I did not go into the question of why the first woman – my first great love – appeared. I immediately had a powerful visceral bond with my current wife, and it was the same for her. The new woman kept forcing herself between us. This scenario was repeated several times.

In the meantime, I saw myself as a huge and mighty eagle gliding over a beautiful mountain landscape, observing its eyrie from time to time. I took great pleasure in the freedom. The feeling of gliding high above everything was indescribable, but the knowledge that I was protecting the eyrie and that I could go back there gave me a certain sense of security and belonging.

2006, 2nd set of case notes: MDMA and LSD

Intention question: What is preventing me from opening myself and my heart up to others? Why is everything I do, not quite the way it might be?

I realised relatively quickly that my grandfather's hatred, resentment and mistrust of other people was the barrier. So that's what's in my way! When I realised this, I asked my grandfather to take back everything that I could see belonged not to me but to him. He accepted this willingly. I felt lighter from that moment on, and could feel an immediate opening up inside.

I looked at my family. My wife was standing a little way away in a black veil and it was obvious that this had nothing to do with me but was created by her ... In the meantime, my grandfather kept on appearing, and seemed to look happy at getting back what belonged to him. I somehow had the feeling that he was blessing me.

The next constellation with my father happened in exactly the same context. I was able to acknowledge all of his hard work, the pain of being in exile and loss of recognition for his professional skills on our behalf. I felt the pressure lift.

... When, still deeply moved, I told my wife about what I had seen, all I got was a sceptical look. She can't see the link between my ancestors and Now ...

2006, 3rd set of case notes: ayahuasca

Intention question: When and why did I close up and how can I open up inwardly and outwardly? How can I be totally myself again? How can I get back my self-confidence?

Music, questions, nausea. The statement came quickly: you can only take if you have let go. And I was allowed to take, I earned it and am allowed to reap a little on behalf of my ancestors. My mother appeared to me, I hugged her and she disappeared, giving me a benevolent look.

Here is a long description of physical complaints.

... The music had stopped in the meantime and I wasn't getting anywhere. I was lying there with a terrible pain in my stomach and had no idea what to let go of in order to move forward. I went to the loo again. I wasn't sick but it came out below this time, giving me the certainty that it wasn't controlling everything and that my ancestors' unresolved crap had to come out. Everything that we had to swallow but couldn't digest – in the widest sense.

I already felt a lot better, more relaxed, lighter, but letting go of the physical stuff wasn't the only thing I had to celebrate. The psychological process of letting go was not over yet. I lay down and the pains in my stomach came back. I wanted to be sick and tried again, this time with success. All of the crap that my ancestors and I had swallowed and not been able to digest came out. What a great feeling – I even enjoyed being sick. I was able to let go and felt extremely free, I had taken the first step – I had been able to let go in a physical sense, too.

Day two:

... Resolution came. I could flush it all away by being sick and nearly crapped my pants. The great battle started on the loo. The pain increased. Stomach cramps, discomfort, sweating and demoralising thoughts: what am I going to find out today?

I started to have thoughts about the huge battle in The Lord of the Rings. I was a knight in shining armour who knows that he has to go in a certain direction but doesn't know the destination. Many monsters have to be slain on the way. I felt a sense of relaxation in my body every time I brought one of them down. But I had to leave my seat to be sick several times. I had terrible stomach cramps. I seemed to be the only survivor of the battle between Good and Evil, and it kept on starting up again. After a long period of suffering and emptying myself, I was tired from all the fighting and I realised that this was not the way to win the battle. I stuck my sword in the ground and went off to find another way. To my astonishment, nobody grabbed me.

... What exactly is it that I have to accept today? I tried to relax, with some success, and felt a little better in my body, too. Bingo!!!!! Male strength!! That was it. That's what I had to accept. But how?

I received a warm welcome in the work-space that F. sets aside for people who feel stuck, and was able to go over to X. I was able to dock on to him and accept and fill up on all of my ancestors' male strength through him, this time for real and something I could really feel. F. also made herself available and filled me up with female power, too. What bliss, what peace. I lay there enjoying my new energy.

2007, 4th set of case notes: ayahuasca

Intention question: How can I open myself up further – to my sons, wife and patients?

I asked to be allowed to feel my mother's love physically.

... Then my grandfather on my mother's side appeared. He took me by the hand and showed me various joyful, life-affirming rooms and artistic scenarios, telling me several times that I should now live my life. My ancestors were now much more reconciled than I had known them to be before, and I saw the sequence of their lives. This showed me that my male ancestors stand for male strength. They were muscular,

powerful, intrepid warriors with a strong connection to me. My grand-father on my mother's side stands for the artistic part of me. I put my mother on a pedestal, telling everyone: "This is my mother, look at her." This was a significant step for me, I was standing totally by my mother. I was a little ashamed of her before. I did the same with my father, which also did me some good. A feeling of well-being flowed through my body. I also introduced my wife to my ancestors and they nodded with approval.

But right after that the plant told me that I should leave my wife behind and continue on my journey. I was terrified. Does this mean divorce? I interpreted it on an intellectual level.

When I was in the work-room I was able to express that I didn't know exactly who I was. The constellation work showed me that I am a Czech with a Swiss passport. I was able to stand by my Czech roots for the first time and feel that I have found my rightful place in Switzerland. A warm feeling, a feeling of peace and security came over me.

Day two:

I came across an event in the kitchen in P. My grandmother and mother were laughing about me. "How cute, how sweet!" I interpreted it as "mockery" and started to cry. This made them laugh even more. The conclusion that I made as a child was that I would be mocked if I show my feelings. Now I had found what I needed to find in order to free myself and open up.

But I noticed at the same time that the origin of my inability to show my feelings went much deeper. I took a booster, a second dos-age, and a battle began, similar to the one in the previous session. I hugged the toilet bowl – but I had to get help after a few hours. F. led me away.

There was a moment when I felt really happy. I had never expe-rienced such a feeling of happiness before. I knew it: this was the moment of conception. Then a little later (weeks?), I experienced an external change of state, energy-wise: my mother realised that she was pregnant. I could feel it quite distinctly. The shutters went down. Bleak. I recognise the abrupt change from an extreme feeling of hap-piness for no particular reason to closure and not feeling anything anymore only too well from my everyday life.

Later on, I didn't actually want to leave the womb. It was dark in here, and it felt incredibly pleasant. Security and protection. I had to leave that situation and I didn't want to. I knew what was waiting for me.

2007, 5th set of case notes: 2CB

Intention question: What do my fears and resistance consist of?

... It took me back to my grandfathers again. Is this where the fear and resistance come from?

I couldn't see anything concrete. My parents are almost not present at all, I can't make any connection. I don't trust other people. I am unable to surrender myself. The film is playing in my head. I am out of it. The question is: where am I then?

2008, 6th set of case notes: 2CB, MDMA, LSD

Intention question: I would like to look at the issue of respect. My wife keeps treating me disrespectfully. What does this have to do with me?

It soon became clear to me that women had hardly any respect for men on both sides of the family i.e. my side and my wife's side. My wife was already like this with the grandparents. I felt this strongly as soon as I met my wife's parents. I couldn't work it out back then, but I understand the context now.

The problem on my side starts with respect for my grandfathers. My mother's father was in a concentration camp for about a year. He was tortured physically and mentally while he was there, to the point where he lost all self-respect.

My father's father was arrested and interrogated by the Gestapo and later by the Communists. Things happened to him there that destroyed his personality. I saw that he had to allow himself to be raped by someone; a man was holding a pistol to his head. They did this to humiliate him, as he was a strong man and was not willing to betray his ideals so readily. Denunciations had led to his arrest. These actions had made my grandfather feel disgust for other people and I think that this was the lump that I kept feeling in my stomach.

Both of my grandfathers were castrated in this way – they were robbed of part of their masculinity and male strength. The fact that they couldn't act or defend themselves just in order to survive and had to allow themselves to be continually degraded meant that they became deadened, continuing to allow themselves to be treated without respect – castrated and powerless. The constellation with my male ancestors enabled me to become thankful and respectful to them: if they had not behaved exactly in the way, they would not have survived. And there would be no me. Their loss of masculinity meant that I could live. I had inherited their attitude and preferences, taken them on, experiencing them and making them my own.

2007, 7th set of case notes: 2CB, MDMA, LSD

Intention question: I want to look at my parents, their relationship and the parallels with my current relationship. Respect was one aspect of this. I had little if any respect for my father or myself up to that point. I wanted to know where and how this had been lost.

... Arriving on the plateau, I asked myself the original question once again. I immediately saw myself kneeling down before my father, listening fearfully to his harangue and waiting for the expected blows. I also knew right away that this was the moment when I lost all respect for my father and myself. I also felt a bit of a coward, that I had simply given up without a fight, but what was I supposed to do against my stronger father?

I decided to go into the fear state and associated feelings. I slipped back into being the little Y. To my surprise, I achieved this state very easily and the picture changed abruptly. It was bright and I was totally free from fear, very relieved and a little proud, and somebody said: "You're doing well." I can't say if it was my father, as I couldn't see anyone any more. As far as I can remember, it was the first time in my life that I was really able to accept praise.

I wanted to look at the whole situation again and find out whether I still had any emotions about it. I now saw myself on my knees before my father, waiting for the blows; I saw myself kneeling for punishment in the corner and it didn't trigger any emotions anymore. I had got over the event.

Using the second substance, I understood that I have to assert my side of things to my wife if I don't want to lose respect for myself again or my sons to lose respect for me. I realised that it is wrong to put our relationship as parents above our relationship as a couple. I decided to change this. In the constellation work, I was able to face my wife with my father behind me and make it clear to her that I would no longer put up with her destructive criticism, and that I would move out if the situation between us didn't improve. My quality of life was important to me now.

Later we did a constellation of my sons and I. I made it clear to my sons as well that I am their father and they are my children. Then we did a constellation of my father and I again. I was asked if I believe that I am doing better than he did. As I confirmed this, I noticed that

I was putting myself above him, despising him. This became clear to me: my father demanded a lot from me. He wanted me to achieve a lot so that I would have it better than he did and he had somehow demanded that I did things better. So I fulfilled his wish. This is an expression of my love for and loyalty to him. Substituting my father revealed the difference: then I said: "In honour of you, I am making something good of myself and having things better than you did", and then my father felt respected. When I said: "I'm doing better than you", he didn't feel respected. I fulfilled his wish. I am allowed to and ought to do better than he did. The second revelation of the evening came to me in that moment.

Up until then, I had seen my father with dark hair and a lot younger than he is now in all of the pictures. This image disappeared at the moment of revelation and an old man with white hair stood before me. My feeling of superiority had disappeared. I can now accept my father as he is. I approve of what he did and how he did it. He did what he could. I can now accept him as the elderly man he has become, I no longer need to put myself above him, and I can also see what he has achieved. It is a relief that he can be the father and I the son.

2008, 8th set of case notes: MDMA

Intention question: I would like to look at my sons.

I can distinctly feel my pelvis opening up today.

The older son demands the male components from me. The younger one needs the artistic side.

2008, 9th set of case notes: ayahuasca

Intention question: Who am I and who am I in different life situations?

I didn't get a direct answer to my question. Instead, I saw people walking past me, in a field surrounded by a see-through fence, like a thin sheet of glass, on which they seemed to be walking and which seemed to "hover" beneath them. A second field was plotted on this field, a different size for each person. It was immediately clear to me that this was a general representation of people with their potential and different opportunities. The coloured field stood for what they are prepared to share with others. The plant told me that the people used other people to see and perceive themselves, and that, by and large, the individual phenomena had little or nothing to do with me personally.

*I understood that I am not responsible for what happens to other peo-
ple. I also understood that I shouldn't keep undermining myself all the
time.*

*This made me realise that I have led a kind of second-hand life: I
have done a number of things just to belong. My soul feels good if I
pursue MY goals. If I don't do this, my soul doesn't feel good and it's
as if I am cut off from myself ... I can't make a clear decision as far as
my wife is concerned. I have an idea what's wrong but I keep blotting
it out if it seems negative ...*

*I have realised what levels I can meet my wife on and the levels
on which it doesn't work. She gives what she can as a mother and a
housewife. I find her role as my partner only partially satisfactory. If
this part becomes more important to me, there is a danger that I might
need someone else for a different kind of interaction. Or I can accept
it and look for what's missing in other people. I haven't decided yet.*

Day two:
Intention question: How can I feed my unrealised potential into everyday life?

*... As time passed, it dawned on me what was missing. It was clearly
male strength ... I don't do male strength. What's stopping me? Gag-
ging, sessions on the loo with diarrhoea. It then became clear to me
that it was to do with my grandfather on my father's side. He had
been tortured, lost his masculinity and somehow castrated. I realised:
I have taken on the castration and related shame. Over the next few
hours the diarrhoea started to have blood in it and I felt like death
warmed up. I worked on sensing my grandfather, wanting to have contact with him and obtain permission for assuming my male strength. I
could hardly feel my testicles. I was struggling with death, "fighting
for my life", and saw blood running from every orifice.*

*Finally I get help. L. conducted a shamanic ritual and my stomach
relaxed a little. It suddenly hit me like a bolt from the blue: I couldn't
let go because nothing would be coming after me. I've been vasectomised!!!! I had myself vasectomised!! The tension was gone. It is
clear to me that I have to reverse it, or I won't assume my strength. I
slowly went back through the situation again once more: I could now
leave my grandfather to his terrible fate. He gave me his blessing and
I can now assume my own strength.*

Case notes from the follow-up session:
*I am still completely shaken, I feel like a dog that's been beaten today,
a failure. I still don't know what I am supposed to do about it (to get*

away from the thought). I need help with becoming a man. I'd like to practise it at home, as I think it's a good place to practise. And because of my sons. Unless a miracle happens, we'll see ...

... I will just follow my own programme, without wondering all the time what she might be thinking now or whether things are OK. I know that she thinks it's just another bunch of crap and disapproves of my actions. It doesn't matter what I do, even if it's for the family, like going to work, for example. I find it terrible living with someone like that. It really upsets me that my son sees me like that. I really don't know how I'm supposed to behave. I need to let things settle.

2008, 10th set of case notes: 250 micrograms of LSD

... I met my "entire family tree", all of my ancestors right back to the Slavs, seeing them metaphorically. They were mighty warriors but pursued no aggressive policies, just calmly went on their travels and ruled. They were actually repressed by other groups, which annoyed me, as I had the feeling that they didn't fight back. Their behaviour was aimed at the well-being and survival of the people. There wasn't any expansion. Prosperity and contentment reigned.

... I perceived energies, saw souls. I was overwhelmed by the amazing power of being. Later on, I felt a strong energy in my pelvis. I saw myself and my sons in a vertical line, which I considered as important. Although there was also gratitude towards her, my wife played an insignificant and subordinate role. My intuition (or was it my interpretation?) was that I should get a divorce if I wanted to make progress in terms of relationships. I need to take the time to do this.

I still have an overwhelming sense of what I have seen and energy in my bones. I see the world a little differently, perceive it differently. I see into people's souls and try to look beyond what is on the outer surface. I feel humility within me and gratitude for the opportunity to find this out. I feel calmer and more certain and it also occurs to me that I can feel that all of my ancestors are behind me, right back to the beginning. A great feeling, and one that I had not experienced with such intensity before.

2008, 11th set of case notes: 2CB and LSD

Intention question: I would like to look at my self-esteem and understand why it is so low.

... I saw the concentration camp scenes very quickly, my grandfather on my mother's side appearing in them. The central scene showed a

guard sexually abusing my grandfather. I understood that your self-esteem would be low after experiencing something like that.

I asked for this to be staged.

2009, 14th set of case notes: 2CB and LSD

Intention question: How can I stage the fact that I finally love myself, and how do I realise my full potential?

I came across my grandfathers again, who were totally subject to out-side control. Both of them had already been through the First World War. One of them spent a year in a concentration camp in World War Two and the other one had not talked under interrogation by the Gestapo and the Communists and had to dig ditches for the rest of his life. Both of them had opted for survival and not fought back; both were broken inside. There was no acknowledgement of their terrible fate. They just functioned as broken men.

The staging revealed my inability to show aggression and my block about it and my powerful control over aggression. Fear and aggression lie close together deep inside me. I almost didn't make it. I feel like the underdog at home ... my wife has the money ...

The staging also revealed that I still despised my grandfathers for not having fought back. I do exactly the same thing. I don't defend myself when my wife insults me and I see myself as a wuss. I didn't manage to react to my wife's "insults" in the staging. I dissociated whenever she humiliated me in front of the children. The only thing that I can think about is what the people around me think of me.

I bow down to the terrible fate of my grandfathers, but I still despise them a little for failing to rebel. I know that I have no right to, but there is still a feeling that things get really extreme if I do this to them: I feel deep hatred for myself.

I can see it now: my grandfathers' fear and aggression live on in me. The instinct to defend myself turns into self-hatred if self-defence is not possible.

I hate
– having to continuously adapt to survive;
– subservience to authority (and the secret feeling of superiority);
– the everlasting and ever-present mistrust;
– the resulting solitude;
– the fear of confrontation;
– the feeling of being controlled from outside, helplessness and "being on guard".

2009; 15th set of case notes: 2CB and MDMA

Intention question: How do I get out of this? What is my mission in life?

I waited. NOTHING happened. Or did it? What was there? Pressure started to build in my stomach and a desire to throw up rose within me. I felt worse and worse and then felt pain, too. My ancestors came briefly to mind, but I suppressed the thoughts. Never again.

I decided to perceive the pain and nausea completely consciously. I felt disgusted. On closer inspection, I saw that it was the disgust of my male ancestors. Disgust over what had happened, and with themselves for not having fought back or made a fuss. They had to save their skins – it was about pure survival. It was also a little like grief. Grief because their suffering had not been seen. I had constantly condemned them myself for giving up.

I was asked to find out whether I could engender aggression and was prompted to do so. Nothing happened. Staged aggression just wouldn't happen for me. It didn't come or stay with me until I was able to say: "Come to me, I need you". I feel a little lighter after this.

When I was standing in front of the mirror a few days later a fit of aggression came up within in me that I had never seen in myself before. I could have screamed. I tensed my muscles and my face became a grimace, radiating pure aggression. I didn't recognise myself anymore. The actual trigger that brought me to this point was a situation at home. Was that the moment when the aggression came to me – did I integrate some of it? It seems so.

A similar thing happened a few days later: I had to go straight to my weights machine to calm down. It was boiling away inside me – I could have killed everything in sight and threw the dumbbells about ...

2009 16th set of case notes: MDMA and LSD

Intention question: How do I get on with my life? I ask to see my Higher Self.

A wonderful ascent – I was held gently. The pain in my right shoulder blade migrated throughout my whole body (with ayurveda, your right side corresponds to male behaviour), and I was taken back to my grandfathers again. I was able to bow right down before them and thank them for what they did for their family and for coming back to ensure our continued survival. For the first time, I was also able to see what my father did for us: he had the courage to emigrate so that we would have a better life. He left his family and friends behind, gave up his job and travelled to a foreign country where he did not speak the language. This filled me with pride and gratitude. What a fantastic feeling. And now I could finally say YES to myself for the first time – without any ifs or buts. Now I can get on with my life.

I sense that my wife and I are a little closer.

2009, 17th set of case notes: 250 micrograms of LSD

Intention question: I ask to be healed.

Images of war and erotic scenes – threatening and overpowering. I was entering deeper and deeper energy fields and was a little frightened of where this might lead. But it was clear to me that I can only enjoy healing and spiritual experiences if I am trusting and give myself up to the event without resistance. So I allowed myself to be drawn down into the maelstrom.

It seemed like I was travelling back through history. Images and stomach pain came back from earlier sessions. I was spiralling down and down into something. Suddenly I saw a form that looked like DNA. My DNA? I felt like I needed to go to the loo, at the same time seeing dirt and brown impurities dropping from the DNA. I went to the loo. As I sat there, the image became stronger and as I evacuated my bowels the dirt fell from the DNA as a kind of "energy soup". A moment of great release. The DNA was radiating beautiful colours, and a bright energy twisted "up" from the depths of the dark energy soup.

Concerned, the group leader brought me back into the room. The stomach pains had passed and the process of "recreation" continued. I passed extremely threatening energy fields that seemed dark and powerful. I kept seeing the bright energy twisting upwards. Then I reached the point where I had the choice to connect myself with something. I also felt respect here, but my faith in a positive experience ultimately made me embark on this adventure. I connected up with the energy. I felt like I was totally disintegrating at that point. Not a word, not a sound, no more thoughts and no more me. Pure consciousness. I was at one with everything. I stayed in this state for a while and the thought flashed through my mind as to whether I would ever get back.

We sat up. When asked, I couldn't say who I was. I couldn't perceive or remember the past that had shaped me from the field where I was. The question did also seem a little trivial after being connected to pure Being. I felt like saying: "I am a being of light, energy, Being". But I was afraid that people would laugh at me, and carried on searching for an answer to the question of who I am. I couldn't hook up with anything anywhere. F. took me by the shoulders and moved my body about in a gentle spiralling motion. A light rose within me and every subsequent spiral took me closer to the light. It was as if I was being reborn from darkness into the light. Who am I? I am who I am and my name is Y.

A new feeling gradually came over my body. It was as if I had been emptied. I searched for familiar patterns and emotions but found nothing. I could feel a slight, relatively pleasant vibration throughout my body. It felt like I mustn't do anything. I was vibrating gently, felt empty but also increasingly felt that I had the power and strength to finally take hold of the reins of my life. I realised that I was in the process of re-defining myself.

I have to get used to this state at first, as it is totally new and unknown to me. Have I now come into myself? *I am experiencing myself and my body in a different way to before. There is also great peace within me. I look at the earlier issues, my grandfathers, parents and wife. I can simply look at them without having to know all about their family background or any difficult emotions. I think that I am looking with love for the first time.*

2009, 18th set of case notes: 2CB and LSD

Intention question: To take another look at my present family.

When I was in the ascent I had another glimpse of the scene when I had to kneel in the corner and suffer being hit by my father. I let it be. Then the archetypal "man" flowed into my genitals and my entire body through the first chakra. I was strong, male and full of love. I now bear the responsibility for everything I do. I am with myself. I realise that a good part of the journey is behind me.

The constellation with my wife has resulted in us having no loving feelings for each other anymore. She doesn't have much left for me and feels that I could be earning more money. She treats me like a fool and provokes me by her constant denigration. I think that there is nothing more to be done about this, that I should go and that I actually will. But I would have to discuss the When a bit more. It will probably happen sooner than planned. I believe that we make each other unhappy and hold each other back. We can probably get on better again alone. This new power, which I obviously need to keep nurturing, enables me to give a better account of myself at home and practise my new behaviour.

Reflection on the process undergone by Y.

Y. came to therapy with an obvious problem in his marriage. The actual issue that had led him to therapy came to the fore during the first session with consciousness-expanding substances. Important relationships came up. Y. came into contact with his relationship with his wife, which was dysfunctional and caused him distress. But his journey in an expanded range of consciousness made it possible to push the relationship crisis into the background and explore his own patterns. The feeling of freedom unconsciously became a resource – a prior indication of where things might go.

Things then entered the realm of epigenetics very quickly: Y. became able to see what he was unable to see before: the feelings that he had accessed for the very first time through consciousness expansion originated mainly in his grandfathers. It involved trauma-induced changes to the epigenome, which were handed down to descendants – himself and his father. Unfortunately, just knowing about these circumstances isn't enough. They can only be integrated if the material is re-experienced cognitively and emotionally at the same time – experience is more than just intellectual knowledge.

The principal tools in this process were direct insights and modified constellation work. The main issues in the sessions were the grandfathers' traumatising experiences of two World Wars, National Socialism and the Nazi era. Y. recognised himself in his ancestors. He was able to attribute his behaviour, low self-respect, inability to defend himself, explosive fits of rage and other feelings, to the understandable physical and psychological consequences of these extraordinary traumas and the stress that flowed from them. Surrender, putting up with hunger, losing their freedom and suffering became a survival strategy for his imprisoned grandfathers, which was reflected in a physical, mental and spiritual immobilisation, resignation and numbness.

Personalities had then evolved from the situation of not being allowed to protect themselves, in which masculinity, aggression, pugnacity and creativity could no longer be perceived within the self. Degradation, torture and sexual abuse had led to feelings of shame and worthlessness. We also had to consider a perpetrator introject – identification with the perpetrator. The fact that Y. had no access to his feelings at all before working with consciousness-expanding substances implies dissociated transgenerational trauma.

Before we could focus on the issue of their marriage, he needed to reconnect with his father: an initial loving assessment made way for his own painful past experiences. His mother's embrace and benevolent regard provided healing energy. This meant that the mother issue could be explored with a basically empathetic approach. The experiences in the womb, especially his mother's horror at discovering she was pregnant, explained his difficult, rather insecure relationship with her. This seemed to explain his occasional rapid switch from feelings of elation to desolate darkness.

It took Y. from September 2006 to September 2009 to realise that he was the one allowing *himself* to be treated with disrespect. And it took a while longer for him to see that he had not yet been capable of an appropriate physical and emotional reaction to such behaviour. Integrating the substance of his experiences and relocating his own authentic personality finally brought him back to the place where the journey had started; he saw that he had sought out the woman who could trigger the issue within him. He acknowledged his part in the failure of their relationship; his inability to perceive feelings, his outbursts when insulted and his self-subordination and surrender. All these aspects of his emotional life and behaviour started to make sense.

He went through all stations of the therapeutic process in the course of his psycholytic self-exploration. In his case, special importance could be attributed to the influence of epigenetics and transgenerational trauma. But other issues also contributed to the overall picture and his dawning understanding of the issue that had led him towards therapy. In the end, it was a spiritual experience supported by Live-Body-Work that led to the healing turning point: re-linking (*re-ligio*) with his inner core, separating his ancestors' emotions from his own and the life experiences of his forefathers from his own experiences. Experiences working at a deep level included purifying his DNA, disengagement from normal consciousness, entering a pure state of Being and going back into his body.

Our work together ended at this point.

Mo's story

The therapeutic process in this example is totally different from the previous one. But Mo. still "goes through" all of the stations and progresses sequentially towards the overall objective of uncovering her authentic personality.

Report on the overall process

I was looking for a lady therapist because I wasn't able to send out invoices for work that I had done, so I was barely surviving. I was in the red, I had nothing left to live on, my bank account was empty and I was a single parent of two children. A well-meaning colleague came to me, saying he had got to know a lady who wasn't bad, so I thought I'd better give it a go. It was you.

After I'd told you my personal history, you looked at me over the top of your glasses and said: I think we need to look a little closer – and then you sent me to the first systemic family constellation with M.

My protagonist collapsed screaming, lay on the floor and was unable to move. Nobody knew what it was about. A parcel of blame was handed back and forth. Nobody wanted it. We let things stand.

I dreamt of battlefields and blood that night ...

...

I went back to you with these results, and you suggested the other therapy relatively quickly after that. "Have you heard that there are other ways, too?" I said: "No, how, what?" Then you told me about the "other work". I thought about it very briefly and decided to do it. I was then able to go to the first session.

First MDMA session: *I was eaten up by anxiety. I was all anxiety. I had a whole load of weird images: a red horse, a green dog. No love or opening up of the heart, but straight to panic and pain.*

I had endless anxiety after this experience. I didn't want to continue. Then you said it was a shame and that it was almost normal. You suggested another individual session.

We used MDMA first in the next session. This caused me to panic again, with extreme pain throughout my body and in the heart area and I thought I was going to die. I screamed. When I heard that this was my heart opening up and "It will pass", I just thought good, OK then.

I didn't notice anything else in the beginning. All I know is that it was awful. Then I took a very tiny piece of LSD (25micro) – I said to myself that things couldn't get any worse, so I might as well continue. I also felt that, if I didn't do any more now, that would be that and then it would get worse. With LSD, I got into the situation that I still had much later – I couldn't work out where I was. Everything was oscillating and I couldn't make anything out clearly, it was all distorted and I couldn't fix my gaze or focus on anything. This went on for years; if I looked at something, I always saw what was next to it really clearly. I felt "misaligned", noticing in the end. Later, we discovered after a lot of delving that the misalignment had occurred because I had no reference point within me that I could attach anything to. The situation at home, where inner perception did not coincide with external reality, was a source of continuous incongruity. Outside, my father was a dedicated and caring doctor. At home, he was a tyrant [meta level: the tyrant is afraid!!!!]. *My mother's unspoken command was: you are not allowed to like your father. As a small child, I was my father's favourite and adored him. I have lots of internal images and there are also plenty of photos with me sitting on his lap. But in addition to this, he was the tyrant who beat my brother. I had a clear picture of my brother getting a beating. I had two fathers! And then there was my mother, who denied everything going on at home. This skewed everything.*

And there was the general atmosphere, suggesting that there must be more to it and something was not quite right: an atmosphere that communicated annihilation and the killer instinct. I could perceive this but couldn't pin it down, not trusting to my own powers of perception. As time passed, I got closer and closer to my father in the sessions, discovering that he had a Nazi past. I knew that he'd been in the war, but he never talked about it. It turned out that my father had been extremely violent [children have images of their parents in their head], *man to man and with Jews. He stomped on them – and I realised that I had long identified with the victims – even until quite recently. I experienced this physically in the sessions.*

I was always "askew" at the sessions. I understood and didn't understand at the same time, and always had a headache. Then F. said: you look like a victim. We had always worked with MDMA and LSD up until that point. I came to 2CB quite late. But I looked at this under the influence of ayahuasca: I saw the man lying on the ground and boots stomping on him. I was this man and I felt the pain. [This was genuine identification with the victim, as is often the case with Nazi families.] *When I was working through my father's Nazi period, I reached a point with LSD and 2CB where it was a case of kill or be killed. It was the same feeling going back and forth. It was one and the same thing. But I had to decide whether I wanted to kill or be killed. I stood opposite my interlocutor and had to decide: am I the one who dies or am I the one who sticks the knife in? I had to go into this decision consciously and assume the energy of the ability to kill as my own. I consciously chose life in the role of perpetrator but had to keep on looking at that role and accepting it – better to agree: I am also a perpetrator. I have realised that the perpetrator then naturally becomes the victim – just as the victim naturally becomes the perpetrator. It took me a while before I could fully accept my role as perpetrator.*

Did things go better with sending your invoices after that?

Things went better with the invoices from the moment I was allowed to sit on my father's lap.

The issue of my bulimia ran in parallel with other issues: we never addressed it as the sole issue. We addressed it implicitly as we worked through my relationship with my father. We discussed and processed the bulimia in connection with my father: when I had to/was allowed to sit on my father's lap, I was able to tell my mother that I like my father and accept things from him. I was only able to address these regression issues with LSD. Later with 2CB, too. It was hard with 2CB – there was massive resistance. The issues were my resistance against being German, being the perpetrator, and against aggression. I would always have liked to be a bit better.

When it came to the issue of survival, I could see that the ovum is fertilised by the sperm during the act of conception and that one sperm hits the target and thousands fall by the wayside. Even this is highly aggressive. Killing is implicit in creation. I had these realisations with 2CB. When I say yes to life, I also indirectly say yes to death and anni-hilation. Everyone carries this within themselves.

Back to the eating issue again: a fellow traveller fed me on one occasion! L. fed me under the influence of ayahuasca. I had to under-stand that living means "nourishing yourself", eating and breathing. Affirming these processes consciously, accepting that this is what it's about. This went on from session to session: just say yes to eating and breathing and that it's OK. [Mo. breathes and eats, obviously. The former is a reflex that we don't control ourselves – we can't delib-erately hold our breath until we die: we let go first and take a deep breath through instinct – it breathes for us.] *For me, it was a ques-tion of entering my body consciously and accepting life – that I have been living for some time now already! My resistance came from the unconscious and I actually believed that I could decide whether to live or die. So it was all about acknowledging that I had already said yes to life! In addition to the father issue, a refusal to live had also mani-fested itself through my bulimia.*

Then there was my mother: my mother had lost her first fiancé in an air raid on W. and part of her died with him. Accept life, even though my mother wasn't really there anymore from the beginning – we didn't really develop a bond with her. This was the next issue for me. (Under the influence of 2CB) I perceived the attempted abortion – as a big sharp object coming towards me but which I also managed to avoid. Every time somebody addresses me directly, speaks to me or calls me by name, I give a start and my senses fade.

I made these realisations when I asked the intention question "Why do I give a start when someone addresses me directly?" As soon as my mother realised she was pregnant, she was completely terrified and simply tried to abort me. She was talking to me here. So I am terrified every time someone talks to me. Both of these facts mean that I didn't really have my mother, and the bond between us wasn't really there, either.

I didn't just have the first realisation that "My mother didn't want me" by myself – she also told me as much herself – that I actually shouldn't exist, but my father wanted me very much. [Pleasing both parents by existing and not existing is a very tall order for a child.]

At a relatively early stage when I was about five years old my mother started telling me things that I shouldn't really know about. I was like a friend or partner to her. She told me terrible things about my father – that he was unfaithful, for example; today, I would describe this as emotional abuse. This triggered tensions in me leading to bulimia, as I had idolised my father and wasn't allowed to anymore.

The most significant thing I realised about why I looked at things in such a distorted way was that the problems between my parents were very difficult for a small child like me to understand. But I continually tried to understand. But I was much too young to understand anything. So I had always been at a level where I couldn't move at all – an adult level where I couldn't understand anything. The more I accessed my child level through the therapy work and was allowed to see that I couldn't understand anything, the clearer I became. I still realise that it was difficult for me at first to agree that I can't understand anything and don't even have to understand anything. This triggered anxiety at first. But this also led to great relief and something that "de-stressed" me. And I accessed myself as the little Mo. My mother was a gifted doctor but was never allowed to work after she arrived in Switzerland. As I see it now, she only really ever felt alive if she was able to work. Her exam qualifications were still not recognised at the time and my father didn't want her to work and become better than he was. He also didn't want her to find out what he was doing – he was cheating on her with the nurses. He worked at the hospital. In spite of receiving a good offer, he didn't have the courage to establish himself. The fact that my mother was no longer able to work made her ill. She died of breast cancer at the age of 71 when I was 34 years old. I loved her very much and am a very faithful daughter. The almost unbearable pain was mainly due to the fact that I never really had her.

Then there was the business with my brother. We discovered that he is only my half-brother. As a child, I suspected that something was not quite right, but expressed it in another way: are you sure that I am one of you? So I related this "There is something not right here" to myself.

Then my father became the issue again. My father even has the persecution and hatred of the Jews in his bones. Under the influence of LSD, I realised at some point that my ancestors on my father's side are of Jewish origin. The hatred that my father has for the Jews has therefore lasted to this day. My father doesn't know this. Like Hitler? Yes, like Hitler, whom we now accept as being one quarter Jewish and taking revenge on his heritage through the persecution of the Jews.

It is an inner instinct within my father to take revenge on the way his life was shaped in this way: My grandfather (Jewish doctor) *cheated on his wife with the servant girl. She became pregnant and was driven out of the house when it was found out.* [Mo.'s father is therefore the child of a servant girl and a Jewish doctor. The "person driven out" then married another man, whom Mo. took to be her grandfather (meta level: you shouldn't look at things in a distorted way...). *My father was brought up as a cuckoo child, so he didn't really know who he was. My father doesn't know who his real father was and my brother is just as ignorant of the fact that he is also a cuckoo child.* (meta level: Mo.'s father did the same thing as his dear father, whom he didn't know; the basic pattern is epigenetic!) *He got even with the Jews, at least with the father he didn't know, and also struggled with it himself.*

I then understood everything about why I had sought out my husband – I sought out a man like my father: he despises people, women. He is incredibly aggressive, brutal, possessive and intelligent.

What realisations led to breakthrough and change?

Recognising and accepting the Nazi in me. It was a tough period, requiring a series of sessions – at least 4 or 5. There were many people with the same issue back then. It was almost a group issue. I was able to affirm everything by the end; I am also what my father did – I didn't do it myself but the principle of the action is within me. In order not to do the same thing, I have to affirm that I am "made up out of my father" and my mother – as he gave me life. He is just my father and nobody else!

It changed my life: I can now admit who and what I am. As a child in Switzerland, I didn't speak Swiss German for a very long time – six years and two years at nursery school. But I denied that I was German at the same time. That I understood! I now know who I am and where I come from. I feel no guilt or reluctance.

What persuaded me to continue with (psycholytic) therapy?

I stayed with it out of a survival instinct, as I definitely gained something that I would not otherwise have gained. There was nothing enjoyable about the work! I asked myself again before every session:

*why am I doing this? And right until the last day, it was always con-
nected with a lot of respect and a little anxiety, too.*

*What made me anxious? I knew full well that there were many things
that I had not re-experienced yet and that might also be unpleasant,
such as my birth, for example. I know that I was dismissed at birth,
but I haven't got there yet. I also noticed that I was feeding my dreams
with material; this also made me anxious. The worst realisation came
when I discovered that I am totally made up of anxiety. That I am full
of dread and in fact* am *dread. I noticed this every morning when I
woke up, linked to the question of purpose. All of my mother's terrible
images, the bombing of W., looking for her fiancé in the ruins – these
images were an integral part of me and I unconsciously defined myself
through them. This is who I am.*

Terrible feelings disappear more quickly when they are integrated.

*What spiritual feelings did I have? I saw myself in a realm of God,
a really peaceful space where there is nothing but light and love ...
no, not even love anymore, just Being. Being, which we identify as a
state of love because of the peace and absence of anxiety and thought.
The absence of anxiety releases the feeling that we call love. Not the
sweetness that is usually foisted on the word love. It is not euphoria, it
is nothing at all. You can't describe it – it is Being.*

*Did this have any effect? Yes, it made me calmer and means that I
am not searching so much.*

[My theory about this is: We can achieve *improvements* through
therapy work; *healing* is on the next level and is not within the hands
of doctors or therapists.]

*Mo.: This is just the realisation that it is what it is. The moment
when you say this is an affirmation of life that encompasses death.
Not even that it is* good, *but simply that it* is. *(It = life, the situation ...)*

*What changes were there at work? I am now a lot more reserved,
I go with the flow, and don't have the aim of helping people anymore; most of all, I am empathetic and go with the flow. I ask the
world for things to be done. In the past, I always thought: I have to
do something. I have stopped doing things, and prepare the ground
for something to happen instead. I am much more reserved, I don't
have to keep giving good advice anymore; I simply reflect what I see
... This has lifted the pressure. Having to do things and make things
happen – yes of course it's nice if you do well, but I have realised that
it's actually out of my hands. This has reinforced the realisation that
if I do things to the best of my knowledge and ability, then I have done
enough.*

Reflection on Mo.'s process

The therapeutic learning process has taken a different course here – but we can still identify all of the "stations".

In Mo.'s first session with me I realised that it had to be an issue relating to systemic entanglements. The constellation revealed that blame was involved and nobody was accepting it, and that it had to be about the war. Both parents are Germans who fled from the former GDR (East Germany). The father is still convinced that the Nazis were a good thing.

When she told me about her dreams about violence after the constellation, I suggested psycholytic therapy to her. Her first experience with 90 mg of MDMA was unusual: there was no loss of anxiety, no relaxation or any kind of pleasant feeling. She even suffered anxieties after the session that she had never had before. She wanted to stop the therapy.

I was sure that we would achieve at least a temporary loss of anxiety if we did another session, and didn't want to leave her vulnerable with her anxiety. So I suggested a second session with MDMA 6 weeks later, and we worked together closely in therapy. She was given 120mg of MDMA in the second session and experienced a painful opening up of the heart, which she had never experienced in this form before. But, in spite of the unpleasantness, Mo. established that she could bring hidden material out into the light with the substance, so she stuck with it.

I brought her into the group after the second session. It was particularly noticeable with her that she was unable to stay balanced with a very low dosage, which worked at the lower border of efficacy in her case. She was particularly incapable of having clear thoughts with LSD. Session after session, it was an uphill struggle to find out where the cause of this might be located. Once we had worked out that her inability to describe her own condition, make a statement about herself, locate or name a feeling within herself– that this inability was precisely the issue and that her "confused" circumstances were not about an intolerance or excessive dosage, we were able to work in a targeted fashion.

A major part of ego development had clearly not happened, meaning that she had no reliable reference point for herself within her system. Her "misalignment" was the expression of a phenomenon where she had no relation with herself in close relationships, such as with her mother and father. She really didn't know who she was. We were also able to identify this phenomenon in her ex-husband, who was like her father and whom she had almost not been able to let go of, even though violence was involved. Using modified constellation work, we put the focus on her mother first and Mo. learned to lie in her mother's arms as a daughter. She was initially resistant to allowing herself to be held, then sensed mistrust for her mother and her inability to relax. This was gruelling work, as she kept drifting away and it only worked for brief moments. We then tried the same thing with her father – she was supposed to see herself as her father's daughter. It took many attempts until she had the vague feeling of being Mo. the child. She finally sat before her parents when she made the realisation "I am Mo". She kept dropping out of the situation, asking "Who is that?" when she looked at her parents. She felt dizzy. The "misalignment", as she called it, didn't appear in any other context.

We found the way to her own self with an attempt to put her in touch with her mother. Using a constellation of her dead mother and suitable music, she was able to cry on her mother's death bed. This grief put her in touch with her own feelings: I cry, therefore I am. It's my mum, she's dead. She started to realise how much she loved and missed her mother. We then went on to deal intensively with the issue of her mother and her fate. Mo. had her mother's experiences and images inside her, the terror of the bombing raid and grief for her fiancé. We worked through the identification with her, which was reinforced by the fact that she had chosen the same profession and also married a violent, two-faced and hard man. Again using constellation therapy, we dissolved the identification and child's loving allegiance. Mo. saw herself as the loving daughter, who had done the same as her mother with every fibre of her being and who now wanted to take her life in her own hands.

We addressed the father issue in a similar way. We focused on the violent father first. We had to consider the family situation: the atmosphere at home, which was not only marked by the difficult relationship between her mother and father, but also by the war and their flight from the GDR. It was then about the father who cheated on the mother – this involved a differentiation from the parents issue with the mother as friend, until we were able to carefully create a relationship with him as the father. By being allowed to sit in his lap with her mother's permission and daring to accept nourishment (= life) from him, she came a little closer to her personality. After this sequence, we could see the way ahead to the other aspects of the parents and her own suffering. We were then able to look at the different aspects of her father once again from this standpoint.

As time passed, the issue of war came into her consciousness. She began to confront the issues of the Nazi era, war, the Holocaust, being Jewish, blame and the roles of victim and perpetrator in the context of her father. The integration of the dark side, in this case being a Nazi and having Jewish ancestry at the same time, was a significant further step towards authentic personality.

After these issues, nearly all of which became group issues during this period, she had a number of insights into her mother's reaction to the pregnancy, and she felt the attempted abortion once again – viscerally. She also found out in this session why she always got a fright when somebody addressed her directly. These body memories caused Mo. to grieve deeply over how little she had known and sensed her mother, and she saw all her efforts to get close to her mother from another angle. Understanding the "misalignment" became easier and easier: her mother hadn't wanted her but her father had wanted her very much. Her mother wanted to block the good relationship between father and daughter, so the daughter longed for the father but stood by the mother. The impossibility of pleasing both parents and the attempt to understand the whole situation as a child resulted in hopelessly excessive demands on the little girl, and the inner conflict produced the symptom of "misalignment": "I can't see or understand anything but I'm trying really hard."

For Mo., writing invoices didn't mean: I have worked and I deserve to be paid for it. She allowed the real job of demanding something for herself to slip into child mode, where she was convinced she "couldn't do it", wasn't up to it, and didn't understand anything ... and definitely that she had no right to demand anything.

We didn't discuss the problem of "writing invoices" – it resolved itself. The bulimia that Mo. had developed in her youth also went away without us working on it explicitly. She was able to see bulimia as an attempt to solve the problem of being there and not there at the same time, thus pleasing both parents.

Mo. is also one of my clients who would have liked to continue the work for a while at the end of my psycholytic therapy. Mo. was allowed to realise that spiritual experiences have a special effect.

There were a number of close links between the realms of the various stations here: personal history – especially the view of her parents – was essentially connected to epigenetics, and to a point where the client was unable to develop her own personality. The work was demanding where the individual issue – being a Nazi, for example – also begged to be and needed to be processed as a group issue. The influences in the womb, not being wanted and the attempted abortion had a direct impact on the unborn child, which had clearly made itself felt in her life. Overall, Mo. can look back at the work she did and say it was fruitful.

Case notes: ayahuasca, Brazil

Request to the plant: Please heal me of my trauma.

About an hour after taking it:
The plant comes to me and asks: are you well?

I say: I am asking you if I am well now and what I still have to do in order to be well.

The plant says: if you think you are well, then you are well. Are you well now?

It takes a while for me to answer. Everything that we worked through in the afternoon goes past me: my guilt, my responsibility, my hurt, the abuse towards me, the intention to destroy me, the period of shock-induced paralysis, the chronic anxiety ...

I acknowledge: it is my decision to be well. I say: yes, I am well now.

I shake for hours after this. I experience everything all over again: right from the beginning – insights and feelings, things overlooked, things neglected, rage at the abuse, the intention, the dissociation and the distortions ...

All I can do is agree and say: yes, exactly.

In the meantime, the plant keeps on saying: I cannot heal you – it's up to you. I also keep saying: please show me everything, I have to be well again. Then my senses fade. The attendant Shaman fetches me back from the realm of the dead.

Being healed means that I don't have the "disease" anymore, that I am in the convalescence phase and have to rest.

A wonderful song is being played outside. I am flooded with a deep and unending gratitude to everything and everyone. My heart is touched by a breath – I am in God's hands, I am lying in them as if in a huge cradle – life flows into and through me again.

Very slowly, I begin to understand the lesson. I am healing means: I have seen everything, perceived everything consciously once again with the plant's protection, it is past. I must therefore decide not to look at the old stuff anymore. I must appreciate my new state and continue to heal by integrating it within my consciousness and my body responsibly.

Now the plant shows me how hard I am still making it for myself to recover. I see myself going about my everyday life. I decide to learn how to go shopping again. The fact that I can listen to other people again is a sign of the healing recovery.

Now the path leads to tranquillity. My breath is freer. For a while, I am hovering as if in Nothingness, without feelings or thoughts, but still fully conscious. I am. I am here.

I feel freer, but still a little flat.

... It's really interesting: it has passed, but my brain keeps going back. This means I am responsible for my thoughts. I can guide them. I decide not to let the emerging thoughts of the past develop any more. I relax my shoulders quite consciously and feel the connection between

my head and my heart. This is the immensely deep bond with my family and my work. It heals and relaxes me. And this is the affirmation of all that has been.

There is a fundamental love within me, not making everything sugar-sweet, but where my heart is wide open and I can look at everything. This is healing.

The actual healing process begins when I say I am healed. It's like the words in the Bible: "Rise and go. Your faith has made you well". I understand the message. Standing up means walking again: because, trusting in myself, I have decided that I can do it, I can do it. Because, trusting in myself, I have decided to heal, I am healed. I allow myself to be healed.

These case notes deal with the issue of "healing". An internal psychic event manifests itself without any therapeutic guidance. The dialogue with the teaching plant reveals a process, the healing effect of this process consists of getting through what happened followed by the spiritual experience of coming back to life from the realm of death. This leads to the experience of safety and security in God's hands. Life flows and the ego is reborn.

CHAPTER 10

Dangers, Risks, Side Effects and the Law

In this chapter we look at some of the more technical and controversial aspects of therapy with substance:

- The dangers, risks and side effects of the actual substances used in the controlled setting
- The "bad trip" where the substances are taken in a non-controlled setting is compared to the challenging experience in the controlled setting of psycholytic psychotherapy
- How to ensure a safe self-awareness session with the triad of dosage, set and setting
- The dangers, risks and side effects of therapy in general and substances in particular – from various standpoints
- Phenomena encountered while working with psychoactive substances
- Potential dangers for clients
- Dangers for the therapist
- The issue of "illegality" and my personal experience
- The advantage of illegality
- The concept of "error" in therapy is discussed both in general terms and from the standpoint of illegality
- The concept of success and failure

Risks associated with the substances in the controlled setting

The danger for clients and therapist associated with the substances is almost negligible in a controlled setting. **There is no risk of addiction.** By this I mean that the substances have no risk of physical dependence in themselves; although it is possible to get "hooked" on the good feelings and wonderful insights. But psychoactive substances don't allow this for long; they simply stop "delivering" these good feelings after a while. There were no instances of this kind of "psychological addiction" in our setting.

LSD, mushrooms, 2CB and ayahuasca do not have problematic pharmacological effects in themselves. But anyone using these substances
should thoroughly research the latest information concerning drug interactions, possible contra indications or side effects. For example people taking lithium should not take LSD.

MDMA can increase blood pressure by 10 mmHg. There is now a list of
medications that should not be combined with MDMA (SSRI antidepressants, asthma sprays, beta-blockers, HIV medication). I asked clients over
the age of 50 to provide me with the results of an exercise electrocardiogram,
as MDMA has a physiological effect that is similar to walking up a hill.

Health incidents

There were no health incidents during my therapy; but we always had one
or two doctors in the group and were equipped with an emergency kit and
defibrillator.

There was one incident involving circulatory collapse with ayahuasca.

Dangers of taking the substances described in a controlled setting

This is the only section of the book where I do not rely on my own experiences. It seems to me to be important to consider the issue of the so-called
"bad trip". However, I have deliberately chosen not to discuss this phenomenon under the heading of "Dangers to clients" as I have found the risk
of a "bad trip" is almost non-existent in a controlled setting.

A search engine provides the following definition: "*Bad trip* is the col-
loquial term used for a very negative drug experience, which can lead to an
extreme state of anxiety. It can occur under the influence of various psychotropic substances, especially psychedelics. In certain circumstances,
people who experience a bad trip can have panic attacks, the feeling of
being all alone, crying fits, paranoia or fear of death." How do we explain
the occurrence of such a state, and how does a person get into such a state?

In my opinion, the choice of the words "take a trip" or "trip" and the
term "intoxication" already indicate an attitude to the substances that helps
us understand a bad trip; a trip in the sense of a brief journey to pleasure
that should take us to the land of entirely positive feelings. If this kind of
brief journey ends in terrifying experiences, the vehicle gets the blame.
This is unfortunately the logic applied by some people so that LSD and

MDMA are therefore classed as dangerous. Ignorance and flippancy are the quickest way to a "bad trip".

In the "Bluebeard" fairy-tale, the Princess opens the forbidden door with the key entrusted to her and is confronted with a horrific sight. But is the key responsible for what she sees? As keys to the unconscious, psycho-active substances cause all sorts of material to emerge. But everything that emerges on a "trip" is still your own personal material. You may see your own personal heaven or hell. If you assess your own material as "nega-tive", projecting it outwards in the form of anxiety, terror and isolation, you will describe it as a "*bad trip*". In the worst-case scenario, the "horror" can be expelled by a sedative. But, suppressed in this way, the material persists, stuck half-way on the road to awareness and demanding to come to the surface in the form of depression, anxiety disorders, psychosis and the like when the effect of the sedative wears off. If uninformed, this leads to the opinion that these substances could trigger psychoses. Psychoses occur in people that are prone to psychoses and who unfortunately tend to "con-sume drugs".

The significance of emotionally intense experiences in psycholytic therapy

Difficult and overwhelming experiential material that is described as a "bad trip" in an uncontrolled setting is exactly what is wanted in a con-trolled setting. It is precisely this difficult and powerful unconscious psy-chic material that is begging to and should be rendered conscious and integrated in psycholytic therapy. Psycholytic therapy is essentially based on bringing precisely this unconscious material out into the light in order to destroy its hidden destructive power. Processing and integrating trau-matising and formative childhood experiences constitutes the essence of the work. According to Stanislav Grof, "bad trips" with LSD are merely an indication that psychological material yet to be processed has become accessible. The cure consists of making the person feel the material that has been brought to the surface by LSD.

The route to a safe self-awareness session

I personally ascribe the occurrence of a bad trip to poor practice and a violation of or disregard for the guidelines of the triad of **dosage, set and setting.**

It is worth reminding ourselves once again of the criteria for a safe substance experience carried out in a secure setting as a way towards self-awareness.

Dosage, set and setting are closely linked.

The **dosage** needs to be decided by the therapist together with the client.

The "**set**" needs to be taken into consideration for determining the right dosage. The set covers everything to do with the client. It is ultimately the safe **setting** that is able to give the client valuable experiences, irrespective of their content. The dosage needs to be:

- Not too much
- Not too little
- Exactly what the client needs

The client and dosage

Is the client familiar with the substance? The dosage should depend on their previous experience and the quality of this experience. If they are not familiar with it, the dosage is kept low.

The client's attitude

What is the client expecting from a substance session? If they are expecting to experience "positive feelings", you will need to talk to them about "addiction to good feelings".

Has the client come up with a clear intention and expressed it?

The client's level of knowledge

Does the client know how psychoactive substances work? Are they aware that they will only encounter their inner selves? If they are still unaware of this and haven't processed it yet, they need to be informed about the nature of outward projection.

The client's level of ability

Is the client capable of introspection?

Is the client capable of observing their own internal process under the influence of a psychoactive substance? (See the sections about primary and secondary school pupils.)

Is the client in a position to surrender to the substance and guide the process with their "self-reflecting I" at the same time?

Is the client in a position to call for help if they enter a situation in which they feel out of control?

Do they realise that they may experience some emotional instability after a session, and are they able to get support?

The combination of set and setting

The client is responsible for choosing a setting that appeals to them, which feels safe and supportive and where they want to and feel able to engage. **The management of the setting is entirely the responsibility of the therapist.**

The therapist and the dosage

Is the therapist familiar with the substances? Have they had personal experience of it? Are they keeping the individual client's experiences in mind at all times and are they in a position to set an individual dosage?

The therapist and the client

Does the therapist know the client, their personal history, current circumstances, problems and chosen issue for the session?

Is the therapist aware of the client's attitude towards taking substances, and have they briefed and informed them with regard to knowledge and ability?

Do therapist and client have a relationship of trust? Are there any undeclared issues between them?

The therapist and the environment

Has the environment been set up so that the client can feel safe and surrender to their internal process?

The therapist as "mountain guide": requirements of the therapist

I used this metaphor in a lecture in England in 2011 and found the same analogy in a book written by a colleague. I continue to use this image because I think it must be particularly apposite if two therapists use it independently of one another.

Substance-based psychotherapy is like climbing a mountain, for which you need a mountain guide. Everyone involved needs to agree on the objective. There has to be total clarity as to which rules apply and who has overall responsibility during the climb. The mountain guide needs to be acknowledged unequivocally as the expedition leader. He or she needs to be an experienced mountain guide who has personally reconnoitred the area, who knows the heights and beautiful views as well as the crevasses and views into the abyss. He needs to be able to assess the equipment and fitness of the members of his group and be aware of the weather conditions. He must know what to do if there is an accident. Finally, he has to be clear about why he is doing this particular job. It cannot be about him and his needs but there needs to be a sense of vocation about properly guiding people into unfamiliar territory for their benefit. He must love "soul work through expansion of consciousness".

In psychotherapeutic parlance, this mountain guide must have psychotherapeutic training, including specialisation in various procedures and facilities, a huge amount of self-experience with and without substances and the skills for guiding a group. There has to be a high level of commitment and in my case, willingness to take a risk – which doesn't just mean the illegal aspect. During the course of the self-awareness group analysis, which I had to do to qualify as a psychotherapist, I personally revealed almost nothing about myself, therefore learning hardly anything about myself. I have also encountered similar resistance to personal engagement in other therapists during supervision sessions over the years. I am not talking about this brand of "self-awareness" here.

On the contrary, any therapist wanting to lead substance-based therapy needs to experience, process and integrate deep, genuine feelings of all kinds, their dark side, trauma, experiences of hell and healing – the whole gamut of human suffering and joy – for themselves in order to be able to identify issues in the client and carry them with them with as little projection as possible. The openness that develops carries a danger of the therapy becoming contaminated with his own issues if he hasn't prepared beforehand. He will only be able to identify difficult feelings, resistance and projection in the client with rapidity and assurance and deal with them in a professional way after going through a sufficient amount of introspection beforehand. It is not that he isn't allowed to have pleasant feelings, but he cannot be caught up in them.

In this kind of work, it is only from experience that you can know when it is right to intervene and when it is advisable to leave the client alone. Although the therapist is a therapy tool himself, he also requires a box of tools. There is potential for danger if the therapist does not have the essential mountain-climbing equipment.

Side effects of therapy

I found the following interesting statement about the "**risks**" of effective therapy in the information sheet of a Berlin psychotherapist:

> Therapy can only be of any use if you are prepared to take the following risks: improvement of symptoms, changed lifestyle, uncertainty about previous points of view; exploring your own part in perpetuating your problems.

In pharmacology, **side effects** are defined as "unwanted effects". But which are the effects and which the side effects in psychotherapy? My view is that it is difficult to keep them apart in psychotherapy. Is changing current relationships an effect or a side effect? Is changing trusted but also are harmful behavioural patterns an effect or a side effect? What is the appropriate term for the intervention whereby a positive feeling that occurs in the context of the self-damaging pattern, becomes no longer available? In what circumstances does intervention constitute manipulation? Who defines whether an intervention in a psycholytic setting is called "manipulation" or "support"?

In any effective form of psychotherapy, developmental processes will be initiated that may or may not please the people around the client – does that make them effects or side effects? In actual fact, the risk inherent to any therapeutic approach is a change that does not please all or some of the people around the client. The passage of time generally brings everyone involved, if not to an agreement with a change, at least to a certain acceptance of it.

Risks and side effects of therapy with substance

Where a change does not please all or some of the people around the client, the unwanted change arising from the psycholytic therapy is rapidly and vehemently attributed to the substance or blamed on the therapist. People say that the client is being manipulated or that they were intoxicated by the drug. The tendency is the same if the change is defined as positive. The error is twofold here –change is due to neither the substance nor the therapist. The change is made by the client alone and is entirely real; he or she is the only one who can make this happen. Each individual follows their own instinct – even though it might appear from the outside that they are being influenced. Whoever leaves a place has to take themselves, their body and their baggage along with them – nobody can do this for them. These factors may seem simple, but they are very important. They appeal to the client's sense of personal responsibility.

The house key opens the front door. Which room the person enters, whether he leaves again or stays, takes something with him or leaves it there – none of this points to the power of the key but says something about the person turning the key and entering the house.

Phenomena encountered while working with psychoactive substances

There are many issues that can lead to difficulties for the client on the one hand and the therapist on the other. The therapist's position as leader during the session may open up issues concerning power. The therapist needs to be capable of critical self-reflection in order to identify any narcissistic tendencies they might have in this role. But they have to assume clear leadership in the session in order to provide a safe vessel during any potentially difficult phases. This can be a difficult balancing act for inexperienced therapists, especially if the client has problems with authority.

Particularly at the beginning of therapy, clients have a tendency to idealise the therapist, which might "feed" any unidentified narcissism and their sense of power. It is a primary task of any therapist to recognise such projections, observe and address them if this phase persists. Of course this is an important part of traditional therapy too but the power of the psycholytic state amplifies this tendency. I believe it is vital to approach these matters on a highly individual basis – a child who grew up without a mother sometimes needs a "substitute mother" for longer than another person does.

The personality may become destabilised at the start of therapy as the client's neurotic system becomes activated. The client is keen to locate an external, identity-defining structure in the person of the therapist at this juncture. Vigilance is required here; it is sometimes enough to recognise the situation and be aware of it.

The high degree of openness under the influence of substances, the body-work, the highly variable roles that the therapist assumes during a psycholytic session, together with the closeness experienced in the house reduces the distance between therapist and client. The tension between proximity and necessary distance can be discussed in a number of different ways – in any case, it is a factor to be included and not to be neglected. It can become a "hazard" in terms of how therapy is judged from the outside.

An equally difficult issue, but one that I will only touch on briefly, is that of friends taking a substance to achieve self-awareness. It definitely does happen during this kind of experiment that difficult issues emerge and one of the group members makes a well-meaning intervention or observation which is not well judged or therapeutically orientated. This may lead to discord within the group. These issues require the leadership of the therapist and must be addressed to maintain the safety of the setting.

Potential dangers for clients

When considering potential dangers for clients, the observer's perspective is a decisive factor in this perception. There is no danger *per se* but nearly everything can be interpreted as one. If something is supposed to change, maintaining the status quo is the danger. If I am not allowed to change anything, change is the danger. If a result fails to meet expectations, the thing or person at the root of the difference is the danger. So where does the client himself see danger? What do they consider to be a danger? Where can they see it? The answer lies with them and their interpretation of what they perceive.

Where does the environment before, during and after personal development of a close person detect and interpret danger? Depending on whether they are judged positively or negatively, the outcome of therapy and changes that have taken place over time are easily perceived as a "danger".

In my opinion, the potential dangers for a client arise if nobody is there with them as they go through their process or if there has not been adequate preparation of the patient or the setting.

To put it succinctly, danger exists wherever dosage, set and setting or elements of this triad are not considered or handled with enough care.

The context of illegality

By their very nature, all therapists live dangerously to some extent; there is an element of risk built into their professional lives. This danger is much greater where psychoactive substances are used. As already discussed under the heading of "Effects and side effects of therapy", difficult situations naturally occur in the course of traditional therapy. A client may become suicidal, suddenly split up with their partner or have a secret affair. A partner may be unhappy with the therapy because the result does not meet expectations. In cases like this, the therapist is often quick to be blamed for the situation or outcome and branded as being biased or unprofessional. Wittingly or unwittingly, they often become the object of transference and involved in systemic entanglements.

In traditional therapy these difficulties are normally resolved over time to the point where everyone involved finds their own suitable form of reaction to the circumstances causing the turbulence.

On the other hand, illegality provides the opportunity to withdraw from this process of working through grief, processing shock and overcoming other problems. From this point of view, the client and the people around them hold the therapist's fate in their hands because of the illegality. Thus the therapist may be held responsible for a separation or unhappiness or blamed for other unpleasant emotional states. Because the therapist is working in an illegal context, they can be denounced or slandered without being able to defend themselves. Because their behaviour was illegal, the public and the client's relatives think that it must be intrinsically bad – it can't have been in any way beneficial or professional because it was illegal. This logic is not only to be found in the therapeutic context. According to the British psychiatrist Professor David Nutt, its impact is felt equally in the field of research. As Nutt points out, sometimes the results of research into psychoactive substances are not even published if they fail to confirm negative expectations.

Illegality creates an invisible bond between client and therapist. From the outside, it might appear that the therapist is holding the client in his hands or manipulating them. It might be said that this bond makes the group into a secret society, and people soon start talking about sects in this context. You could describe the leadership of a psycholytic session as the wilful influencing of a guru-like person. Such labels are more likely to be used simply because this form of therapy is illegal.

It isn't easy for a therapist to expose himself to these eventualities, even if it is his own choice and they take responsibility for it. It means that the therapist has to have a high degree of self-awareness. And, as for any other person, it is a huge challenge for a therapist to deal with the intensity of the criticism and prejudice of inexperienced people.

The literature on the subject of "illegal drugs" and "drugs and illegality" is easily accessible and almost infinite. That is why I won't be discussing it in any detail here. But I would like to draw particular attention to

LSD in this context. The substances that I have described are illegal in the eyes of the law under the Narcotics Act. "LSD is a narcotic." The Narcotics Act relates to dependency-inducing substances. Trafficking them in the broadest sense of the term is liable to prosecution.

This represents a complex problem. First of all, LSD does not intoxicate; it expands the range of consciousness. Secondly, it is demonstrable that LSD is not dependency-inducing. The legislation is aware of this. But it is given the status of an intoxicant, bringing it under the Narcotics Act. This is how things stand. To polarise or polemicize would not be in keeping with the actual issue of the effect of psychoactive substances, and nor would it be appropriate within the context this book.

Illegality is the one extreme – legalisation would be the other. I cannot speak of the total legalisation of "drugs". But I am of the opinion that there must be a legislative connection between the hazardous nature of a substance and its classification. This needs clarification. In a lecture he gave in 1995 or 1996, Hans Carl Leuner called on the German Federal Government to authorise research and teaching relating to these substances again. He used an image and made an analogy: "It's like this with substances: tickets are sold down at the bottom of the ski lift and take skiers up the mountain. When they arrive at the top, there is nobody there to tell them how to get back down again. So they just travel or speed back down and there are many accidents on the way. The paramedics are ready at the bottom to take the accident victims to hospital to be patched up again. What we need are not paramedics at the foot of the mountain but ski instructors up on the mountain to teach skiers, accompanying them safely down the mountain." I remember the standing ovation from the audience when he issued this call, and I too hold the view that highly trained escorts are indispensable when taking the psychedelic path.

Research projects and many other activities carried out by younger people with commitment are a light on the horizon, confirming that a change in attitudes to psychotropic substances is in sight.

My personal experience of illegality

In the light of the illegality of the substances I used, it might seem surprising that a book like this, with such content, exists at all. I had to take personal responsibility for the illegality involved in my work. There can be no doubt that I put myself above the law. My current ability to write about my work free from fear is down to the fact that we – my husband and I – were betrayed. I was tried for an Offence against the Swiss Narcotics Act and was sentenced to 16 months in prison, suspended for two years. Because I was able to prove that I had worked in a controlled setting, I was acquitted on the grounds of conducting therapy.

I give details of my motivations for starting this work in the first few chapters and the subject of this book concerns the way in which I conducted my work. On a personal level I was obviously aware that handling psychoactive substances is illegal, but, looking back, I saw a big difference between knowledge and experience. Illegality was somehow an abstract concept. The ruling of "Offence against the Swiss Narcotics Act" that was issued did not come within the sphere of my personal experience. I had not been able to anticipate the full extent of the possible consequences of the term "illegality". I saw myself as a therapist using not narcotics but psycho-integrative substances to help people to achieve helpful insights about themselves and improve their quality of life through consciousness expansion – in the widest sense.

Had I been truly afraid of the illegal aspect, I would certainly never have taken this path at all. I can still clearly remember my initial hesitation – it took a while until I arrived at an inner stance that I took to be conviction. My arrest, my time in custody and my trial turned out to be a rich chapter of my life, where I learned what it feels like to have the status of a criminal. The judge's view that I was "a person acting from their convictions" identified and gave a name to the essence of my illegal behaviour.

In hindsight, this conviction masked the risk of betrayal or of being discovered. I naturally considered the foreseeable risks there might be relating to the dosage and client's state of health. My previous experience as a doctor in an intensive care unit seemed to me to be enough. The setting was established, the environment was ritualised and discipline reigned. Due to the composition of the group, there was also usually a doctor amongst us. We always had an emergency kit and respirator ready. I provided this mainly for Holotropic Breathwork, as I considered that this approach put more strain on the circulation than substance work.

One problem that I didn't pay enough attention to, was the fact that group members became used to the protected environment, perhaps forgetting that our work was actually illegal. Although we went through a little ritual at the start of every session, where we agreed not to disclose "the location, people present or substance", people started to talk about the work in an open and uninhibited way after a time. This had its dangers, and occasionally led to me being asked about the work by people who didn't belong to the group. Looking back, I might also have lost sight of the threat posed by the illegality of it as I worked to perfect the setting and develop my skills as a therapist with the substances.

The advantage of illegality

Illegality also had its advantages in my setting: the people who came to me had to address this issue even before therapy began, coming to me of their own accord. Nobody could say that they hadn't wanted or known this. There were also clients to whom I had offered this type of therapy, but who did not dare to do something that was illegal. My clients knew what they were letting themselves in for.

Actually taking the substance was always a personal decision, which I emphasised occasionally by adding, "I know what I'm doing here and I take personal responsibility for it" to the ritual before taking the substance. One client remembered me telling her "You don't have to take anything, of course" when she "grumbled" so that it was patently clear to her that she and not I was responsible for the decision.

So the problem of "illegality" became an important step towards commitment and engaging with the process of change.

It is not always completely clear to begin with whether something is an advantage or disadvantage – it may become clearer later.

The danger of errors

In the illegal setting, every error is magnified. Where and how do errors happen?

I made errors as a young doctor because I had little experience and simply didn't know certain things. The same applies to psychotherapy – with or without substances. So when I started my work, there simply wasn't the knowledge about the contraindications of the substances that is available now. I definitely made "errors" when selecting a few of my clients. The failure to spot a borderline disorder due to an incorrect diagnosis is one example of this type of error. It also turned out to be an error to invite a client's partner along to a session in one instance, and *not* to invite them in another.

So what is an error in therapy and when is it an error? Without illegal elements, this is also a tricky subject. For me, an error is when I have not followed the prescribed principles for fulfilling a task. For example my procedures and ideas for couple therapy may be very different to those of another therapist. The approach of any therapist will be either "right or wrong" depending on the school of thought and the perspective of their training. If an undesired result occurs in the illegal psycholytic setting, it could be more readily argued that the fault is in the approach itself.

But a relationship separation has very little to do with psycholytic therapy itself. Experiencing a substance merely deepens what was there anyway, maybe accelerating the process of realisation. But if you add the context of illegality, it has powerful potential to put therapists in danger! When I asked her about mistakes I had made, a good friend of mine said: you told some clients the truth when they were not mature enough and didn't want to hear the truth. I had to admit she was right. An excessively provocative approach over-extends the client, so that they don't feel understood, and not just in the illegal setting. Excessively clear statements on my behalf have also led to people stopping therapy in the traditional setting, but have also had the exact opposite effect, leading to the comment: "At least you speak plainly."

I can imagine that other therapists working underground as I did could describe my entire approach as wrong. This alone is a reason for me to keep emphasising in this book, perhaps redundantly, that I am only talking about my own experiences, procedures and results. In my opinion everyone who has had a psychedelic experience knows that the interpretation of the message lies with the recipient, that beauty is in the eye of the beholder and that everyone is only responsible for their own perception. Realisations of this kind lead to greater tolerance and better results from experiences with substances. I personally had a wide range of experiences as a participant in a variety of settings, and do not presume to describe my own as being any better than anyone else's.

With regard to "errors" in therapy: even here, illegality has the potential to tip the scales. What leads to mere irritation in the normal setting can attract betrayal and slander in an illegal setting.

Failure and success

Describing something as a success or a failure always says something about the person doing the describing. If the therapist has failed to "produce" the desired result, some will see this as success and others as failure. Even here, there is no such thing as success or failure *per se*. For me, psycholytic therapy is successful when the issues that the client has brought with them to therapy have become integrated in everyday routine. This is a sign of what I call "success". It is important to be aware that success or failure is not apparent immediately, but only after a considerable period of time.

In general, I consider the most serious failure of psychotherapeutic work to be the failure to encourage clients to assume personal responsibility and having to watch them continue to blame others for their lack of well-being. Continued damaging behaviour, the persistence of the same old relationship squabbles and neurotic behaviour also indicate to me that a therapy has failed to work. I also call it a failure when such behaviour can still be found after psycholytic therapy work.

My psycholytic therapy has never resulted in a sustained deterioration of the symptoms. I have already talked about an "initial worsening". Psychotherapy always has a catalytic effect; it accelerates a process that would take place anyway. You therefore have to ensure that you establish causal links. If a couple in crisis begin therapy that leads to separation, it is easy to blame the therapist for this and interpret the separation as a failure. What separation ultimately means to an individual no longer has anything to do with success or failure.

Some clients stopped therapy with me in the years when I was practising psycholytic therapy. I went ahead too quickly in two cases and – in hindsight – I didn't clarify the severe symptoms sufficiently from the start. This is where error and failure coincide. A series of clients stopped the therapy after working through the problem that had brought them into therapy. This is common in traditional psychotherapy but was unusual in our work. Most of my clients stayed after the resolution of the presenting problem, to continue tuning into themselves and continue the path towards self-awareness. So I can't interpret these cases as either a success or a failure, given that the determination of what is successful in therapy is extremely varied, and its interpretation can fluctuate wildly over a person's life.

If I view success in terms of the quintessence, the *quinta essentia*, success is achieved in working with psychoactive substances when the authentic and autonomous way of life merges with everyday routine.

Supervision, intervision and exchange

As is recommended for every therapy method, supervision or intervision is also indicated for underground work, and it does take place. But it throws up the same questions and doubts that I have always had about supervision in general, and which I have formed in various contexts down the years. Psychotherapy is like a laboratory situation; client and therapist are both outside their own environment and have a "relationship" with each other. The way the individual relationship is shaped through the verbal and non-verbal, interventions and much more is an "artificial one-off". How this is achieved is closely related to the nature of the psychotherapy training, the stage of development of the therapist and the client's own idiosyncrasies.

When you describe a difficult case, you are bombarded with good advice and suggestions that come from other people's toolboxes put together in a different way. You can definitely assume that the advice is well meaning. Apart from the fact that the supervisors were not there at the time, have different tool boxes and their own personalities, it can easily happen that the problems described are viewed with a critical eye and that the approach is assessed and judged. In this way, a kind of defensive stance is engendered imperceptibly in the person doing the judging, who has probably tried a few things himself; maybe he even feels like a failure or burnt out. If the group succeeds – and this does definitely happen – in locating the blind spot and the supervisor is able to acknowledge this, the support is genuine and expedient. Real help also consists of watching a video recording of your own therapy session with colleagues and getting feedback. You feel understood right from the start and it is easier to accept suggestions and advice.

In any event, what always proves to be fruitful and encouraging in psycholytic therapy work is the shared development and exchange on the subject of general stumbling blocks. Knowledge transfer is also useful and necessary. But some form of supervision, intervention or exchange with a trusted colleague is still always a must.

I need to mention one more point: psycholytic therapy is not a method that has developed its own "school". There are no "Hofmannians", "Grofians", or "SAEPTs" [Swiss society for psycholytic therapy]. This fact makes exchange more difficult. And this is why I keep emphasising that it is purely about the setting evolved through my work, that other therapists may organise their psycholytic therapy work totally differently and that I would not presume to judge other ways of approaching it.

CHAPTER 11

The Parallels of this Work with Shamanism, Healing and Spirituality

Chapter eleven looks at the parallels of the work that I have described with the shamanic approach. An outline is given of my understanding of healing and spirituality in the psycholytic setting.

Parallels with shamanism

I discovered similarities between the shamanic approach and the psycholytic process while I was compiling the material for this book. I always avoided using the term shamanism in the early days. I felt very wary of anything related to shamanism, perhaps I was prejudiced against it. The participants in the first self-awareness group always referred to me as the "psychopomp". This term meant nothing to me at the time, they used it in a jocular fashion and in my ignorance of the origin of the term, I also found it rather funny. Later on, I discovered that psychopomp (from the Greek, *psychopompos*) is the name for the "guider of souls" who accompanies the souls of the deceased to the Other Side. These guiders of souls were present in many ancient cultures, and the concept stems from archaic shamanism.

There is no denying the similarities between some of the elements of psycholytic therapy generated in our setting and those of shamanic traditions. In hindsight, my own experiences, my discovery of the well of forgetfulness in my first encounter with ayahuasca, experiencing the death of the ego in my hellish near death experiences, contact with ancestors and spirits, encounters with entities, events in Brasilia around my betrayal and out-of-body experiences, all show strong similarities with the shamanic initiation process. In common with the shamans, I also took the same substance as the other participants at sessions, enabling me to "look inside" the people seated before me to seek to identify the problem.

The shaman's task is to "Access the spirit world, fulfil the intention and return to the normal world". And the fact that it became completely natural for me to be available for every one of the "people entrusted to me" at all times is also the nature of the relationship a shaman has with his "patients". I am still of the opinion that true shamans should be left in their traditional environment, but also believe that something like a "shamanic principle" is also needed for our time, stage of development and culture. In this respect, the "know thyself" (*Gnōthi seautón*) of the ancient Greeks would seem to me to be the necessary exhortation encouraged by the current zeitgeist.

Even if the shaman doesn't exactly use the terms "dosage, set and setting", the corresponding concepts still form the basic structure for his activity. As with shamanism, we always consumed substances and plants as part of a ritual within our own setting. We developed and expressed an intention before taking anything. Shamans place a high value on the expression of the intention, as it is the purpose of the session. With shamanism, a substance only works if you use the right words. We listened to the teachings of the substances and plants. We made contact with our ancestors with the help of the substances and modified constellation work. The substances helped us to remember. We used Live-Body-Work to facilitate body memory, which determines our mental state.

It was mystical experiences that re-connected us with the divine or cosmic order in the sense of *re-ligio*. Like a shamanic re-membering after a dis-memberment, they brought us back to our true nature, inner core and cosmic order. This re-union enables us to live harmoniously with our partners, neighbours and fellow human beings.

If the individual wishes to learn how to reflect upon himself and perceive himself as the centre of the universe, he needs to practise centring himself, maintaining balance and learning to be with the substances assisted by breathing techniques. When a person is supported by the knowledge that he is the centre of the universe, he will also regard others in terms of this state of being.

As we practised it, the mindful use of psychoactive substances is one of the major aims of shamanic practice. The shaman lets the substance guide him, sings and uses certain methods to transcend darkness and turn into light. We also allowed the substance to lead us, discovering that the intention helped to determine the direction, even or especially when we let go of any intentions when in the ascent (see iterative integration cycle).

We learned how to master the substance, as dictated by shamanic tradition. For us, this meant simply looking and not reacting under the influence of the substance with the "observer" and later the "benevolent, empathetic observer". The tools of psycholytic therapy could be compared with the methods of the shaman. All in all, it seems to me that we have returned to the original principles of shamanic activity using the resources of our own era.

Healing

One of my aims at this point is to present my ideas about healing and spirituality. As I have also pointed out in other contexts in the book, I do not presume to provide any cut-and-dried definitions or criticise others. I would also repeat my basic tenet that terms are not the things themselves and it is always about how they are manifested through us as we go about our daily activities.

In my setting and my work with and without psychoactive substances, "healing" occurs when a psychic problem is fully resolved at its most fundamental level in one's innermost being. The basic requirement for healing is first and foremost the intention to make a change; the person seeking healing must engage with what comes along, assume personal responsibility, staying with and in contact with the process. Self-awareness and self-knowledge are the ultimate healers. What else helps with healing?

Freedom from fear is healing, touching, being held, crying and laughter, contact and resonance, openness, understanding, listening, confronting, honesty, holding – all of these things are healing.

What is healing?

Prayer is healing. So is believing, humility, gratitude, affirmation and re-connecting (*re-ligio*) with that which is greater than us. Being in the right place and respecting your parents is healing. Understanding, insight, mindfulness and caring for the environment and ourselves are all healing.

What is healing?

An authentic approach, having authentic feelings and handling them responsibly are all healing.

Being present is healing.

Love is healing.

Grace is healing.

This is the way to spirituality.

Spirituality

Spirituality manifests itself through consciously taking responsibility for leading your own life, in "becoming who you are" every day and showing who you are through your behaviour. In concise terms, this means – do your job and follow your heart – earn money, enjoy success, have courage, be competitive – whatever comes along. "Wash your bowl", as the Zen saying goes. Look after your things and care for what belongs to you. Don't waffle on about something you should or have to do – just do it, live your life. Have children or travel abroad, split up or have a relationship, but do it in the knowledge that things might not go according to plan.

Living spiritually does not mean remaining aloof or feeling better, wiser or nobler than others. It does not mean living or not living as a vegetarian, nor does it mean walking around dressed in white. It simply means doing what you do with heart and soul, love and understanding in relation to yourself and whatever you do. It means: solve your problems right where they are and don't store them up in a separate space.

Wanting, thinking and acting, bearing the consequences of this and holding your heart in your own hands – this was the meaning of spirituality in my setting.

Spirituality is essentially what heals us.

CHAPTER 12

Conclusions – Looking Back and Looking Forward

Looking back

There came a point when this type of work had to end. The first participants had just matured into "school leavers". A person who came into therapy because of their suffering became a *normal* person who was happy and no longer suffering. Achieving adult autonomy is the essence of this therapeutic approach: The therapeutic learning process of taking the person who is suffering at the start of the therapy to their authentic personality at the end, which evolves over time through the integration of issues as various stations are passed. In this way, the journey becomes the destination. Not all of my clients matured to the status of school leaver, but all of them achieved a new state of knowledge specific to them.

Through realisations, re-experiencing, corrective new experiences and achieving spiritual wisdom, what started out as a problem related to their personal history ended up producing the therapeutic arc to the next station, revealing other areas of interest. Understanding and benevolent empathy with regard to one's self and others brought a change of perspective. The integration of the issues that emerged during the process ultimately set the pace.

Recognising the coherence of body, mind and soul, we dedicated ourselves to processing obvious emotional problems and difficulties. Substances opened the gates to the unconscious; the use of various tools and relentless self-exploration led to concrete statements and results on each of these three levels. Along the way, we realised that nearly every issue had manifested itself at various levels of life and therefore had to be processed several different times. We could only advance step by step to start with, trying to heal what had just been identified as the problem or issue. This demanded hard work and critical examination on many occasions. Driven by therapy, dynamic changes took place in the intervals between sessions. The integration of what had been experienced in everyday life ultimately opened the way to a dawning spirituality.

In hindsight, operating from an initial state of suffering, a pattern of parallel development processes helped each person towards the end state, where many of the goals had been reached:

- Handling substances: from the person who has taken a substance to a person with expanded consciousness in their normal state.
- Individual process: from understanding to integration via insight.
- Development from beginner to school leaver.
- From psychological methods to spiritual healing.
- Group process: from individual group members to group identity.
- Cognitive process, organisation of developments: from the cellular biochemical to the psychological process.

Looking forward

The question of how things would continue came up again and again in our group. We faced the issue of what to call what we had "experienced" together. If it was no longer therapy, then what was it? It became necessary to find a guiding term that could lead to accessing and exploring new and higher levels. We were unable to come up with an answer and nobody took it up again. But this much was clear:

The last part of the learning process needed to come into being in an atmosphere of peace and shared communication, and without any therapeutic intervention from me. Even if the journey continued to be the destination, we knew that this would involve future levels way beyond therapy and the personal, and might even defy description. The ground had been prepared for shared, collective and universal insights and realisations. It was clear that the next step would and should not involve an "esoteric event". In terms of its description and semantics, the step from "healing" to "hallowed" – for example – already harbours the risk of sliding into orthodox/religious and esoteric ideas, suffering from the lack of terminology available in this field.

Social conditions allowing, where could the path to the integration of all biographical subject areas lead?

- From the artificial persona to the essence?
- Towards an integral world view, self-realisation and universal common good?
- Towards a more spiritual/religious attitude?
- To new observations on consciousness and perception?
- To philosophical and/or scientific findings?
- To the affirmation and experience of death and dying as part of life?

Would it be too daring to envisage a conceptual model that begins with dysfunction in everyday life but ultimately leads towards spiritual development – a better life and a better death? I am not sure if this will happen in my lifetime, but I can hope for it.

Let us close with a quotation from Albert Hofmann: "I think that in human evolution it has never been as necessary to have this substance LSD ... It is just a tool to turn us into what we are supposed to be."[4]

---

[4] Speech given on his 100th birthday.

Bibliography

Grof, Stanislav 1975 Realms of the Human Unconscious
Grof, Stanislav 1988 LSD Psychotherapy
Grof, Stanislav and Christina 2010 Holotropic Breathwork
Hofmann, Albert 1983 LSD – My Problem Child
Henrik Jungaberle 2008 Therapie mit psychoaktiven Substanzen
Hüther, Gerald 2013 Biologie der Angst
Hüther, Gerald 2012 Das Geheimnis der ersten neun Monate
Levine, Peter A. 2013 Sprache ohne Worte
MAPS Multidisciplinary Association for Psychedelic Studies
Möckel-Graber, Claudia 2010 Eintritt in heilende Bewusstseinszustände
Roth, Gerhard 2014 Wie das Gehirn die Seele macht
SAEPT Schweizerische Aerztegessellschaft für Psycholytische Therapie
Samuel Widmer 2002 Ins Herz der Dinge lauschen
Psycholytic and Psychedelic Therapy Research 1931-1995. A complete
    International Bibilography. Tosten Passie MD, MA. Lauemtius Pub-
    lishers
Passie, Torsten – Dürst, Thomas 2009 Heilungsprozesse im veränderten
    Bewusstein. VWB – Verlag für Wissenschaft und Bildung, Berlin
Porges, Steven 2011 Neurophysiologie der Selbstregulation Vorträge

Made in the USA
Las Vegas, NV
19 September 2022